Sylvain Chomet's Distinctive Animation

Animation: Key Films/Filmmakers

Series Editor: Chris Pallant

Titles in the Series:

Sylvain Chomet's Distinctive Animation

From The Triplets of Belleville to The Illusionist

Maria Katsaridou

BLOOMSBURY ACADEMIC
NEW YORK • LONDON • OXFORD • NEW DELHI • SYDNEY

BLOOMSBURY ACADEMIC
Bloomsbury Publishing Inc
1385 Broadway, New York, NY 10018, USA
50 Bedford Square, London, WC1B 3DP, UK
29 Earlsfort Terrace, Dublin 2, Ireland

BLOOMSBURY, BLOOMSBURY ACADEMIC and the Diana logo are
trademarks of Bloomsbury Publishing Plc

First published in the United States of America 2024

Series design by Louise Dugdale
Cover image: The Triplets of Belleville (2003) © Sylvain Chomet

Library of Congress Cataloging-in-Publication Data
Names: Katsaridou, Maria, author.
Title: Sylvain Chomet's distinctive animation : from The triplets of Belleville
to The illusionist / Maria Katsaridou.
Description: New York : Bloomsbury Academic, 2023. | Series: Animation : key
films/filmmakers | Includes bibliographical references and index. |
Summary: "Examines key works of the distinguished French animator Sylvain Chomet and their
importance for the study of contemporary animation"– Provided by publisher.
Identifiers: LCCN 2022049145 (print) | LCCN 2022049146 (ebook) | ISBN 9781501363993
(hardback) | ISBN 9781501374562 (paperback) | ISBN 9781501363986 (ebook) | ISBN
9781501363979 (pdf) | ISBN 9781501363962 (ebook other)
Subjects: LCSH: Chomet, Sylvain, 1963- | Animators–France–Biography. |
Animated films–France–History and criticism.
Classification: LCC NC1766.F82 C495 2023 (print) | LCC NC1766.F82 (ebook) |
DDC 791.43/34092–dc23/eng/20221220
LC record available at https://lccn.loc.gov/2022049145
LC ebook record available at https://lccn.loc.gov/2022049146

ISBN: HB: 978-1-5013-6399-3
           ePDF: 978-1-5013-6397-9
           eBook: 978-1-5013-6398-6

Series: Animation: Key Films/Filmmakers

Typeset by Integra Software Services Pvt. Ltd.
Printed and bound in Great Britain

To find out more about our authors and books visit www.bloomsbury.com
and sign up for our newsletters.

For my grandfather Andreas Katsaridis and
my husband Makis Stergiou.

Contents

Figures

Tables

Acknowledgements

The creation of this book would not have been possible without the contribution and support of several people whom I would like to thank. I am deeply grateful to Sylvain Chomet for his invaluable contribution to this book and his kindness in answering all my never-ending questions about his works. Additionally, I owe many thanks to Sally Chomet for our fruitful discussion concerning production practices. I am immensely thankful to Aton Soumache and his team for their substantial help. Special thanks to Antoine Delesvaux for his time and support.

I would like to express my gratitude to Prof Alexandros Ph. Lagopoulos and Karin Boklund-Lagopoulou for their support. I am very grateful to Maureen Furniss for her generous help, from practical information to theoretical discussions, and, moreover, for her much-needed positive and constructive approach concerning my research on European animation in general and Sylvain Chomet's works in particular.

Moreover, I wish to express my deepest thanks to Chris Pallant, the editor of this book, for his significant contribution, help and support. Additionally, I would like to sincerely thank Stephanie Grace-Petinos, Erin Duffy, Katie Gallof and everyone at Bloomsbury that made this book come to life.

I would like also to express my special gratitude to Sophie Vandorpe for her help when most needed.

Last but not least, I want to express my gratitude to Makis Stergiou, my husband, for his multilevel contribution, which expands from creating the film charts to always being at my side. Without the help of all of you, this book would never exist.

I thank you all from the bottom of my heart!

Introduction

Sylvain Chomet is a versatile French artist known for his successful career in comics and animation. He also made his live-action debut in the film *Paris, je t'aime* (segment *Tour Eiffel*, 2006) and later, in his feature film *Attila Marcel* (Chomet, 2013). All his works deserve particular attention and analysis, however, this book focuses on his animation films and his contribution to the evolution of contemporary animation.

From his first short animation film *The Old Lady and the Pigeons* (*La vieille dame et les pigeons*, Chomet, 1997) to his feature films *The Triplets of Belleville* (*Les Triplettes de Belleville*, Chomet, 2003) and *The Illusionist* (*L'illusionniste*, Chomet, 2010), Chomet's works were nominated and received many awards at renowned international festivals, such as the Cannes Film Festival, BAFTA, Annecy International Animated Film Festival and Academy Awards. The films were immensely successful at these festivals, garnered rave reviews and gained a devoted audience. They have often been described as 'poetic', 'surrealistic', 'unique' and 'quirky' by critics. Nevertheless, what makes Chomet's films so unique? And why are they considered particularly essential for the study of contemporary animation?

Although Chomet's animation films have a recognized artistic value, the relevant literature is limited to an excellent quality but modest number of academic articles, including Richard Neupert's 'The Triplets of Belleville' (2005:38–42), Daniel Goldmark's *Drawn to Sound: Sonic Nostalgia and Les Triplettes de Belleville* (2010:141–56) and Pierre Floquet's 'What Is (Not) so French in Les Triplettes de Belleville' (2006:8–13). This book seeks to provide the reader with a systematic study of Chomet's animation films, mainly focusing on his features *The Triplets of Belleville* and *The Illusionist*. We further aim to acknowledge his works' importance for the study of contemporary animation. As demonstrated in the following chapters, the answers to the questions listed above lie in the successful combination of many parameters, some of which include the aesthetics, technique, narrative and themes used. In addition, it is believed that the films must be viewed through the lens of their historical and socio-economic context. Furthermore, special attention has been paid to the production processes, which play a significant role in the final result. Some of the topics covered in the book will be briefly mentioned below.

Chomet's choice to make films that appeal primarily to the adult audience has resulted in his aesthetics, themes and storytelling being significantly different from what we have been accustomed to in most popular animation films, which are usually aimed mainly at the children's audience. Moreover, Chomet has a distinctive style of animation. He states: 'It's a hybrid really because my style is a "French comic book" – the Belgian/French kind of comic books – *Asterix & Obelix* and more adult comic books. And that's my style really – Franco-Belgian with English techniques' (Chomet in Arts University Bournemouth, 2018). Indeed, as presented in the following chapters, the tradition of the French school of comic art, along with an indisputable Anglo-Saxonic influence, is very evident in all his animation works.

First and foremost, the comic book aesthetics, expressed, among other things, that the extensive use of exaggeration in his characters' design and animation, is accompanied by the complete absence of the use of anthropomorphism,[1] which is vastly present in Disney-like animation. Although he highly admires early Disney animation films, his work is substantially different. Another fundamental characteristic is his technique, deriving from his background as a comic artist and his early career in London as an animator. Chomet uses mainly 2D animation, with some supporting implementation of 3D technologies, such as in background objects and vehicle animation. Moreover, as Richard Neupert notes in his article 'The Triplets of Belleville', the 3D images were reworked in order to blend in better with the 2D figures and backgrounds, resulting in a seamless synthesis that refuses to follow the industry norms for 3D, which typically impose a hyper-realistic Pixar style devoted to mirroring live-action (Neupert, 2005:42). For Chomet, the technique is crucial, not only in how he expresses himself but, more importantly, in what he expresses. There is, therefore, a strong interconnection between the technique and the meaning defined in his films, which is clearly highlighted in Philippe Moins' notes from his interview with Sylvain Chomet at Animation World Network: 'For Chomet, animation is like a manifesto – technique and message come together' (Moins, 2003).

Another aspect that distinguishes Chomet's films is their narrative and original and powerful storytelling, which are not based primarily on dialogue, but mainly on visual and auditory systems of meaning. In other words, Chomet heavily relies on motion, image, design, sound and music to communicate with his audience and move the narrative forward and not on dialogue. Finally, as discussed in the book, the films are characterized by recurrent themes addressed with great social sensitivity. Although some of the themes are serious and dramatic, Chomet often chooses to present them comically through his distinctive humour.

Apart from their many similarities, the films vary greatly from each other, not only because they are two distinctive texts, but also because they differ in the process of their materialization from the very beginning. For example, while *The Triplets of Belleville* is based upon Chomet's original idea, *The Illusionist* is based upon a script written by Jacques Tati as a script for a live-action film. By analysing both films, their differences and similarities are addressed in order for more accurate results to be reached. In summarizing, Chomet combines all the aforementioned elements in his own unique and very successful way, judging by the result.

The reason, however, that Chomet's films are considered to be important is not limited to his being a virtuoso of the animation form. Chomet, in our opinion, belongs to a small group of artists who create and give the necessary impetus to an 'other' kind of animation, equally different from non-narrative experimental films and mainstream animation. As Chomet states: 'my feeling that animation was either something very commercial with no real value or something very intellectual. I told myself that there was no third way when Nick Park's *Creature Comforts* came on. From that moment on, I knew what I wanted to do ... I wanted to make animation films like Nick Park did' (Moins, 2003). In other words, Chomet decided to make films of unique artistic value which would appeal to a broader audience.

Since no film (or text in general) is produced in a cultural and social vacuum, for this analysis to be complete, the study of the films should be articulated with their social, historical and economic contexts. In other words, the films' analysis is associated with their material production and the socio-economic conditions in which they are produced. Additionally, some information related to the artist is to be discussed, such as instances of his life, previous works and influences, all of which can be traced in his films. Moreover, the conditions that prevail in contemporary animation and the most common ways of funding and production are to be mentioned.

Much of the information concerning his early life, the production process and any data that were not available in the existing literature[2] come from Sylvain

Chomet himself, who kindly replied to all our questions in a discussion that took place in Bayeux, France, from 3 October to 6 October 2019. The conversation is recorded and the audio file is approximately eight hours long. The recording was transcribed and an indicative part can be found in Appendix 1 at the end of this book. Due to the recording size, it was impossible to include it all, and, consequently, I tried to include most elements mentioned in the chapters, with few exceptions. Furthermore, wherever possible, I utilized material from interviews he has given in various media; Appendix 2 contains a non-exhaustive list of Chomet's interviews for further reference.

In order to address all the aforementioned aspects, our theoretical approach is multidisciplinary and it is mainly grounded on animation theory, history and production, film theory, narrative analysis and semiotics. Concerning the films' analysis that is presented in Chapters 4 and 5, our methodology is based on the French semiotic school and, more specifically, on Algirdas Julien Greimas's theory and methodology. Greimas's methodology analyses in parallel the narrative and the meaning of a text. Namely it is a semio-narrative methodology. His *generative trajectory* starts from the surface, the figurative level of a text, where the plot unfolds, and goes down to its thematic, abstract level. Thus, our approach is not limited to the surface level; it also applies to the deep structure of the films. Our meaning analysis is based on the Greimasian concept of *isotopy*. Greimas and Courtes define isotopy as a semantic category in the syntagmatic sequence that aims at the homogeneity of the discourse and the cohesion of reading. In every semiotic system, isotopies are organized under semantic codes that convey meaning, function and the relationship between notions. Isotopies consist of *oppositions* (antitheses) from which meaning is produced, for example *life* vs *death* or *countryside* vs *city*. It should be noted that these oppositions are specific to every text and they do not apply undifferentiated to other texts. That is to say, every text/film has its own isotopies grounded in their own oppositions and thus, they carry their own meaning.

Additionally, as mentioned above, it is of pivotal importance that the connection and interrelation between the films' semiotic systems and their material production be considered. This articulation is possible through social semiotics. More specifically, to study the meaning and ideology in animation films, the movies need to be connected with their production and society (for more on French semiotics and social semiotics, see: Alexandros Ph. Lagopoulos and Karin Boklund-Lagopoulou, *Theory and Methodology of Semiotics: The Tradition of Ferdinand de Saussure*, 2021).

Moreover, it is vital all the elements of a film be considered together, as a whole, as well as the relationships between them, in their synchronicity (e.g. within the context of a scene or a shot) and our analysis not be focused on individual systems of meaning, even if these are the dominant ones in the respective film. For this reason, for every film, we have created a chart of both its colour and sound/music that can simultaneously show the interrelation of these elements, their connection to key narrative acts and indicate the duration of the shots and their transitions (see Figures 3, 8 and 18 and Tables 1.1, 4.1 and 5.1). Each movie is presented in a circular fashion: it starts on the top-most part of the circle (12 o'clock) and continues clockwise. It consists of (a) the external colourful ring, which depicts the colours used in each frame of the film, sorted and ordered by luminance, hue and saturation. Additionally, it provides data about the duration of the scenes and the editing of each film, (b) the inner, smaller black and white ring, which is the waveform of the audio, in order to visualize the 'louder' parts that often include music and the 'quieter', mostly including sound effects and rarely dialogue, parts of the films and (c) the colour palette in the centre made by using a single dominant colour for each frame. The brighter dots are situated closer to the periphery, while the more saturated ones closer to the centre. The hue spreads around the circle in a clockwise manner. By averaging and limiting the colours to one per frame we achieve a better visualization of the stylistic approach followed by the artist, concerning the colour. This is not as accurate as the coloured ring, but if every colour of every frame was used, it would probably cover the entire spectrum and it would not fulfil its purpose. (d) The markers outside the chart, namely the black circles with numbers, denote the corresponding parts of the film in relation to main narrative sequences or acts. Their description can be found in the table following each chart (Tables 1.1, 4.1 and 5.1).

Finally, the term *context*, as it appears, for example, in Chapter 2, is used for both denoting (a) the relationships of the films with other texts or phenomena and (b) their relations with their historical and social context – that is, the circumstance under which they have been produced and screened.

The book is divided into seven chapters and two appendices.

The first chapter, 'The Early Years', focuses on the artist, his studies and early works, and various factors that affected his later career. More specifically, it is relevant to his life, his studies, his works on comics, his collaboration with meaningful partners, along with influences on his works, such as music, Jacques

Tati and comic artists. A sub-chapter is devoted to his first short film, *The Old Lady and the Pigeons* – a superb, highly acclaimed and award-winning film *per se*. It can also be considered as the herald of his first feature film, *The Triplets of Belleville*.

In the second chapter, 'The Films in Their Context', the historical, social and economic frame in which Chomet created the films is discussed. In addition, the dominant ideologies concerning animation and the various practices and policies concerning funding, producing and promoting contemporary animation films are presented.

The third chapter, 'From Concept to Manifestation', follows the long journey the films made, from being just an idea to being shown on screen. It includes details from the conception of the idea to the materialization of the film, such as collaborations, economic data, production practices (such as co-production or/and recruiting a considerable number of freelance animators to work on one film) and, finally, data concerning distribution and screening of the movies.

In Chapter 4, 'The Analysis of *The Triplets of Belleville*', we refer to the various aspects of the film, such as (a) the technique, the aesthetics, the design, the animation, the sound and the cinematography, and (b) the narrative and the storytelling. More specifically, we analyse the film's narrative as far as its structure and plot are concerned. We discuss the characters, the roles that they have to undertake to advance the narrative, and the distinctive way Chomet deploys image and animation, as well as sound and music in a complex system, to tell his story. We focus on (c) the themes and the meaning that the film has brought forth. Namely, we look at the film's surface and deep structure.

Chapter 5, 'The Analysis of *The Illusionist*', follows the same structure as Chapter 4. It addresses the same aspects: (a) the aesthetics, the design, the technique, the animation, the sound and the cinematography, (b) the narrative and the storytelling analysis, that is the analysis of both the structure and the plot, by analysing cinematic, auditory and visual elements of storytelling and, as in the previous chapter, we focus on (c) the themes and the meaning of the film.

In Chapter 6, 'Conclusions', we summarize and discuss the findings from the analysis of both films, taking into account all the data presented in the previous chapters.

Last but not least, in Chapter 7, 'Beyond *The Illusionist*', we briefly refer to Chomet's works after the period that this book covers, in order to highlight both the continuity and the advancement of his art and outline the need for further study of Chomet's existing and upcoming works.

After the bibliography and filmography sections, the book includes two appendices: (a) *In Sylvain Chomet's words*, with an indicative part of the transcribed audio archive, and (b) 'List of Sylvain Chomet Interviews'. The list is not exhaustive and intends to provide additional sources for further study to interested scholars.

This book aims to address many aspects of Chomet's animation works. In addition, the book applies a methodology for animation film analysis grounded in the French Semiotic Tradition. Most importantly, a heavy load of field-specific terminology has been avoided, as much as possible, without resorting to oversimplifications. Where needed, the chapters incorporate a comprehensive theoretical/methodological framework, either in-text or as endnotes. We hope that animation scholars from various specialties, such as history, aesthetics, theory, scriptwriting, and researchers from other domains interested in animation in general and Chomet's works specifically will find it interesting. On a final note, we wish to point out that, despite this being an academic text, we always take into consideration Chomet's animation admirers, given that a book about Sylvain Chomet could not bypass one of his core principles: his respect for his audience.

The early years

Childhood and education

Sylvain Chomet was born in 1963 in Poissy, in the west suburbs of Paris. His father, Raymond, was an engineer working at the local Simca (then Chrysler) car factory, while his mother, Josiane, stayed at home to care for Chomet and his sister Lysiane (Figure 1), who was ten years older than him. When his sister left home, he was still quite young and spent most of his days in the company of his mother, a woman of a very artistic nature. She can be credited as his first inspiration, nurturing his interest in drawing and painting. According to Chomet:

> She was an artist; she was very skilful. She could paint and she could also rebuild a wall. She could do a lot of things. I remember, one day, she took some plaster and some plastic, and she put the plaster on the plastic and it became a kind of a hard surface and she started to paint a fresco – a prehistoric thing. It was beautiful! Absolutely beautiful! And it looked like a cave work.
>
> (Appendix 1)

As a boy, Chomet observed his mother closely and when he was two-and-a-half years old, he drew his first picture. Of course, the infant's drawing was very simple but it was a rather detailed picture of the family's television.

> The first time I had this pencil in my hand, I drew the television we had in the lounge. And on the television was a statue of a character with a big moustache. And I drew that too! I even drew the open door of the television cabinet and all the buttons. It's a very basic drawing, but everything is there.
>
> (Chomet, Appendix 1)

His mother kept the drawing and dated it. Over the years, she continued to date all of his early drawings, which are still preserved in Chomet's archives. Ever since that first drawing of the TV set, Chomet has continued to draw prolifically. From the age of six at primary school, he was drawing during lessons – especially

Figure 1 Young Sylvain Chomet with his parents and his sister. Courtesy of Sylvain Chomet.

in the boring ones – which didn't go unnoticed by the staff. Chomet remembers that his head teacher had the best response: 'He knew I liked to draw, so he asked me to do this big drawing of all the people from the school. I've kept it actually.' (Appendix 1).

Just as Chomet expressed his talent for drawing from infancy, he also demonstrated an early passion for music, which is evident in all his films, where music and sound play a vital and evocative role in the storytelling. Whilst music and sound generally constitute systems of meaning in films, they invariably also complement the dialogue and the visual systems. However, in Chomet's films, natural language is a secondary system replaced by music and sound. In other words, in his films, music and sound are not secondary systems of meaning. On

Figure 2 Young Sylvain draws at his desk. Courtesy of Sylvain Chomet.

the contrary, combined with the visual systems, they constitute a concrete entity far stronger than in other contemporary films that rely more on natural language and dialogue in order to convey their messages.

In 1973, ten-year-old Chomet and his parents left the Paris suburbs for life in the Normandy countryside. His parents bought an old country house; it was a ruin that his mother completely rebuilt. But in time, the new home was filled with bright and pleasing colours and during the summers, Chomet went to an art school in a nearby village where he learned pottery and sculpture. In many ways, their new life in the country was idyllic, as it is described in his interview. Indeed, in later adult life, he returned to France from Canada, bought back his childhood home, which had since been sold, and lived there for a couple of years with his wife, Sally. But living in the countryside proved a lonely experience for young Chomet, who lacked the regular company of playmates. So, he found a way to overcome this by drawing some imaginary friends for himself, who soon became real for him.

> I was kind of a lonely child. There was my mother, who really loved me, but as a child, I was creating my own friends in a way and, for me, that was real … Every time I was drawing something, it came to life! Every time I started a face, I had

to finish it because I didn't want to leave them without a face as I had a feeling that they were real. 'Yeah, they do exist! They do exist! You have to find them, but they exist.'

(Chomet, Appendix 1)

It is possible that his need for friends, his habit of consistently designing characters for himself and his belief in them inspired the future characters that manifested as 'real' and plausible – albeit extraordinary – in his films. In Chapter 3, we see that while Chomet's characters are exaggerated, and their stories often surreal, they still manage to seem 'real', giving the viewer the impression that the character has a life, an 'existence', a past and future outside of the film, providing a welcome suspension of disbelief for the audience. Indeed, the influence of Chomet's early childhood, his family and his life experiences are evident in all his films (see Chapters 4 and 5).

Chomet's mother not only nurtured his artistic skill, she encouraged his early appreciation of comic art, when she began buying him comics magazines like *Pif Gadget*,[1] that he found totally enchanting, leading to his lifelong enthusiasm for comic art. Whilst many mothers all over the world buy comics for their children, for young Sylvain, who was already drawing obsessively and creating his own friends and adventures, the discovery of comics was life-changing. As Chomet describes it:

> It was fantastic! It was basically a little magazine with a lot of comics stories in it. But really great comics! It had Hugo Pratt! It had some really amazing stuff, all kinds of styles. So, I started to get in my head I wanted to be a comic book artist. So, that was it. That's what I wanted to do!

(Appendix 1)

At school, when he was asked to write down what kind of job he wanted to do in the future, a common practice at French schools in that period, young Sylvain answered: a 'dessinateur humoristique' which means a cartoonist, someone who wants to draw something which is funny. Accordingly, he followed the young artist's path, obtaining his baccalauréat in Fine Arts in 1982, and then building a portfolio of work at preparation school. It was there that a supportive and talented art teacher, who taught the life drawing class, gave Chomet the confidence to realize that he really could draw. After performing brilliantly in his admission examinations for Higher Education Art School, Chomet was on track to realize his dream to be a *dessinateur humoristique* – until, quite suddenly, he did a volte-face by applying to fashion design school! His change of heart stemmed from his new enthusiasm for fashion as performance rather than knowing anything about fashion school.

> It was the beginning of Jean Paul Gaultier ... and his shows were like performances with great people of all shapes, and I saw one of them on television, with the music and everything, and I was fascinated by it. I thought: I want to do that! It's amazing! So, I went to this school in Paris, but I soon realised it wasn't my world ... I really liked the fashion design side of it but when I was designing my mannequins with the clothes, mine had Tintin heads on.
>
> (Chomet, Appendix 1)

At fashion school, one of the main activities was sewing and while all his classmates knew how to sew, Chomet had never sewn before and wasn't particularly interested in learning how. Disappointed by the course and realizing that fashion design was not for him, he switched to a course on illustration for advertising. Even though this new course focused on drawing and was better suited to Chomet's talents, he still wasn't happy with this choice, because it wasn't what he really wanted to do. Fortunately, though, one of his illustration teachers was the well-known comic book artist Georges Pichard, who understood Chomet and told him about a new school for comic art that had recently opened in Angoulême. After visiting the comic school, Chomet knew instantly that he wanted to study there. But to apply for the next round of admissions, he had to produce an entire comic book for submission. So, abandoning his advertising course, he devoted all his time to creating a fifty-page comic book. The following semester, he started at the Ecole Supérieure de l'image d'Angouleme, where he found himself part of a community of like-minded students.

The biggest influence for Chomet during this period was the French comic artist and researcher Daniel Goossens. The art of Goossens is a mixture of surrealism and realism. He uses a semi-realistic drawing style to manifest strange characters and stories containing odd twists and a very distinctive sense of humour. His stories have been compared to the absurd sketches of the British comedy group Monty Python (Lambiek, 2016). Concerning Goossens's influence on Chomet, he points out:

> The biggest influence on me and also on other people around me when we were at the school is the French comic book artist Daniel Goossens ... And the way he draws, and his stories and his sense of humour, I think he is a genius. I'd say

his style, when I was reading his comic books, that's what influenced me to go in my realistic caricaturised style. But most of my culture in cinema didn't come from animation at all.

(Chomet, Appendix 1)

It is worth explaining that the French-Belgian comic tradition is quite different from both US comics and Japanese Anime traditions. Bandes Dessinées (BD), the sequential art popularly known in the United States as 'comics' and in Japan as 'manga', have a long history and have made a significant contribution to cultural production and revenue. Moreover, they have been characterized as 'the Ninth Art' (Beylie, 1964; Lacassin, 1971). For more on BD, see Grove (2013). They encompass a vast variety of genres, media and styles, and are not limited to children: there are BD for all ages. As noted earlier, Chomet's style has been influenced by Daniel Goossens, and Chomet especially admires Goossens's slow animation timing. Chomet's other influences include the Ligne Claire (Clear Line) style of work, such as Tintin (Hergé) and Asterix (Uderzo and Goscinny). As its name suggests, Ligne Claire is characterized by the precision of its linework, along with geometrical features slow pacing and realistic character proportions – a trait that Chomet doesn't completely adopt in his exaggerated style. Whilst Chomet's animation design has been influenced by the various artistic styles of BD, ultimately, he has created his own unique style. It is worth noting that his focus on creating animation films for adults aligns with the tradition of French comics. However, it is interesting that this comics tradition didn't apply to French animation for many years.

In terms of early cinematographic influences on Chomet, his family didn't really go to the cinema for entertainment. Although his mother did take him to see some animated films, like Warner Brothers and Disney movies, Chomet's main experience of cinematographic culture as a child was based on late-night French television programming, which at the time was dedicated to screening great directors and films. So, Chomet stayed up, watching films by renowned directors like Jacques Tati, Federico Fellini and Luis Buñuel. It was these directors who made a profound impact on him and shaped his cinematographic culture: 'It was total revolution! I'd never seen anything like that!' he recalls (Appendix 1). Many years later, the cinematic influences of these live-action films – rather than animation films – went on to influence him as a director of animation films, which is discussed more extensively in Chapter 3.

Chomet started watching more animation films and attending animation festivals, such as Annecy, only after going to London and working in animation.

He speaks in interviews of his admiration for early animation such as Fleischer's animation and some early Disney features, particularly the *101 Dalmatians* (Geronimi, Luske and Reitherman, 1961), which he cites as his favourite animation film of all time.

During his studies in Angoulême, Chomet published his first comic book *Le secret des libellules* (The Secret of Dragonflies, 1986), which was also his first transmedia project, long before transmedia storytelling became a mainstream practice. At that time, there was a children's play revolving around a book. That book didn't exist in reality and the publisher asked Chomet to 'invent that book'. Chomet did it and that's how his first book came out. So, apart from a stand-alone book, he also created a unique story that was connected with the play's storyworld.

At the same time, he collaborated with Nicolas de Crécy on the adaptation of Victor Hugo's first novel, *Bug-Jargal* (1826), into a comic book, where he did 30 per cent of the coloured pictures. Chomet collaborated with Nicolas de Crécy on many works, such as on the comics series *Léon la came* (1993–8) in which Chomet wrote the scripts, a work which was highly accredited both by the public and the critics and in the film *The Old Lady and the Pigeons* (Chomet, 1997) to which we will refer more extensively below. He also wrote the scripts for Hubert Chevillard's comic book series *Le Pont dans la vase* (1993–2003).

After finishing the school, Chomet continued to create and publish comic books, and at the same time he started working in a company which was doing layouts for animation series in Angoulême. At that time, there were some animations companies in Angoulême which produced animation TV series. Most of their employees were graduates from the Comic Art school of Angoulême. Chomet was not happy with the quality of the work he had to produce, but he went there, as all the other graduates did, to earn his living. As he describes, his work there was less than satisfactory: 'I was really frustrated and miserable there, because there is nothing more painful for someone who knows how to draw, to have to work on bad drawings. This is absolutely physically difficult. Really challenging! After some quite disappointing events I felt like a lion in a cage!' (Chomet, Appendix 1).

It was during this time that something happened that ultimately steered Chomet onto his path towards animation. He had heard about another studio working on a far more interesting project based on *Rahan*,[2] a comic hero created by Roger Lecureux and Andre Cheret that Chomet had enjoyed as a child, not layouts like the company that Chomet worked for. So, Chomet decided to try his luck and apply for a job there. And, in the manner of one of his own character creations, he grabbed his portfolio, climbed out of his office window (he had his own room on the ground floor, with a window facing the park) and paid a visit to the animation studio. He showed them his drawings and they were impressed by them. But since he had never tried his hand at animation before, he was asked to do an animation test of the main character, along with a dope sheet (a traditional tool in animation for the animator to instruct the camera operator how to shoot the animation). Chomet had never seen a dope sheet before and he didn't have a clue what to do with it. So, whilst he sailed through the test drawings, he put them in the wrong place on the dope sheet. When he handed in his animation test, the studio owner liked the drawings, but burst out laughing at the dope sheet. Then, to make matters worse, he called in his colleagues to take a look at the Chomet's first dope sheet. Poor Chomet couldn't understand what was so funny until somebody explained. In the end, he didn't get that job and feeling rejected and deflated, he ended up quitting his job at the other studio. He had decided to give up on animation altogether, leave France and move to London to become an illustrator. Ironically, it was this rush decision that edged him one step closer towards his exceptional career in animation.

London: 'The best artistic period of my life'

Chomet arrived in London in 1988, in the midst of a boom time for British animation in advertising and cinema. It was the year of the release of *Who Framed Roger Rabbit* (Zemeckis, 1988) and the film's animation director, Richard Williams, brought its animation production to London. *Roger Rabbit* played a pivotal role in the animation renaissance of the 1990s, altering preconceptions by audiences and production companies about the scope of animation. Indeed, 'before Roger, if an animated feature just made its money back, it was considered a success' (Anderson, 2019). Yet *Roger Rabbit* was the highest grossing film of 1988 and also won three Oscars. But when young Sylvain arrived in London, carrying his portfolio, he was oblivious to the fact that he had just landed in a flourishing world of animation. He still imagined he was about to embark on a new career as an illustrator, despite not knowing a soul in the city or having the slightest idea where he was going to sleep, let alone where he would find a job.

He remembers his first night in London vividly:

So, it was the middle of the 1980s when I arrived in London, and I didn't even know where to sleep. I just took the train; I came; I didn't know where to sleep, it was in the evening; actually, I bumped into a French person who said, 'oh, you can stay at the French institute,' which was very cheap, and it was a horrible place, but at least I had a bed and a place to wash, and I slept there.

(Appendix 1)

Then, the next day, he walked randomly into Soho in central London, where most of the animation studios were located. Of course, Chomet didn't know that then; he was waking up to the realization that he had arrived in foreign country, without any useful names or addresses in his quest to find a job. He found himself on a bench in Soho Square, wondering: 'What am I doing here? I'm completely mad!' (Chomet, Appendix 1). Then he stood up, walked down the first street in front of him and started looking at the doors on each building until, finally, he saw a company name that sounded as if it might have something to do with graphics. After ringing the doorbell, he explained he was a French comic artist. The company turned out not to be a graphics business, but it did specialize in lettering, but they were so impressed by his drawings that they tried to help him find work by going through their contact books. Chomet left the building, armed with a few contact addresses and heartened by their generous attitude, which contrasted sharply with his experience back at the animation company in Angoulême.

Nonetheless, it still proved difficult to find any work as an illustrator, so it wasn't long before someone suggested that he should try one of the animation houses. Most of the London animation companies were working on commercials then. And despite Chomet's reluctance to return to an animation studio, he was so desperate to work that he decided to give it another go. Fortunately, this time, he passed the animation test and landed his first job as an in-betweener[3] at Richard Purdum's studio.

I didn't really want to do animation. I started working in animation because I had to earn my living, but I still wanted to do comic books! But then I started to discover the world of animation and meet people like Oscar Grillo and Michaël Dudok de Wit, and I became friends with Dominic Buttimore, who was a young producer then … And we made some beautiful commercials there. Very clever commercials, like the English do so well. They were stylish and very funny.

(Appendix 1)

The atmosphere in London animation studios back then was both creative and cooperative, which suited a creative person like Chomet who wanted to learn. During this time, he met a range of people whose work he admired, such as the animation director Oscar Grillo and he also befriended Dominic Buttimore, a young producer at the time (with whom he later started a collaboration on *Familiar Things*, an animation feature film based on South Korean novelist Hwang Sok-yong's acclaimed book of the same title).

In the nurturing atmosphere of London's animation studios in the 1980s, Chomet was keen to learn as much as he could, as quickly as possible. He realized that to get up to speed and develop his own style, he needed to put in the extra hours at night after his day job. Chomet worked for two years in order to define his personal style in animation. Chapter 3 discusses how he managed to adapt his comic book style to animation whilst preserving the characteristics he takes from the Franco-Belgian comic book tradition. He also began attending industry festivals, like Annecy, where he saw the British animation movie *Creature Comforts* (Park, 1989) before it was on general release. It was after seeing *Creature Comforts* at Annecy festival that Chomet started to realize the importance and the impact that a good animation film has on the audience.

> It was then that I started to realise that I could have my own style. When I saw *Creature Comforts*, I saw the power of a good film, what it can give to people … And, you know, that's the most exciting thing for a director: to be incognito in a theatre and see if people are laughing at the right place, if the thing you've been thinking is actually working.
>
> (Chomet, Appendix 1)

Nick Park is an animator that Chomet greatly admires (Dobson, 2020:58) but, apart from a brief social encounter, Chomet and Park had never properly met until around the time of writing this book. Although the two animators belong to very different animation traditions – Park uses stop motion/claymation technique – Chomet thought that *Creature Comforts* was excellent and was impressed by the impact the film had on the audience at Annecy, that comprises hard-to-please industry people. Since that screening of Park's film in 1989, Chomet has always set great store by sitting in a theatre alongside the audience – whether it's industry or the general public – to observe people's reaction to his films.

In London, Chomet recalls, the animation studios were mostly working on commercials, 'but very beautiful commercials, very clever commercials, like the English can do, beautiful styles, very funny, very well animated, very artistic'

(Appendix 1). And at the centre of all these studios was one name: Richard Williams, the animation director behind *Roger Rabbit*, who Chomet was keen to meet.

> Richard Williams had this big studio and I wanted to go there because for me and everyone else, he was the core of animation. Basically, he was god. His level of animation was fantastic! So, for me, I thought that guy was a god! But I thought I would never meet him because they were still finishing Roger Rabbit. They didn't have much animation left to be done, just in-betweens, and I had a director's job in a studio making commercials, so I didn't have the chance to meet him then.
>
> (Chomet, Appendix 1)

Although their paths didn't cross for another several years, Williams' spirit of creativity and collaboration that prevailed over the animation houses of London in the late 1980s shaped Chomet's own attitudes and ideals about animation and filmmaking, rooted in the pursuit of excellence and cooperation. And his earlier dream to become an illustrator was long forgotten:

> I fell in love with animation, really! And it made me even more mad about the way I was treated in France, because I saw the way people were working in London and their dedication about doing their best job, and the level of excellence that was there. It was very uplifting. And I kept that in my studio and in my films. Obviously, when I would open my own school, I would basically keep this English mentality, that mentality from the eighties.
>
> (Appendix 1)

Another animator credited by Chomet for having an influence on his work is Bill Plympton: 'He is so productive. He has a fantastic style. He was someone who also actually influenced me – his style, with a bit caricature to it. He is a great animator' (Chomet, Appendix 1).

The Old Lady and the Pigeons

The Old Lady and the Pigeons (*La vieille dame et les pigeons*, Chomet, 1997) is the first short film written and directed by Sylvain Chomet. The film has been characterized by scholars as a 'masterpiece' (Hernández, 2019) and it was highly appraised by critics. It won, among many other nominations and awards, the Grand Prix for best short film at the Annecy Festival, the British BAFTA Award and the Canadian Genie Award for Best Animated Short. It was nominated for Best Animated Short at César Awards 1998, and for Best Animated Short Film at the 70th Academy Awards (Oscars).

In terms of storytelling, the influence of Chomet's childhood, his family, his experiences of solitude and his personal observations are evident in all of his films, including his first short animation, *The Old Lady and the Pigeons*.

The idea for the film came to Chomet when he was sitting on a bench in a London park with a colleague, noticing the pigeons around them.

> I was looking at the way pigeons move and I said: 'What … it's complicated!' because the head is not moving at the same time with the legs and it seems to be like a mechanism. So, there are two head movements for each step … So, we said: 'Why don't we do an animated film?'
>
> (Chomet, Appendix 1)

In the end, Chomet went on to develop the idea on his own, writing the story and making a storyboard and designs for the two main characters and pigeons. The story is about a hungry, emaciated Parisian policeman, who sees an old lady feeding cakes to pigeons in the park. He decides to take advantage of the situation and goes to her house, disguised as a pigeon. The old lady welcomes him and feeds him every day for weeks. Every day, he goes up flights of stairs to the woman's apartment and, every time, he passes a maid cleaning the floor. Over the weeks, the policeman grows fatter and fatter and, gradually, it becomes more difficult for him to climb the stairs. In the end, he discovers that the maid is the old lady's pet cat in disguise. Then the old lady tries to kill him with a pair of shears to feed him to her cat. When he tries to remove his fake pigeon head to show her that he's human, it won't come off. In his effort to avoid becoming cat food, he falls off the window, landing among a flock of pigeons. The film closes with the policeman, skinny once again, but now dressed as a human, behaving like a pigeon in a park in front of the Eiffel Tower.

So, that simple observation on a park bench evolved into a wonderfully complex and surreal, internationally acclaimed animation film. Whilst the importance of *The Old Lady and the Pigeons* is undoubtable now, it took Chomet nearly six years to complete, because of funding problems and some narrow ideas about animation he encountered along the way.

His first setback was the discovery that while he could create beautiful animation in the UK, it was 'almost impossible' to have his own film produced. So, just as he had to take a different route when he sought work as an illustrator, he decided that to be able to make an animation film rooted in a French sensibility, he would have to return to France.

In Montpellier, in the south of France, he found work at an animation studio that was making TV series. Although it was hardly interesting work, he stuck with it because he wanted to find a way to produce his film. A highlight of this period was when he was asked to teach animation to students of different ages and backgrounds, which he found rewarding. The aim of the one-year course was to give students a sufficient background in animation for working on the TV series. Chomet, however, wanted to teach them more than that:

> The idea was that these people after a year would be hired to work on the tv series. But I thought to myself I wanted them to do their own little things as well. I taught them animation, I taught them to a standard that was higher than the company required. I managed to make a couple of people do their own films and go to the festivals. I really liked it! That's why I really like to teach. I like to teach to people who are really enthusiastic and I thought it was really nice!
>
> (Chomet, Appendix 1)

Unfortunately, in his second year of teaching, the company told Chomet to stop asking his students to make their own films. As a result, he turned his back on the company that year, 'because I was not happy with that, it was not nice … so, yes, they found a job in tv series but that was not at all what animation is (Chomet, Appendix 1)

In the meantime, he met Didier Brunner (producer at *Les Amateurs*) through his friend Hubert Chevillard. Brunner was looking into potential projects and was interested in Chomet's short film. Over the next two years, they tried to secure some film funding until, finally, they received development money from the French National Centre of Cinematography (*Centre National du Cinéma et de l'Image Animée*). The only setback was that the money covered just four minutes of production while the entire film was about twenty minutes long. So, they agreed to produce just the first four minutes of the film and use this as a pilot to seek more funding to complete the rest of the film. Chomet worked in his apartment with an assistant doing the in-betweens, while Nicolas de Crécy, his fellow graduate from comic school, did the backgrounds. The three of them worked on the first four minutes of the film, which remained the first four minutes of the final film – nothing was changed – and they shot the sequence at Folimage Studios in Valence. Brunner eagerly showed these first four minutes to potential investors in France, but Chomet describes the disappointing response they received:

It was a 'no' from everybody. They all said: 'That's weird' or 'It's a bit sinister'. They didn't think it was for children. They didn't like the colours: 'It's a little bit too dark'. 'It's going to be scary,' they said. But we told them: 'It's for adults!' But then they said: 'Animation is for children!

(Appendix 1)

From the start of his career in animation, Chomet had sought to make animation films that were not constrained to a children's audience. What's more, he wanted his films to be seen by the general public and not just by industry audiences at animation festivals. As Maureen Furniss notes: 'In every type of cultural production, there are dominant forms of expression that tend to define it within the minds of people in the general public, if not specialists in the field' (Furniss, 2008:13). Furniss explains that in the case of animation, it was Walt Disney who defined this 'type of cultural production' from its early days as a genre for children. This narrow idea of the audience for animation had become fixed in the minds of the animation industry and the general public. Also, Chomet's animation was judged to be 'too French' since it was clearly grounded in the tradition of French comics and not in mainstream, popular – and more profitable – US animation. Although French animation has always carried a high intrinsic value – animation, after all, was born in France – at that time, other French animation films were heavily influenced by other countries, such as the United States and Japan. In time, however, that trend did shift (see Chapter 2). But in the face of such resounding rejection for his first short animation film, Chomet left France once again. This time, he decided to move to Canada.

By the time he arrived in Montreal, he had abandoned the idea of making his own films and started working for a commercial studio. Meanwhile, Didier Brunner hadn't given up and he went to England to talk to Colin Rose, Head of Animation at BBC Bristol, about their short film. Rose had set up the BBC's Animation Initiative in 1991 to commission and produce/co-produce high-quality animation for adult and family audiences, with independent animation companies. This initiative led to successful productions, such as *Wallace and Gromit: The Wrong Trousers* (Park, 1993). Brunner believed that Rose's focus on producing animated films for adults as well as children meant that he would appreciate *The Old Lady and the Pigeons* on its own merit. Chomet recounts what happened at that meeting:

[Colin Rose] looked at the first 4 minutes and laughed and said 'that's fantastic! Yes, we are going to help you produce that!' As soon as the BBC got involved, the French TV channels said: 'oh, yes, we will contribute too.' CNC, the French National Centre of Cinematography was ok, because CNC gave us the first money to achieve the film.

(Appendix 1)

Finally, they had the money to finish *The Old Lady and the Pigeons*. What's more, the commercial animation studio in Montreal, where Chomet had been working, agreed to co-produce the film and he opened a studio in Montreal and they co-produced the film. By then, Chomet was no longer the only animator on the film; he also enlisted Gérard T. Goulet, who animated much of the rest of *Pigeons*.

Once work on *The Old Lady and the Pigeons* was completed, it was entered into animation festivals. They sent it to the Ottawa festival, but it wasn't selected. On reflection, Chomet thinks that the rejection might have stemmed from a disagreement between the French-Canadians and the English-Canadians on the panel. But when it happened, he lost all confidence in the film.

> They saw the film; they didn't select it. It was a big shock! I said, that's it. It's a bad film. And this lovely person, Colin Rose, came to Montreal and we screened the film and he saw the film and he said: 'Sylvain, you and me know it's a good film.' I wasn't very sure about that because I hadn't made a film for just the two of us. I wanted everybody to like the film. But I thought at least I did it – I got to the end of it. I tried to live the dream. But it's not happening; it's rubbish. Ok, that's it. The end.
>
> (Appendix 1)

After the film's failure at Ottawa festival, Chomet relocated to Toronto and started working at the new Disney Animation Studio, developing a character for the sequel to *Hercules* (Clements and Musker, 1997). In Toronto, Chomet received a telephone call from Brunner telling him that *The Old Lady and the Pigeons* had been selected for screening at the World Animation Celebration Festival in Los Angeles. Chomet hadn't even known that the film had been submitted. He describes what happened next:

> We won! We won the first prize at World Animation Celebration. So, suddenly, my film – that nobody wanted – got one of the biggest prizes in the US! I couldn't understand it! Then, a couple of days later, I got a call from Colin Rose who said: 'Congratulations, you've been nominated for a BAFTA award.'
>
> (Appendix 1)

Rose suggested that Chomet attend the awards' ceremony in London to represent the film, but he couldn't go because of his job at Disney in Toronto. But before the ceremony, they spoke and Chomet joked to Rose: 'Give my regards to the Queen!' The following day, Chomet received a call from Rose saying: 'Congratulations, the Queen is giving you a BAFTA!'.

From that moment, the film's success was unstoppable. It won, among other awards and nominations, the Genie Award for Best Animated Short Film; the Grand Prix in Hiroshima International Animation Festival; Grand Prix for Best Animated Short Film at Annecy festival; and Cartoon d'Or at Cartoon Forum, Europe. It was also nominated for an Academy Award for Best Animated Short Film, in the US (Oscars) and for Best Short Film (Meilleur court-métrage) at the César Awards, France.

Whilst this book focuses mainly on the analysis of Chomet's two animation feature films, this chapter briefly covers some of the characteristics of *The Old Lady and the Pigeons* that are shared by Chomet's later films. Undoubtedly, each of the films is as distinct as the different creative periods in Chomet's life. His art changes and he offers his audience something different every time. Yet, there is an affinity – a continuity – that is always present in his works. Some of these elements are intrinsic and unique to Chomet's films and will be discussed in detail in later chapters. As mentioned earlier, *The Old Lady and the Pigeons* narrates a story with an abundance of realistic and surreal elements, intertwined in a concrete entity. It discusses serious matters, but the narration is mainly comical.

Chomet's first film bears the mark of his early influences, including the heroes of silent movies and the French film director Jacques Tati, since apart from opening and closing sequences in which American tourists are rambling about their visit to Paris, the film is dialogue-free. The time period of the film is fairly ambiguous: the American tourists appear contemporary, but the policeman's uniform could date from the 1950s or 1960s. The film features a hungry French police officer, and this *hunger* vs *food/feeding* theme suggests a post-war era after the food shortages during the Second World War. The policeman's story is tragicomic, so that while Chomet ensures we empathize with him, we also laugh at his sufferings because they are too exaggerated and unpredictable. Indeed, all the characters are exaggerated at the same time as they are recognizably realistic.

As Pierre Floquet notes, Chomet uses cultural clichés and stereotypes, like the French view of obese American tourists in the opening and closing sequences, parenthesizing the events that occur in Paris. This American caricaturization counters the eccentric and neurotic stereotypes of the French policeman and the old lady. All the characters are ridiculed, whether they are tourists or French citizens. Hence, Chomet's obese Americans are not necessarily illustrative, they are factual components of 'a parodic world' (Floquet, 2006:8).

The personal style of Chomet's comic books has been expressed in the film through beautiful character animation, according to both scholars and film critiques. Maria Lorenzo Hernández notes: '*The Old Lady and the Pigeons* is one of the last hand-drawn animations where the characters are still drawn in pencil and later scanned on cels, where the drawn construction lines are still visible, as can been seen in Disney's *101 Dalmatians*, with which Chomet's work has more than one parallelism' (Hernández, 2019:118).

However, the world of this film is not like Disney's 'plausible impossibility' (Bendazzi, [1994] 2006:65). *The Old Lady and the Pigeons*' characters occupy an '*existing*' world, both familiar and unfamiliar to the audience. It's a world that might exist here and there, somewhere and maybe nowhere at the same time, a liminal space, as this is first defined by anthropologist Victor W. Turner (1967) and then used by numerous scholars to describe an 'in-between' place, a 'doorway' to something else. In other words, it is the world of adventure, of the heroes' trial, a world that exists but is invisible to us until the director allows us to enter it; whilst ensuring that although we empathize with the hero, we can also laugh at his sufferings. At the same time, the film is tragic (since we can relate to the heroes and their sufferings) and comic (as it is too exaggerated and unpredictable), enabling the audience to leave the theatre having lived a unique experience, something that we will discuss further in relation to Chomet's feature films. As well as exaggeration, the film contains disguise but not anthropomorphism. The pigeons remain pigeons and the old lady's cat may be disguised as a maid, but she is still a cat. An important element of the plot is that none of film's characters ever achieve their goal. The police officer stays hungry. The old lady, although she feeds him to fatten him for her cat, cannot feed him to her cat. The cat fails to eat the police officer. The situation remains unchanged for the pigeons as they keep eating carefree in the park. The story is also full of secrets and deceptions. All the characters, except for the pigeons, have a secret and deceives for their own gain. Finally, it unravels when all the secrets are revealed. Chomet's interesting story didn't appear as a surprise. He had acquired extensive experience in script writing and storytelling from his comic book works, some of which are referenced above.

The chart given in Figure 3 illustrates the film's visual and auditory systems, showing various elements of the film (see Chapters 4 and 5 for similar charts

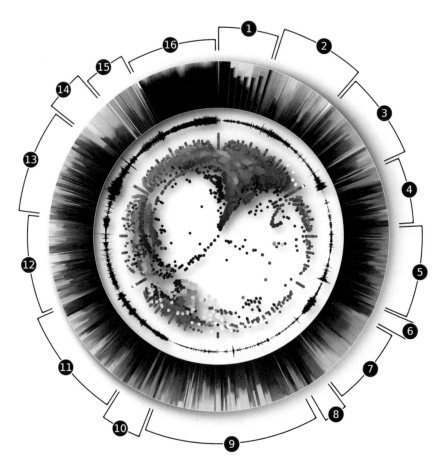

Figure 3 *The Old Lady and the Pigeons* colour and audio chart.

created to analyse *The Triplets of Belleville* and *The Illusionist*). As mentioned in the *Introduction*, in the chart, the colour circle presents all the colours per frame. The second circle represents the volume of sound and music which, in conjunction with the colour circle, provides information about the development of the narrative plot. For example, the volume of sound peaks in scenes related to important narrative acts and also at the end, at the final stage of the plot and the narrative resolution. The colour shades related to each hero and each location are specific (e.g., the park, the old lady's house, the cat's room). The policeman's dream has distinctive hues, differentiating it from reality. Also, the hues seem very carefully selected; the colour palette is limited to certain hues and shades of intensity that unify the whole piece. This harmonious use of colour owes much to his experience of comic books:

I'm coming from comic books, so I've got a sense of illustration … the importance of the light, the dark places, the colours … It's nice to have a harmony of colours for a scene … So, [the scenes] all have a unity of colours.

(Chomet, Appendix 1)

The rhythm of the film and turning points in the narrative can also be understood from colour changes and variations in the level of sound/music that correspond to different scenes (see Table 1.1).

Table 1.1 *The Old Lady and the Pigeons*: the main sequences/narrative actions that correspond to the chart's sections (Figure 3).

1. Titles with polaroid photos. Introduction.	9. He goes to the old lady's house dressed as a pigeon. She feeds him because she thinks he is a pigeon.
2. Establishment of the policeman's situation. The hungry policeman walks on the street of Paris and watches the obese tourists eating.	10. He returns home happy.
3. At the park, he sees an old lady that feeds the pigeons.	11. He goes every day to the old lady's house and she feeds him. He becomes fatter and fatter. This everyday routine 'closes' with the image of the pigeon that had been captured, lying dead on the floor, with cockroaches running away from its dead body.
4. At his house. He eats a simple meal and sleeps under a police-themed poster.	12. It's Christmas and he eats at the old lady's house. He discovers the old lady's secret, which is that she tries to fatten him to feed him to her cat.
5. His dream turns to nightmare.	13. He tries to reveal his true nature, that he is a human, not a pigeon, to no avail. The old lady tries to kill him with a pair of shears. He fights with her in order to save his life.
6. He wakes up, with nothing much to eat for breakfast.	14. He falls from the window and lands among a small flock of pigeons.
7. He stalks the old lady. He catches a pigeon.	15. At a park in front of the Eiffel Tower, the policeman is skinny again. He is dressed like a human, but he is behaving like a pigeon.
8. The policeman is disguised as a pigeon.	16. End titles.

The Old Lady and the Pigeons was produced during the cusp of a new era in animation and was one of the last films to use a slow and labour-intensive traditional animation technique that involved drawing the animation on paper, then photocopying the drawings on the cel (celluloid), and then painting it on the other side, with special paint, so that it stuck to the celluloid. The backgrounds were drawn onto paper and, finally, they shot the frames with a rostrum camera (a special camera for shooting animation; see more in Chapter 3).

Yet, even during production of his first film, Chomet was open to new technology in animation. It was the time when Pixar was moving towards the extensive use of 3D animation. Although *The Old Lady and the Pigeons* predominantly used traditional 2D techniques, Chomet describes the only scene that was created in 3D:

> The only thing in CGI that we did was right at the end of the film, when the fat pigeon goes to the window, and we have a view of the glass falling towards us. [But] because we were actually working on rostrum camera, we had to print it on paper, then print it on celluloid and then paint it on the back, of course. So, there was integration. But it was really cool because at least it was quite effective and it would have taken someone months to do all those little pieces of glass. So, that was the first time I put CGI into one of my films.
>
> (Appendix 1)

After the eventual success of *The Old Lady and the Pigeons*, Didier Brunner went on to produce the hugely successful feature animation *Kirikou and the Sorceress* (Ocelot, 1998), and he asked Chomet to work on two more films featuring the character of the old lady, which led to Chomet's first feature-length animation, *The Triplets of Belleville*.

The films in their context

Sylvain Chomet's *The Old Lady and the Pigeons* (1997) and his first feature film *The Triplets of Belleville* (2003) were created on the eve of what is considered the 'revival of European animation' (Neupert, 2011). *The Triplets of Belleville* was the first animation feature of this period aimed primarily at adults. *Kirikou and the Sorceress* (Ocelot, 1998) signified a momentous shift in the history of French animation, leading many scholars to distinguish between a pre- and post-*Kirikou* era. 'Michel Ocelot paved the way for what at first seemed like "a production model" for other French animators, as a small, but unprecedented cadre of animators began to produce feature films in France' (Neupert, 2011:139) and 'Chomet became a strong force in the revival of European animation' (Neupert, 2011:142).

One of Chomet's greatest achievements is that his films prove that it is possible to make animation that diverges from conventional notions about what constitutes animation and who it is for, thus freeing other animation directors to be more creative, whilst producers too have become more open to a wider range of animation projects. Even so, Chomet and Ocelot still faced problems regarding resources, funding and distribution. Neupert notes: 'Ironically, what would become the lead example of "French" feature-length animation [*Kirikou and the Sorceress*] required financial investments and talent from beyond France's borders. […] In the end, there were eight co-producers and five nations involved in the production' (Neupert, 2011:128–9). Similarly, *The Triplets of Belleville* was a co-production between several countries: France, Belgium, Canada, Latvia, the UK and the United States.

As discussed below, at least in Europe, co-productions are a standard production practice. The issue is that directors like Ocelot and Chomet had to struggle in order to secure the necessary funds to make their films. This raises many questions (and possibly the need for an extended discussion) about the criteria, decisions, prevalent ideologies and institutional practices concerning funding for contemporary European cultural production.

In order to fully understand the significance of Chomet's films, we need to place them within the context of animation history, with particular reference to France's pivotal role in the development of animation technique; the dominant paradigms of animation; the prevailing practices and policies around funding; and production and distribution of contemporary animation films.

Animation: The invention of the technique

Since the early years of animation, France has played an important role. More specifically, many significant animation scholars such as Bendazzi, Wells, Furniss and Neupert extensively analyse the efforts made to develop techniques that would allow the production of animated images, which began in the nineteenth century. It was Peter Mark Roget's study *The persistence of vision with regard to moving objects* (1826) that led to the research and development of a vast amount of early animation devices. Roget claimed that the images we see remain for a fraction of a second in the retina of the eye, before being replaced by the images that follow. So, if the sequence of images is fast enough, the viewer has the impression of movement, even if he is looking at still images. John Ayrton Paris, a famous doctor at the time, created thaumatrope (1828) and the Belgian scientist Joseph Plateau created the phénakisticope (1832). Early animation devices that were invented during that period included, among many others, the Zoetrope (Bradley, 1866), the praxinoscope (Reynaud, 1876), the and the phénakisticope (see Wells, 1998:11–13; Bendazzi, 1994:3–11; Furniss, 2016:13–25).

A very important nineteenth-century French invention was Claude Émile Reynaud's 'praxinoscope'. Although it was originally sold as a children's toy, it was the first step towards the creation of Reynaud's *Theatre Optique* (1889). In fact, Giannalberto Bendazzi credits Reynaud as the true inventor of cinema – six years before the Lumière brothers' Cinématographe (Bendazzi, 1994:6).

However, at the time, the public was quick to turn its back on *pantomimes lumineuses* after seeing the Lumière brothers' screenings in 1895. Alan Cholodenko in his article *The Animation of Cinema* (2008) argues that Reynaud's *pantomimes lumineuses* had a great reception from audiences and since 1900 it is estimated that more than half a million people have seen them. Nevertheless, the invention of the film camera took interest away from animation at a time when there was increasing public demand for a 'real' representation of the world, along with the confusion between the notions of 'realistic', 'true' and 'unmediated' representation.

Animation at the marginalia of cinema

Since the invention of live-action cinema, animation films have been defined by their relationship with and in contrast to live-action cinema. From the beginning of its history, animation was perceived as 'the art of illusion', in contrast to live-action cinema, which was named 'realistic representation'. This misconception between the two art forms goes so deep that animation is often believed to represent fantasy, while live-action cinema is often recognized as a 'truthful' recording of reality. Without addressing philosophical theories about reality and representation, this popular – and false – belief that cinema is a referent of the physical (real) world has led to the notion of animation as 'other'. However, the sign of a tree in a live-action film is not more 'real' and 'true to reality' than in an animation film. The only difference lies in its depiction. Nowadays, due to rapid technological advances in production methods, alongside the mass use of animation and visual effects in live-action movies, cinematic signs are all undoubtedly constructed, mediated and processed, making it even more difficult to uphold the claim that the cinematic sign is the unmediated representation of an object as it is. In fact, both animation and live-action can achieve the same level of reference to nature and society. In the history of cinema, animation and live-action films have evolved into two distinctive forms due to historical and social conditions, thereby developing different languages (Katsaridou, 2019). Furthermore, Bendazzi (2004:1) interestingly notes that between 1895 and 1910, the term 'animated' referred to what is now called 'live-action'. He concludes: 'Animation is everything that people have called animation in different historical periods' (Bendazzi, 2004:1–7). So, techniques that were once considered animation were, later, in different historical periods considered live-action.

What's more, many animation scholars argue that live-action is just a form of animation. Alexandre Alexeïeff notes: 'It is legitimate to consider cinema as a particular kind of animation, a sort of cheap, industrial substitute ... which was destined to replace the creative work of an artist, such as Emile Reynaud, with photography of human models "in movement"' (Alexeïeff, 1994: xix and xx in

Bendazzi, 1994). Lev Manovich writes: 'Born from animation, cinema pushed animation to its periphery, only in the end to become one particular case of animation' (Manovich, 2001:302). Alan Cholodenko also notes: 'Film per se is a form of animation' (Cholodenko, 2008:35).

Indeed, Chomet's film practice appears to share this view of the interconnectedness of animation and live-action, and the transferability of one form to the other when one cinematic form is limiting. For Chomet, it doesn't matter if a story is told through live-action or animation. They are both a means to create a fictional world and he chooses the most appropriate form to suit the story he wants to tell. He also breaks the borders between the cinematic forms by applying live-action cameras in his animation films. He states that it is essential for him to choose the best cinematic form for the story he wants to narrate; some are told better with live-action, while others with animation. Additionally, we believe that issues of production time, availability of an experienced human workforce and available funding might have an impact on any director's choice.

Moreover, Chomet's animation manages to tell a story and communicate ideas with strong references to our reality. His creation of the changing skies of Edinburgh in *The Illusionist* is an excellent example. According to Chomet, everybody who lives in Edinburgh and anybody who knows the city recognizes his reference to the city's ever-changing sky, despite it being an animated drawing.

Nevertheless, since the early years, animation suffered greatly from live-action 'reality' related bias that resulted in its devaluation and marginalization as a cinematic form, perceived as appropriate only for children. Moreover, many animators also felt that they had to emphasize that their art was different from live-action. As a result, animation directors, Chomet included, who also made live-action films, were met with scepticism.

Animation as art – the role of France

After the development of early animation devices, with their focus on technique and movement of images, attention turned to the narrative arc and the artistic creation of early animated films. French animator Émile Cohl created the film *Fantasmagorie* (1908), the first animation film according to many scholars, such as Wells, Neupert, C. W. Ceram, Pierre Courtet-Cohl and Bernard Génin.

Despite all the innovations in the early years of US cinema that eventually led to the emergence of the 'cartoon', it is *Fantasmagorie* (1908), by Emil Cohl (1857–1938), with its surreal stick-figure animation, that should be understood as the first two-dimensional cartoon. Its bizarre narrative shows off the possibilities of the newform and signals 'metamorphosis' as the core language of animated stories.

(Wells, 2007:85 in Neupert, 2011:22)

Émile Cohl went on to create over 300 films, becoming a leading light among both French and international animators (see more on Cohl in Neupert, 2011:22–59). By 1919, France already had its own animation studio: Lortac in Montrouge (see more about Lortac and other animators that followed Cohl's tradition like O'Galop, in Neupert, 2011), the first animation studio in Europe. Later, Paul Grimault and Andre Sarrut formed a small production company, Les Gémeaux, in 1936. Grimault is considered one of the greatest French animators and, according to Grimault specialist Jean-Pierre Pagliano: 'His ultimate goal in the 1930s was to make shorts to compete with Hollywood imports, especially Betty Boop … These beginnings bear witness to a strong ambition: to compete with American productions by following original inspirations and within the constraints of his own country' (Pagliano, 1996:10 cited in Neupert, 2011:100). Grimault's first attempt *M. Pipe fait de la peinture* (*Mr. Pipe Does His Painting*, 1937) was unfinished. Neupert writes about this short film: 'Grimault's characters struggle to escape repression, often through creativity, but they never really manage to improve the world around them. There are no Disney endings with a celebration of a new social order. However, the business conditions were also far from Disney's situation, and *Mr. Pipe* was apparently never fully completed or commercially exhibited' (Neupert, 2011:101). Neupert also refers to comments by Henri Langlois, a Cinémathèque[1] founder: 'France would have really benefited from the renewal of animated film. Several valuable French attempts were made during the 1930s to restart animation … But alas, a national plan for animation would have been needed to overcome all the commercial contingencies' (Neupert, 2011:101). So, despite their best efforts, Paul Grimault and his Gemeaux confronted stubborn, real-world obstacles (Langlois, 1986:294 cited in Neupert, 2011:101). Paul Grimault did finish many other films, including the animation feature *The King and the Mockingbird (Le Roi et l'Oiseau*, 1980) in collaboration with the French poet, Jacques Prévert. Grimault and Prévert had previously collaborated in one of Grimault's most successful shorts, *The Little Soldier* (*Le petit soldat*, 1947). The production of *The King and the Mockingbird* started in 1948, but the procurer suddenly stopped its production and the film was released unfinished in 1952, without the approval of its creators. Later, Grimault obtained the rights to the film and made another version in line with their original concept. While it had taken Grimault over thirty years, since production began in 1948 to its release in 1980, the film is considered a masterpiece by critics.

France has a long history of important animators and cartoonists, such as Albert Dubout (to whom Chomet pays a tribute in the opening of *The Triplets of Belleville*), René Laloux, Lortac, O'Galop, Ladislas Starewich, Jean Painleve, Paul Grimault, Michel Ocelot and, of course, Sylvain Chomet, just to name a few. Even so, French animation production gradually focused on TV series and, at one point, even tried to imitate the Disney animation style and production model.

Clearly, France has a rich history in animation going back to the early nineteenth century. But the French contribution to animation is not limited to production; it also extends to the development of major institutions, such as the Association Internationale du Film d'Animation (ASIFA) in 1960, and the academic study of animation. The first serious attempt at the historiography of the genre was made in France by Giuseppe Maria Lo Duca, in his study *Le dessin animée* (1948), with a foreword by Walt Disney. The Annecy Festival in southeast France, established in 1960, is one of the most important festivals for the genre. Considering all the contributions mentioned above, it is clear that France plays a vital role in the development of both European and global animation.

Animation as industry

At a time when France, along with most of Europe, was focused on auteur, art films and experimenting with various techniques closely related to fine arts – whilst also struggling with funding – the United States, in contrast, focused on animation production from the mid-1920s, with the aim of mass and cheap production, which essentially led to 'the birth of the animation industry'.

A leading figure in the United States' animation industry was John Randolph Bray, founder of Bray studios in 1913, who is considered the founder of American animation. Bray was not interested in the aesthetic of animation; he simply saw it as a lucrative business. Not surprisingly, Donald Crafton describes him as the 'Henry Ford of animation' (Crafton, 1993:137), whose aim from day one in the business was to rationalize production, cut back on costs and accelerate production times. This inevitably led to the production of films of lesser aesthetic value at Bray Studios.

Around the same time, a discovery was made that would define animation production for a century. In December 1914, the American animator Earl Hurd patented a technique called *cel animation*, in which characters are painted onto transparent sheets that are then placed over painted backgrounds. By reusing the backgrounds, it was possible to reduce production time and costs. Surprisingly, however, this method was not instantly popular because animators preferred to paint on paper (Maltin Leonard, 1987:9). It was only when Disney adopted cel animation, it became the industry's standard production method. Cel animation improved the quality of the films and minimized the production costs.

As Bray Studios became successful, other production companies started to emerge. These include Fleischer group, Pat Sullivan's group, Terry Aesop's Fables Studio and, of course, Disney, that changed the course of animation. The market expanded, industry revenues increased and new jobs were created, which to a large extent were filled by the large reserve of immigrant European artists. The First World War had a catastrophic effect on the production of animated films in Europe, and many animation artists emigrated to the United States. Soon, Europe had become dependent on importing American animation films, often made by European émigré artists. For example, in 1913, France imported the first animation series in the world, *The Newlyweds*, produced by Éclair, from the United States. The series was based on George McManus's popular newspaper comic, created by the French founding father of animation Émile Cohl (Crafton, 1993:81) who, meanwhile, had also emigrated to the United States.

Disney's diachronic influence on animation

There is an extensive bibliography on Disney, in which his methods are sometimes praised and sometimes criticized. And there is no doubt that Disney defined the genre for over a century. He succeeded in bringing the public back to animation, though this came at the high price of defining animation as a genre aimed exclusively at children (for more on Disney, see Pallant, 2010, 2011).

Disney was a pioneer of technological innovation in animation. Whilst there are too many technological innovations adopted by Disney to list here, he was an early adopter of cel animation, which resulted in lower costs, faster production time and improved quality. As Disney became internationally successful, all US companies were forced to follow the same technique or risk extinction. He was the first to use Technicolor, the three-colour system in his film *Flowers and Trees* (Silly Symphony, 1932), which won an Oscar. It is also worthwhile to mention the Walt Disney Studios' discovery of the multiplane camera that brought a sense of 3D to the films. It was Disney who introduced pose-to-pose animation, in which the key animator draws the key movement poses of characters, and the assistants do the 'in-between' drawings. The visual result

> is the style most emblematic of Disney, symbolizing a measured, industrialized approach to animation that is in direct opposition, both practically and ideologically, to the spontaneous straight-ahead style …
>
> (Pallant, 2011:18)

Moreover, Disney imposed a homogeneous design language for all his animators and a design code for the characters, most of which were cute and child-friendly. He also formulated his twelve principles of animation, a specific way of animating, described in *The Illusion of Life: Disney Animation* (Johnston Ollie and Frank Thomas, 1981).[2] Whilst Chomet admires many Disney animation features, such as *The Jungle Book* (Reitherman, 1967) and the *101 Dalmatians* (Geronimi, Luske and Reitherman, 1961) which, as mentioned before, is his favourite animation film, he disagrees with Walt Disney's unified code of animation:

> Animation is an art that is the process of changing. You often find the solution by accident. I believe that the 12 principles of animation thought up by Walt Disney in the '40s have paralysed animation. For me, it's more about showing that animated characters can also be excellent actors.
>
> (Chomet in Caruso, 2003)

As mentioned before, Chomet doesn't draw the type of 'cute' and 'round' characters imposed on animation style by Disney. His unique style comes from the French comic tradition and he has never dressed his characters up according to a 'universally' accepted code of animation. This, arguably, was one of the hurdles for Chomet in the early days of his career.

Disney's early dominion of the world of animation, followed by Pixar at the turn of the twenty-first century, is undeniable, so the studio quickly emerged as the dominant animation paradigm and for years, it controlled the dominant ideology in animation (see Dorfman and Mattelart, 1975, and Artz, 2003). Eric Smoodin notes that Disney had its corporate finger in more socio-cultural pies than perhaps any other twentieth-century producer of mass entertainment (Smoodin, 1994:2). Disney's dominance is discussed by

Maureen Furniss, who asserts: 'It is safe to say that in no other medium has a single company's practices been able to dominate aesthetic norms to the extent that Disney's has' (2008:107). In other words, 'Disney's orthodox animation is the predominant language of animation' (Wells, 2002:4). Disney's diachronic success has meant that all other animation producers are defined in relation to the Disney model, whether they are trying to imitate it or challenge it. The Disneyfication of animation, with the production of so-called 'popular animation', was responsible for diluting artistic originality, resulting in a tendency towards homogenization and the 'death' of the creator-artist. Disney also popularized the belief that animation was a genre for children, whilst creating a distinction between US industrialized production funded by private companies, and European animation, which relied mainly on state funding. European animators have continued to rely on state funding, sometimes as part of co-production with other European countries and also with states such as Canada, as with Chomet's *The Triplets of Belleville*.

After securing productivity, the animation industry aimed to maximize its profits through global distribution. Maureen Furniss explains that a common practice of production companies aiming to sell to the global market is to hide issues of gender, race, religion or any other sensitive matters like disability and sexuality behind the curtain of anthropomorphism (Furniss, 2008:238–239). In order to avoid upsetting audiences or receiving any threats of legal action, big production companies prefer making animation films that are sanitized and squeaky clean. Disney used anthropomorphism extensively to appease audiences, but sometimes that wasn't enough. The mass consumption of Disney films, along with its global distribution and worldwide success, made the studio apply further restrictions on its films so that they reflected the aesthetic, dominant ideologies and moral prejudices of their audiences and never challenged them. As Terry Ramsaye points out:

> Mickey Mouse, the artistic offspring of Walt Disney, has fallen foul of censors in a big way, largely because of his amazing success. Papas and mamas, especially mamas, have spoken vigorously to censor boards and elsewhere about what a devilish, naughty little mouse Mickey turned out to be. Now, we find that Mickey is not to drink, smoke, or tease the stock in the barnyard. Mickey has been spanked. It is the old, old story. If nobody knows you, you can do anything, and if everybody knows you, you cannot do anything except what everyone approves, which is very little of anything.
>
> (Ramsaye in the MOTION PICTURE HERALD of
> February 28, 1931, in Animator)[3]

The use of anthropomorphism continues today, though with some changes, for companies such as Pixar. But just as Chomet does not adhere to many of the tropes of popular animation, he does not use anthropomorphism. Instead, his characters are beautifully exaggerated though not in the classical sense of beauty. Despite Chomet's appreciation for Disney and Tex Avery, his own animation challenges the dominant ideology that, for decades, has hung over and hindered animation: that it is a genre only appropriate for children.

The role of Japan – Anime

Japanese animation began in 1917 and, during the 1920s, the majority of films were dramatized folk tales. As Japanese society changed, this was reflected in the themes and characters of animation in the 1930s that started to imitate the Western tropes of fast pace and humour. Toei Animation Company was set up in 1948 and its film *The Tale of the White Serpent* (Okabe, Yabushita, 1958) is considered to be the first anime feature film. The most important artist of that era, Osamu Tezuka, who illustrated some of the most famous manga comic books, set up Japan's first TV animation production company, Mushi Productions. His first series, *Astro Boy* (1963–6), was a huge success and led to the creation of three further Japanese production companies.

Anime uses the limited animation[4] technique both as an aesthetic choice and to keep down production costs. Roland Kelts points out that apart from the homogeneous designing code, anime has a wide and non-homogeneous theme pool. Some common characteristics that can be detected in all of its sub-genres are the focus on people's loneliness, and the hostility of the environment where people live (Kelts, 2006:29). The heroes and the anime characters have little in common with traditional Disney animation heroes. Instead of cute little animals, the world of anime is often inhabited by strange creatures, robots and monsters. Fictionalized human characters express emotions and desires unknown to any of the characters featured in popular Western animation films. Some anime includes violence and even sex – a subject Walt Disney dreaded, and made sure it never appeared in his studio's films. Another major difference between anime and Western animation is that anime films are free from the concept of a 'happy ending'.

Anime series became popular in the US and European TV markets and, gradually, anime films started to be produced and they too became globally successful. During the 1970s, these were usually cheap productions mainly made for television. Then, after 1980, anime's popularity rocketed: 60 per cent of the world's animation production in 2008 was anime. As a result, France imposed restrictions on the number of anime films allowed on TV to protect its own home-grown animation industry (Brown, 2008:6). The success of Japanese animation on TV led to a flurry of feature films, such as *Akira* (Otomo, 1988), an international success, and *Spirited Away* (Miyazaki, 2001), which was the first anime film to win an Oscar for Best Animated Film.

Even though Chomet uses different techniques to anime, he is a great admirer of Hayao Miyazaki:

> His stage and path are quite slow, and I like that because it makes a change from these very eccentric and very American things that are speedy. So, he's got great visuals, great writing. The acting is beautiful and he has these beautiful endings as well. They are not happy endings, like in American movies – sometimes they are really sad. There is a poetry to it [Miyazaki's art] and it is very special. I hope, in a way, I'm also poetical in my way of making films.
>
> (Appendix 1)

While both mass-market and auteur productions co-exist under the anime umbrella, Japanese animation challenged the perception of what was considered appropriate for children and also aimed its films at teenagers and adults. According to Susan J. Napier, 'Anime films practically contain everything that the western audience is used to watching in live-action films: romance, comedy, tragedy, adventure, and they might be different from one another in the same way American live-action films are different from one another as far as themes are concerned' (2005:24–5).

Contemporary era – a paradigm shift?

The end of the twentieth century marked a change in the aesthetics and, to a lesser extent, the themes of popular animation films. This change coincided with (a) the radical technological advances in the techniques and methods of production; (b) the globalization, which outsourced production, and the creation of small, interconnected animation units, and (c) technological advances in communication and the use of the internet among production companies and film audiences. At the time that Chomet started to make his films, 3D animation was beginning to replace cel animation as a more popular technique. Pixar became the leading animation company, based on its technological excellence and software development. It had started as a technology company, making computers and its clients included government organizations and some medical companies. Later, it expanded into original software production, which it continued to do, enshrining one of Pixar's traits: technological originality. So, every time a Pixar film is created, new software and coding is produced. Pixar's short film *Tin Toy* (John Lasseter, 1988) was the first film to be created exclusively by computer that won an Oscar. Then, in 1995, Lasseter's *Toy Story* was the first feature film fully created with computers. This event symbolized a change in the paradigm of animation production and denotes the start of the contemporary era of animation. On the eve of the twenty-first century, cel animation had already been replaced by computer animation, at least in terms of industrialized production. However, great animation films are still produced using other techniques and some – including the films of Sylvain Chomet – have been box-office hits and highly acclaimed by critics. Yet Chomet quickly understood the potential of new animation technology. He has embraced it in his films to facilitate his work in 2D animation and sometimes reduce production costs.

In 1997, Pixar teamed up with Disney to distribute its films, but this collaboration wasn't always smooth. Pixar maintained control of the creative department and animation production whilst Disney managed promotion and distribution of the films. The expenses and profits from Pixar's film were equally split, but Disney charged an extra fee of 10–15 per cent for distribution. Moreover, all story rights and sequels belonged to Disney. This arrangement, especially concerning rights' ownership, was unsatisfactory for Pixar. So, in 2004 the two companies had a temporary divorce. Finally, after long negotiations, Disney bought Pixar in 2006. There were terms and conditions in the final agreement that ensured that the purchase did not mean a takeover and that Pixar remained independent. Furthermore, Pixar controlled all decisions regarding the choice and production of films. Additionally, some terms and conditions also made provisions for staff employees. When Disney bought Pixar, it was the most profitable company in animation. So, buying it guaranteed Disney high profits and secured its position on the top of animation industry. Pixar, meanwhile, gained access to a vast distribution system, Disney's film promotion network and franchise opportunities at Disney's theme parks. (For the history of the takeover and the relationship between Disney and Pixar, see Orwall, 2004; Marr, 2006; Catmull, 2008; Alcacer, Collis and Furey, 2009; Pallant, 2011;

Fiascone, 2014.) Whilst Pixar retained autonomy over its artistic production, the merger of the two companies re-established Disney at the top of the industry. 'Disney owned motion picture studios, television networks, radio stations, cable channels, publishers, retail stores, toy makers, resorts, and theme parks all over the world. The big fish keep eating little fish, a practice that continues up the economic food chain in an ever-widening ocean' (Costanzo, 2014:4–5).

So, although contemporary animation might appear to be different since the merger, Disney in reality has continued to have a significant influence on mainstream animation. As Wells notes, adopting the term coined by Shilo T. McClean (2007):

> In the modern era, there is a 'new traditionalism', in which the dominant 3D aesthetics – created in the studios of Pixar, Dreamworks Animation, Sony Pictures Imageworks and other big Hollywood studios – has effectively replaced the 'classic' 2D animation of Disney's studios. The aesthetics, as well as the narration and the themes of these films constitute a 'new traditionalism'. Based on the American tradition of animation, the 3D films created by computer have become the 'new classicism', which other films imitate, reject or criticise, in the same way that animation reacted to Disney's dominance for many years all around the world, a reaction to the style as well as to the company itself.
>
> (2008:23)

However, Shilo T. McClean points out that this 'new traditionalism' is actually based on the tradition of American animation, and more specifically Disney's.

> 'McLean's term reflects the fact that Pixar, while innovating technically, has essentially embraced the well-established "rites-of-passage/emotional journey" storytelling techniques of the Disney studio and the comedic verve of classic Warner Bros cartoons in a contemporary, but essentially traditional, model. Critical mass has now been reached in the computer-generated feature and the "wow" factor of merely engaging with the fact that a film has been made using computer technologies has passed'
>
> (Wells, 2008:30).

According to these academics, there is a historical continuum: the new paradigm does not clash with the previous one; it is based upon it. Although they do not clash, there are still some important changes. For example, while Pixar continues to aim primarily at young audiences, it has begun to address adult thematologies as well, like loss and death in *Up* (Docter and Peterson, 2009) and loneliness, ecological destruction and romantic love in *WALL·E* (Stanton, 2008).

During the same period, the European Union took decisions and steps towards creating a sustainable European animation industry, based upon auteur animation, which is the dominant European model concerning film production and European culture. The EU's decision to create and promote a European cinema industry that funded and promoted national production through initiatives, such as the MEDIA Programme, enabled the renaissance in French and, more generally, in European filmmaking during the late twentieth century. There was a focus on co-productions and films with international appeal. European funding and changes in production processes, new film promotion and distribution networks, and training opportunities also gave birth to new companies that could compete or collaborate with existing established ones. Additionally, many European states offered tax relief schemes, making them appealing locations for producers.

Reflecting on funding and development opportunities for European animation during the period, Yoon and Malecki write:

> 'The transnational character of animation in Europe is promoted by the Council of Europe's Eurimages programme, which supports co-production of animated feature films, and by CARTOON, funded by the MEDIA Programme of the European Union. CARTOON, the European Association of Animation Film, sponsors gatherings where artisans meet for collaboration, knowledge-sharing, and training, including Cartoon Forum, a co-production forum for European animation TV series; Cartoon Movie, a co-production forum for feature-length animation mainly for the cinema, and Cartoon Masters, four training seminars per year, dealing with specialised subjects. These venues and animated film festivals in Annecy and Stuttgart serve as "temporary clusters" for the dispersed network of animators throughout Europe; such gatherings substitute to some extent for agglomeration economies found in Hollywood'.
>
> (Cole, 2008 in Yoon and Malecki, 2009)

According to Masters, it was not only smaller independents that reaped the benefits of state-funded professional gatherings for knowledge-sharing activities. 'The media giants have taken advantage of the innovative animations being produced in Europe, doubtless enjoying as well the subsidies for co-production' (Masters, 2005 in Yoon and Malecki, 2009).

Even so, animation directors like Ocelot and Chomet have had to overcome many exhaustive obstacles in order to produce their films. Producers such as Didier Brunner (producer of *Kirikou and the Sorceress*, *The Old Lady and the Pigeons* and *The Triplets of Belleville*), who welcomed the renaissance in French animation, have also had to endure time-consuming bureaucracy to secure film funding. However, state funding and co-production schemes with other countries have been lifelines to independent animators wanting to produce alternatives to Disney's model of commodified animation. Maureen Furniss observes:

> The styles and content of animation are diversifying as animators in varied contexts find ways of overcoming the hurdles that challenge production and exhibition. More than ever, animation is being embraced as a means of expressing a wide range of social and political perspectives, reflecting the lives, interests and resources of people worldwide. Governmental and cultural organisations have aided this development by providing seed money and institutional support that allow relatively independent creators and small studios to create such works.
>
> (2017:423)

As a result of the global rise in animation production, the practice of outsourcing production to a wider range of countries has benefitted the animation industry, which, historically, was produced at great expense in studios in big cities that had all the funds, the infrastructure and skilled workforce (regarding the culture industries, see Schoales, 2006; regarding technological changes and challenges in animation production, see Yoon, 2009). However, late-twentieth-century trends in computer-generated animation, new technology and advances in communications have made it possible for parts of films to be produced by different companies and countries; some secondary production stages are outsourced to remote, less-expensive companies, in areas such as India or Mexico. This dispersal of production has been welcomed by the foreign countries involved since the films also became products of their respective economies, creating jobs, bringing technical skills in animation and generating profits. Outsourcing production in this way is widely accepted as the most viable and time-efficient form of production method to date. During the interview, Chomet has commented on production difficulties in the past, like having to use regular mail to send drawings and how internet and communication advances made the production process more manageable.

Inevitably, the internet has had a significant impact on the global consumption of films. Larger audiences around the world can now review and critique films; compare them with other films; create groups dedicated to films and, to some extent, participate in the promotion of the film. Word-of-mouth promotion is hardly new but, in the past, it was mostly local or regional. The internet and social media have transformed the role of the viewer. There is greater scope for consumers to be more actively involved in promoting or discrediting films, thereby influencing future productions (Katsaridou, 2019:318). Today, audiences have even greater influence, since they can, for example, form international fan groups, start and contribute to discussion forums, or share their opinions on social media.

Advances in technology have also provided independent artists and smaller production companies with alternative routes to funding and screening films, when previously they might have had little or no access to a wider audience. For example, online film screenings and fundraising for production costs through crowdfunding have enabled independent artists to create films and find audiences for them. As a result, some films that are aesthetically and ideologically different from mainstream ones are becoming increasingly accessible to audiences. However, these options are far from adequate and it is still a struggle for independent animators to try to compete in an industry in which the majority of animation is still aimed at children.[5] Chomet explains:

> I wanted to do things in animation that hadn't been done before. It's a very rigid medium in what people think it should be. It's always got to be for kids. It should bring good feelings, have bad guys and good guys, and end with a moral. But this means there are lots of subjects and things you can't show, like someone smoking a cigarette. With Belleville, the aim was to go against that, and do something that wasn't aimed at kids. It's great that kids can enjoy the film, but it freed us up to go in directions that the animated movie hasn't gone in before.
>
> (in Bullock, 2003)[6]

Chomet still believes that the narrow attitude of the animation industry which has encouraged audiences to have a limited idea of animation has created a closed circuit of continuous reproduction of the same ideology. He refers to a 'fast food' film culture, in which people have learnt to consume tasteless films in the same way that they consume tasteless food. Reflecting on his days at Disney in Montreal, he comments: 'They don't make films anymore – it's as though they make commercials' (Chomet in Curiel, 2003). Chomet's aim is to change people's consumption habits. He always wants to surprise people with his films and serve them something new and unexpected every time.

This, however, requires artistic freedom, which is not always valued or possible in larger studios, even at more creative ones. In contrast, the role of animators and directors in smaller, state-funded or independent productions is paramount, allowing both the expression of the director's *parole* and their non-mainstream themes and ideologies. Yet, of course, the auteur's freedom of expression can also be limited by the lack of funding and difficulties attracting the best skills. Even

Chomet is not immune from this tension. After the success of *The Triplets of Belleville*, he started to receive offers from US studios, but fearing the limitations they might impose on him, he decided to make his next film, *The Illusionist*, through his own Edinburgh-based company, far away from the big companies and their firm grip on animation practices. Unshackled from big studio money, Chomet was free to continue to make animation in 2D, his preferred choice of animation technique, even though he considers 3D as simply another animation technique, and he is a fan of 3D films such as *WALL·E* (Stanton, 2008). As Moins notes: 'For Chomet, animation is like a manifesto – technique and message come together' (2003) and the 2D animation technique best suits the message of his films. Yoon and Malecki, however, point out: 'Theatre audiences prefer CGI.' If big studios believe this, then it becomes a problem for animators who prefer to work in 2D. Yoon and Malecki's view – commonly shared by the industry – is based on a comparison of profits from 2D and 3D animation films made between 1995 and 2006, where the average profit made by CGI films was 230,800,000 US dollars – more than twice the profits made by 2D films (Yoon and Malecki, 2009:249). While the writers provide a credible and clear picture of contemporary animation profits per technique, further discussion is needed to form a conclusion concerning audience preferences. For a more accurate picture of audience preference for 2D versus 3D, profits made by the respective types of films should take into account the number of theatres, the number of screening days and the size of their publicity budgets. For example, the film *WALL·E* was screened in 3,992 theatres during its first week of release, with an average 15,803 US dollars profit per theatre. In contrast, *The Triplets of Belleville* was screened in only six theatres in its first week, averaging a profit of 18,013 US dollars per theatre. According to this method of calculation, *The Triplets* was actually more successful per theatre than *WALL·E*, or to be more precise, it cannot be proven that audiences prefer CGI unless the 2D and 3D films being compared have the same number of screenings, in theatres with similar characteristics, and have the benefit of the same promotional budget. In the United States, as a rule, 50 per cent of a film's budget is spent on promoting it. For example, Pixar's *Monsters Inc* (Docter, 2001) cost 115 million US dollars from which 50 million was spent on marketing and advertising the film (Austin, 2003). *Ratatouille* (Bird, 2007) had a budget of around 180 million US dollars. The cost of publicity equation, however, does not apply to low-budget films like *Mary and Max* (Elliot, 2009) that had a budget of about 6 million US dollars, barely covering its production costs. As a result, lower budget films, such as *Mary and Max* and *The Triplets of Belleville*, gain far less publicity and are much less accessible to audiences. When it is time to distribute a film, the production company deals with a distribution company to determine the number of film copies released, alongside the promotion and screening of the film to potential buyers and theatre representatives. The contracts between production companies and distribution companies can vary. The assumption is: the better the distribution network the production company can access, the more screenings a film will have. And, of course, theatres prefer to screen films with better advertising behind them to attract bigger audiences and profits.

In addition, we should factor in historical changes. Nowadays, the public's enthusiasm for technologically advanced films, which prevailed in the period Yoon and Malecki examine, seems to have begun to subside. So, to suggest that audiences prefer 3D animation is based more on profits deriving from the reproduction of the dominant paradigm, which is largely shaped by audience accessibility to the films, rather than about genuine audience preference. But a superficial reading of the profit margins enjoyed by 3D animation explains the difficulties that auteur directors can experience finding investors.

Despite all the difficulties faced by auteur films – and directors as critically acclaimed as Chomet – their productions and existence are essential not only for the evolution of animation but, above all, for the expression of cultural, political and social diversity. Animation is a cinematic form with a tremendous power to express numerous techniques, aesthetics and ideologies. Within this genre, auteur films and filmmakers like Chomet challenge prevalent perceptions and throw wide the full scope of animation.

From concept to manifestation

Inspiration: The birth of an idea

The most commonly asked question by scriptwriting students concerns inspiration, and it is the most difficult one to answer in any depth. Where do ideas come from? Where is inspiration to be found? Whilst scriptwriting scholars can provide some general advice on the subject, in reality, there is neither a single methodological process nor a universal, one-fit approach. So, any attempt to trace back to the original seed, the first trigger that led to the birth of an idea that later germinated into a film, can be an elusive task though it does also make for an interesting challenge.

Gratifyingly, in Chomet's films discussed in this book, many of the auteur's inspirations are easily identifiable. His films contain key moments and fragments from his own life experiences and his influences that he has transformed into a very different, surreal and poetic artform. Furthermore, through Chomet's lens, it is also possible to view and understand the social context in which the films were created. He himself asserts his desire to be 'in' his films, and he explains that his inspiration comes from his own experience (see Appendix 1; see also *Urban Cinefile*, 2018). This is evident in the characters of *The Triplets of Belleville*, who were inspired by people that Chomet knew in real life. Madame Souza, for example, was based on a Portuguese lady he knew. The character of her grandson, Champion, the kidnapped cyclist, emerged from the artist's encounter with a car mechanic. It is worth remembering that Chomet's father used to work as an engineer in the car industry. Later on, Chomet changed Champion's profession and made him an athlete. The triplets – the three tall singers – were inspired by Chomet's maternal grandmother. Carlos Aguilar notes:

> 'The eponymous triplets were a reflection of his grandmother on his mother's side. She was a colorful character and a strong woman. He never met her, but everyone in his family would tell him anecdotes about her. He grew up

knowing she was a lovely person with a big heart. The essence of the triplets comes from her'

(Aguilar, 2018).

Even Madame Souza's dog, Bruno, is based on a dog he met on the streets of Montpellier in France.

Even when it is possible to trace and combine all these external biographical, social and historical pieces into a film's semiotic system (namely the context and the situation in which the films were created), the reconstruction of the artist's internal creative process leading to their synthesis as a specific whole remains elusive. When Chomet was interviewed for this book about how he creates his films, and where his ideas originate, he responded that he didn't believe that he creates anything new. He believes that he pieces together elements which nobody else has noticed. So, for him it's not a matter of being especially intelligent or gifted, but about having the ability to observe things with sensitivity and to distinguish what is important. He sees himself more like an archaeologist:

> The way I work, it's much like an archaeologist – someone who goes into a desert and tries to find some prehistoric animals that nobody has ever seen before. So, I go there and then you see a little bone just going out of the sand and for everybody it's just another stone. But if you are a good archaeologist, you take a brush and you go around it and you say: 'No, it's a bone actually.' Then you start to find other bones around and then you excavate … And you've got all these bones but they are all not in the right order, and then you start to put them together and then you realise that this is the jaw. When you finish, you've got a beautiful skeleton of a creature. I think that's how I make films. I find little things like that, some little things that people wouldn't take much notice of.

(Chomet, Appendix 1)

The parallel between the way that he makes films and the work of an archaeologist is evident in the fact that many elements of his films derive either from his own experience and memory or from a collective past; a historical era that affected him directly or indirectly. Moreover, the 'little things' that Chomet finds and includes in his work might signify that nothing is just randomly placed in his films; even the little details have significance. Additionally, all his characters are important, with their own story, their own *narrative programme*, whatever the importance of their role in the main narrative of a film. Chomet also implies a belief that all the pieces, even the little ones, have a rightful place within a unique pre-existing structure, and that there is only one way to connect them to reconstruct the 'mythical beast' of any film. This might lead to the hypothesis that for Chomet his films, like his heroes, pre-exist for him and that he 'discovers' and narrates their stories 'as such'. According to Chomet: 'The film wants to exist and it's there, and if it's not in the right shape, it's going to show you it's not the right shape. If you put the wrong bone at the wrong place it's going to be not nice to watch' (Appendix 1). For Chomet, the first piece of the prehistoric creature is arbitrary; he may start to build the whole beast using any piece of it in order to create his final story. A good example of this technique was his observation of the way that pigeons walked, which, as mentioned in Chapter 1, inspired *The Old Lady and the Pigeons*. Another example is the way that two words 'Attila Marcel' went on to become the basis and title for his feature film *Attila Marcel* (2013). Chomet came up with the name during production on *The Triplets*. He started to wonder who a character like Attila Marcel might be and concluded that he might be a brute, a French wrestler. Then he wrote a song called *Attila Marcel* for a scene in *The Triplets*, where Madame Souza vacuums the bedroom, 'singing an Edith Piaf kind of song, about this man called Attila Marcel, who's beating this poor woman' (Appendix 1). After years of developing the story, it finally turned into the film *Attila Marcel*.

The birth of *The Triplets of Belleville*

After the huge success of *The Old Lady and the Pigeons*, producer Didier Brunner asked Chomet to create two more short films featuring the old lady as the protagonist. Brunner wanted a trilogy. Chomet worked on the idea and came up with the concept of the triplets, a story of three identical sisters. Their stories would be different, but the character design would be the same as that of *The Old Lady and the Pigeons*, who would be one of the characters in the trilogy. The triplets were born in Paris in the 1900s and they appear at the beginning of the film in their mother's arms. The first of the trilogy, *The Old Lady and the Pigeons*, took place in Paris; *The Old Lady and the Bicycles* featured a sister who lived in the suburbs with a nephew who loved bicycles; and *The Old Lady and the Frogs* was about one of the triplets living in a remote area in Canada with frogs.

Chomet wrote the three interwoven stories and started on the storyboard for *The Old Lady and the Bicycles*. BBC and Colin Rose were involved in the production, so he went to London to present the storyboard. Rose noted that the existing material was more than enough to make a feature film. Didier Brunner, who was also at the meeting, agreed. At the same time, Brunner had some issues concerning the reuse of the old lady's character with the producer in Canada, so he preferred not to use the same character. Chomet agreed and started to work on the feature, which materialized into *The Triplets of Belleville* (2003) about three, tall ladies, who lived in a vast North American city called Belleville. According to Chomet, he chose a city name that was meaningful to him and imbued with personal memories. In real life, Belleville stands halfway between Montreal, where Chomet lived, and Toronto, where his girlfriend Sally Brown[1] lived. So Chomet was familiar with the 500 kilometres route between the two cities on either side of Belleville. Moreover, Belleville is not just a Canadian city, it is also a suburb of Paris. As Pierre Floquet notes: 'Chomet plays with false clues and pseudo references. Belleville is actually both a working class suburb of Paris, and a Canadian town somewhere between Montréal and Toronto' (Floquet, 2006:12).

The old lady's character continued to exist in some of the scenes, but as a secondary character, not the protagonist. Brunner, however, continued to encounter copyright issues with the Canadian producer regarding the reuse of the old lady's character so, in the end, Chomet was unable to use the character at all. For practical reasons since he had created an entire storyboard with her character, Chomet kept the same dimensions but changed the design of the character. Then he sent his designs to a lawyer in Paris for approval that the character was sufficiently different from the original old lady. However, the design was returned several times because it was still considered too similar. At this point, Chomet became very disheartened.

During that time, Chomet and Sally Brown often went to a Portuguese restaurant that they loved and, one night, Chomet decided that his old lady would be Portuguese and no longer French. So, Madame Souza was born: a petite, old woman, with a strong character and a clubfoot. And she went from being a supporting character in just a few scenes to the film's protagonist. Furthermore, Madame Souza owes her voice to the owner of Chomet's favourite Portuguese restaurant. In a scene where Madame Souza plays the piano as she sings out of tune, it is the real-life restaurant owner who is singing.

Moreover, Madame Souza's Portuguese identity also has two reference points. She is both the Portuguese woman at the restaurant and a nod to the Portuguese, working-class immigrants in Belleville, France, who from the 1950s migrated to France to work typically as builders and cleaners: 'As she is Portuguese, one may easily imagine she works somewhere as a cleaning lady in someone else's home, as many female Portuguese immigrants did and still do in France' (Floquet, 2006:11).

Chomet's characteristic ability to observe and understand diverse cultural behaviours with great empathy means that whilst he is an exponent of French culture, he has also embraced and incorporated other cultures, like English, Scottish and Portuguese into his work. The change of the character's nationality from French to Portuguese called for the development of a different character with a diverse cultural background, attitude and behaviour, resulting in a different design from that of the Old Lady. Once the character of Madame Souza started to manifest, she needed to be 'treated' quite differently. The clubfoot, the unmelodious singing and her other characteristics are unique to her. After designing an image of the character of Madame Souza, Chomet sent it to the lawyer and it was finally approved.

In production

The film is a co-production between France, Belgium, Canada, Latvia and the UK. Most of the animation was produced in a big studio in Canada, with animators from various countries such as Canada, France and Belgium. A great deal of work was done in Belgium, at Walking the Dog, the production company which made the scenes featuring the crowds in Belleville and the overweight people, directed by Benoît Feroumont, for whom Chomet notes, '… did a very good job; it was really a pleasure to work with him' (see Appendix 1).

Over the course of production, film techniques evolved and included aspects of CGI. As mentioned in Chapter 1, Chomet first used CGI in the movie *The Old Lady and the Pigeons* and in only one scene. The incorporation of this scene in the film required a lot of work as they had to integrate the CGI with the hand-drawn animation: 'Because we were actually working on rostrum camera, we had to print it on paper, then print it on celluloid and then paint it on the back, of course. So, there was integration' (for more see Chomet's interview, Appendix 1).

Animation technology was fast evolving. Computers were increasingly advanced and powerful, and CGI software was becoming cheaper and easier to use. Rostrum cameras became obsolete. *Triplets* still used hand-drawn animation on paper that was scanned and then imported on to computers for the colouring process. Working with computer software rather than printing made the incorporation of CGI with hand-drawn images much easier and more effective. As a result, Chomet decided to use CG animation for parts of his films that are difficult or extremely time-consuming to produce, such as scenes with bicycles, cars and the sea. The use of computers released him from some of the technical restraints placed on animators for years:

I think if I had done *The Triplets of Belleville* before that, without these tools, it would have been much smaller. With these, I could have as many levels as I wanted! There is no limitation! In the old technique, when you have the celluloids, you can have a maximum of four layers of celluloid! The celluloid affects the colours. They are not really transparent; they are slightly grey. You have to compensate for the colours and it is madness! Then, we went digital and that was amazingly easy. That was really fantastic!

(see Appendix 1, see also Chomet in Foley)

The film's music was composed by Benoît Charest, with two tunes written by Chomet. Sound and music play a major role in both films under discussion and in animation films in general. As John Halas and Roger Manvell noted in their book *The Technique of Film Animation*, 'The animator is responsible for the vision, the control of the total medium, including sound as well as sight. He must think sound as well as picture. He is only half an animator if his skill is limited to drawing' (1959:81). Chomet's films do not include much dialogue, apart from a few phrases. Instead, music and sound replace the function of natural language systems. In some cases, natural language and dialogue seem like background sounds, deemed insignificant, while other sounds and music come to the foreground, catching the audience's attention and becoming meaningful. As Furniss notes:

> Typically, the sounds deemed most important are made to be the loudest; in most cases, the dialogue is loudest in the hierarchy in order to effectively deliver narrative information, with effects and music recorded at a lower level as supporting elements. However, by changing the hierarchy, perhaps by swelling the music or by including sound effects that are so loud that the dialogue cannot be heard, one can manipulate the listener's perception of what is occurring within a scene.

(2008:83)

Chomet's use of music alongside his film's soundscape demonstrates the early influence of silent movie heroes on Chomet. He chooses to diminish dialogue in order to drive the audience's attention to the animation and the characters: 'I also think that an animation without the constraints of spoken words is stronger. If you have to fit everything to the words, all the gestural movement revolves around the mouth. Without it, you are much freer to create true animation, through animation itself' (Chomet in Moins, 2003). Reviewing *Belleville Rendez-vous*, Foley noted that lack of dialogue might also serve a more practical purpose to 'broaden its appeal to those who might be put off at the thought of having to sit through subtitles' (Foley). Floquet (2006) also argues that limited dialogue allows for an international (universal) element in the filmic discourse, so that the film can be screened and understood without captions or dubbing. In *The Triplets,* there are just a few lines of dialogue at the beginning and end of the film, as well as some radio broadcasts during the *Tour de France* cycling race.

During the making of the film, some important musical elements only appeared by chance. For instance, in one of Chomet's favourite sequences: the sea scene, in which Madame Souza and her dog, Bruno, take a pedalo to follow a ship across the Atlantic to rescue Champion, that is scored by Mozart's C-Minor Mass, was conducted by John Elliot Gardiner. Chomet recalls that Mozart's C-Minor Mass was playing on his headphones while he accidentally looked at a render of the sea sequence. When he looked at it, he realized the music harmonized perfectly with everything in the sequence. Due to budgetary constraints, they tried to use the same piece of music performed by four other orchestras, but none of them fitted with the animation: 'The other pieces were very nice, but I was putting them on and they were not working! It was the same piece! It was amazing! But it was just the one I was listening to that actually worked there.' (Appendix 1). It is worth noting that, usually, in film animation, the music is composed before the animation is produced whilst the opposite usually applies in live-action films.

Another interesting detail in the production of music for *The Triplets* relates to the song for the 'Vacuum Cleaner Cabaret' scene, where the triplets and Madame Souza perform together using household appliances and objects as musical instruments. Chomet, inspired by the group Stomp, suggested that Benoît Charest use a vacuum cleaner, along with other objects like refrigerator grills, which came from Chomet's own fridge, a newspaper and a bicycle wheel to make music.

As Aguilar notes:

The rest of the music was combination between composer Benoît Charest's creations and Chomet's ideas. In order to create the song for the scene known as 'Vacuum Cleaner Cabaret', where the triplets and Madame Souza perform together, the director suggested Chare[s]t used a vacuum cleaner to elicit strange sounds. He played the vacuum's tube as a wind instrument. He would place his hand over the hole to figure out what kind of sounds it would make and he would control the airflow with his fingers. The vacuum cleaner used for the film was eventually named 'Mouf-Mouf' ... Essentially, what the characters on screen are playing is exactly what was employed to construct the track.

(2018)

These natural sounds repurposed and recomposed into music relate both to the film's context (the triplet's household instruments) and to the production practices of the film itself. Moreover, this practice connotes the creativity and collaboration among the film's crew members that reflects on the homologous film's sequence, namely the creativity and cooperation among the singers and Madame Souza. Indeed, although the production company comprised a large staff, the atmosphere was positive, with strong personal relationships between producer, employees and Chomet, which (as described below) turned out to be partially missing from the production of *The Illusionist*.

For Chomet, animation film production should be creative and collaborative, and it's always been the way Chomet seeks to make his films, embracing the values from the 1980s London animation scene. It is testament to this warmth and creative spirit that when Chomet left Canada to do the compositing in Paris, Gérard Goulet, who did the opening sequence on *The Triplets* and had kept all the bits of paper out of the hole puncher used in the animation department, scattered them over him from the building's window as if they were snowflakes. It was a gesture that Chomet appreciated very much (see Appendix 1, for the full story).

His return to France marked a return to his past – not, on this occasion, through the stories and characters in his films, but a real, physical journey to his childhood home, where he moved back in with Sally Brown. While the house had remained unchanged, the local area had become more isolated, which eventually hindered Chomet's contact with the animation world.

The Triplets was officially selected at Cannes. Chomet reflects positively on the experience of screening at the festival:

There was real respect, you know. Suddenly you realise they say thank you for spending all this time in the dark room to do these little characters and it's beautiful, thank you. And I could see people react, I could see people laugh. It was brilliant. It was absolutely fantastic. It's why you do animation as well; it's got something different to comic books. With comic books, you never see people laughing at your work.

(Appendix 1)

The film was released immediately after Cannes with great success. It was nominated and won many important awards (forty-two nominations and twenty-one wins) and was also critically acclaimed, which was significant as the film is aimed primarily at an adult audience. Among others, it was the first PG-13 animated film nominated in the category: Best Animated Feature at the Academy Awards. While it lost the Oscar to *Finding Nemo* (Stanton and Unkrich, 2003), a film aimed at children, the very nomination of *The Triplets of Belleville* signified a shift, albeit a slow one, in the animation industry that was finally starting to perceive animation as worthy of broader audiences.

It took Chomet around five years to produce the eighty-minute-long film, when previously it had taken him ten years, overall, to make his twenty-five-minute short, which was due mainly to the funding issues described in Chapter 1. The budget for *The Triplets of Belleville* was 9.5 million US dollars and it made a revenue of 14,776,760 US dollars, according to Box Office Mojo,[2] which was considerable for a French animation film aimed mainly at adult audiences.

The distribution was very good and the film stayed in cinemas for a very long time. Chomet reflects fondly on the film's distribution company:

> They were fantastic about *The Triplets*! It went well in France because the film stayed a long time in the cinemas. It was really long – for the whole summer. And the people I talked to, the people in the cinema, people who actually screened the film, they said: 'We are so happy to have the *Triplets* during the summer because it was actually one of the only films which was making money.' It lasted for four months! A really long life for a film.
>
> (Appendix 1)

In fact, it was also the highest grossing French film in the United States in 2003.

Meeting Richard Williams

It's worth noting that during this period, Chomet finally met Richard Williams, the person who, as it is mentioned in Chapter 1, has deeply influenced his animation perception. This is an encounter of major significance that led to a long-lasting friendship between the two men. Chomet describes vividly this meeting 'when I actually met God in person!' (Appendix 1). In short, he was invited by Hiroshima animation festival, where they were screening *The Triplets*. He knew that Richard Williams was there, but he was feeling too shy to talk to him. So, Sally Chomet talked with Richard Williams's wife, only to find out that he had seen *The Triplets* and he wanted very much to meet Chomet! They went for dinner in a tiny Japanese restaurant in front of the festival venue, where all the animators had been drawing on the walls. Chomet speaks about him with excitement; he remembers that Williams had an 'amazing energy, he had very blue eyes, you could even see his brain from his eyes'. (Appendix 1) What came as a surprise was that Williams was asking him about the way he made *The Triplets*, about the technique. He had retreated to a place near Vancouver with his wife for ten years and he was just returning to animation. During these ten years, animation production practices evolved more than they did in the last 100 years. Chomet noted that lately he found himself at the same situation, after spending a period in Normandy, in the countryside, far away from animation developments. He asked young animators who were previously working on *The Triplets* and later made their own studio information about the use of tablets for drawing. Chomet and Williams became friends and he later visited Chomet in Scotland, during the making of *The Illusionist*. The last time they met each other was during Chomet's visit at the Aardman studio in Bristol. It was a surprise to find him working there:

> We went into another little building … and we opened the door and it was dark in it. I could see tables with tons of paper on them, and in the corner, there was a little light coming and Richard Williams was there! He was working on his last film basically, a film he was doing on his own. And, you know, talking to him was fantastic! … He was really a passionate person, and he managed to actually transmit his passion to everybody else. To me, he is something of a god in animation!
>
> (see more in Appendix 1)

Still, when he got out of this room, he became a bit sad, realizing that he was not ready to live only for animation, he doesn't want 'to end in one room doing my things … although I really love animation, there is a kind of limit … I am a social guy as well; I don't really like to be just on my own like that … That's why I stopped doing comic books. Because comic books are about being on your own as well.' (Appendix 1). Chomet is a social and collaborative person and he likes to work in a studio, maybe a small studio, as it will be discussed below, but not alone. He cherishes the creative atmosphere and the things that are happening when people work together on a project.

From *The Triplets of Belleville* to *The Illusionist*

During production of *The Triplets*, there was a scene where Chomet wanted the animated characters to watch a live-action film, specifically Tati's *Jour de fête*

(1949). This was hardly a surprise since Tati's film is about bicycles, which are pertinent to *The Triplets*. Chomet is a great admirer of Tati, so he had already incorporated a lot of other elements related to Tati's films. The producer, Didier Brunner, asked Tati's daughter, Sophie Tatischeff, for permission which she happily gave, and she was so pleased with the film that she offered Chomet the rights to a script that her father never made, *The Illusionist*. But Tatischeff explained that she didn't want any other actor to play her father, so it couldn't be a live-action film. However, an animated film, in the style of *The Triplets*, would be perfect.

Tati wrote the script for *The Illusionist* between 1956 and 1959. In 1958, *Mon Oncle* (My Uncle, Tati) was a big success at Cannes, where he took *The Illusionist* script with him in the hope of making the film. It was at the highest point of his career but, instead, he decided to make *Playtime* (Tati, 1967), which became his masterpiece. If he had made *The Illusionist*, it was going to be a very different kind of film without the inclusion of his famous character, Monsieur Hulot. Whilst it is uncertain why Tati didn't make *The Illusionist*, Chomet believes that Tati wanted to play the role of the magician in the film, but he was very clumsy with his hands. Also, an injury from a car accident had adversely affected the movement of one of his arms, making it impossible for him to play the magician. Furthermore, Tati might have been too close to the project because he himself had worked in music halls and he was very sad that the tradition was coming to an end. While he had been able to work in cinema, most of his friends in music halls had become impoverished and he helped them out from time to time. Chomet also believes that the film was written for Tati's daughter, Sophie Tatischeff: 'Because he was doing his films, he didn't spend much time with his family and they really liked each other actually. She adored her father but she has said in an interview that she would have liked to have spent more time with him, but he wasn't always there.' (Appendix 1).

Didier Brunner asked Chomet if he would be interested in reading Tati's script and he agreed that he would once working on *The Triplets* was over. However, at the time, Chomet was not very enthusiastic about directing someone else's script – even if it was written by Jacques Tati – because he had already started working on *Barbacoa*, a project 'really close to [his] heart' that he envisioned as his next film. The story takes place in the Paris Commune of 1871, during a rather dark historical period, when everybody is starving because the city has been sieged by the Germans. There is no food so children are chasing animals, even rats, in the streets, and, ultimately, a revolution breaks out in the city.

Chomet explains *Barbacoa* is a dark fairytale: 'I had this story about animals escaping from the zoo and it was kind of a fairytale because animals would turn into human form and behave like humans.' (Appendix 1). The producer had his reservations because he thought it would be too dark for children. Once again, Chomet contended with the limiting and dominating perception of animation being for children – and not teenagers or adults. From a producer's point of view, Tati's script probably seemed more appealing and more marketable. So, Brunner gave Chomet the script, about thirty pages, written in the style of a novella, to read on his way to Cannes.

> I read it over a couple of hours, and all the time I was thinking in my head: 'I hope it's going to be bad because [Tati] didn't do it first, and I don't really want to do it.' So, I was ready to cheat and I read it with really bad faith, trying to find something wrong about it – but I just loved it! And I said: 'It is a beautiful film.' I had everything when I read it, and I already knew the ending was a musical piece because there was something uplifting in the story as well. It was really amazing! So, I told Brunner: 'Yes, this will be a great idea.'
>
> (see Appendix 1)

Unfortunately, Sophie Tatischeff died before Chomet returned to France, so they were never able to meet. *Les Films de Mon Oncle*, set up by Sophie Tatischeff in 2001, held the rights to Tati's oeuvre. Chomet already appreciated the work of the foundation and this also played a role in his positive response to making the film since he prefers to collaborate with people who understand and value art and don't focus on profits at the expense of quality.

During this period, he was invited to screen *The Triplets* in Edinburgh. It was his first time to Scotland and he liked both the country and its people. Moreover, he found that Scotland shared the same atmosphere as the film, possessing the same light and weather conditions, which are hard to come by. Originally, Tati had set his script in Prague, but Chomet didn't think that contemporary Prague fitted the script. As already mentioned, Chomet likes to work in locations where his films take place and Edinburgh not only looked right, it also reminded him of Canada, of which he had fond memories. So, he and his wife Sally moved to Edinburgh to make *The Illusionist*. It was easy for them to relocate then because at the start of production, they didn't have children and Sally Chomet worked as one of the film's producers.

They found a large, old apartment over three floors and set up Django Films with a handful of people, including Evgeni Tomov, art director on *The Triplets* and animator Laurent Kircher. Initially, the studio made commercials whilst starting on the preparatory work for *The Illusionist* among other films. Chomet enjoyed working in this apartment because it rekindled positive memories of *The Old Lady and the Pigeons*, which also started out in an apartment. Django Films evolved into the biggest animation studio in Europe at the time. During this time, *The Triplets* was released in the United States and was a big success, bringing Chomet to the attention of Hollywood producers.

Working on Weinstein brothers and Universal Studios projects

Chomet had many positive experiences with both Pixar and Disney in the United States. He speaks warmly about most of the people he met there, such as John Lasseter at Pixar, and the old animators at Disney. Unfortunately, however, he also encountered some Hollywood producers who demonstrated the difference between auteur animation and commercialized production.

The first of these were the Weinstein brothers. Bob Weinstein held the copyright to a penguin character that originated from a newspaper cartoon and he contacted Chomet to develop a film around this character. Chomet agreed and he created a department in his studio devoted to this purpose. Although the character was very limited, Chomet created a whole story around him, set in Las Vegas, involving birds that were being captured by people.

> It had these really amazing characters, like a really old lady who had too much plastic surgery. There was also a nasty man who captured birds and kept them in a big cage, renting them to different shows – and there was this penguin inside it. The story was really nice, visually very nice.
>
> (Appendix 1)

Additionally, Chomet's team did some of the designs, backgrounds and made some models that were five to six metres wide. Bob Weinstein came to Edinburgh and Chomet pitched the story with the new characters. The pitch appeared to go well and Weinstein left very satisfied. However, to their surprise, at dinner that evening, Weinstein behaved in a way that Chomet describes as unacceptable:

> We were really in shock because he was really aggressive and the first thing he said, even before we ordered, was: 'Yeah, I'm very disappointed. This is not my film.' But you don't have a film, you have a character, which is there. What do you mean it's not your film?
>
> (Appendix 1)

After a series of unpleasant incidents, Chomet left the restaurant determined not to work with Weinstein. The meeting revealed the stark conflict between the practices of commercial producers and auteur creators discussed in Chapter 2. Weinstein had acted as if the film belonged to him because, in his view, the director is just another hired employee. Chomet as creator, however, could not accept this attitude. And as he often states and, more importantly, proves in his professional choices, he is not just a 'director for hire' (for more see Appendix 1). Happily, for Chomet, the project didn't get any further in development, although he was frustrated because he believed they had done a great job that Weinstein couldn't see the potential of. Chomet adds: 'And then there was a film like *Rio* (Saldanha, 2011) five years later, and I thought I hope Mr. Weinstein realised that he could have had a film like *Rio* – a big box-office hit – in his hands, but he wanted to have his *own* film.' (Appendix 1).

Another difficult incident concerned his collaboration with Universal Studios on the development of an animated film adapted from the book *The Tale of Despereaux* (DiCamillo, 2003). When Chomet had opened his studio in Scotland, he received a telephone call from a producer at Universal, who wanted to adapt a children's book in CGI. Chomet accepted the project even though it was for a CGI film and he didn't usually do CGI. 'I thought: why not? It was another technique and I would have to find the right people to animate it, but why not?' (Appendix 1) Ever since his early days in animation, Chomet has always been open to working with new techniques and new media. Even live-action direction was another technique and another way of telling stories. So, at this point, his studio in Edinburgh was developing *The Tale of Despereaux* at the same time as *The Illusionist*. Different teams worked on the films on different floors. One of Chomet's conditions for taking on the project was to remain true to the darkness of the original book that appealed to Chomet. 'It is about a mouse living in a castle, in medieval times, and it is a very dark book. It's kind of old-fashioned and it takes place in a dungeon. I said: "If you want to keep this darkness, yes, we can do something beautiful."' (Appendix 1). Universal agreed and Chomet started to design the characters and create a storyboard. During this process, a producer from Universal took over scriptwriting and, according to Chomet, brought in a Disney-like script and insisted on character designs that Chomet considered wrong:

> Once again, they bought something and broke it. They actually broke the magical thing that was in the book and it became almost like a Disney movie

and [the writer's] reference was Beauty and the Beast ... The villain in Beauty and the Beast is a tall, very masculine guy, called Gaston. The [writer] had that in mind and I said: 'I'm sorry but the guy in this book is a sailor and he's got a rat on his shoulder. He can't be this strong guy because everybody is laughing at him as his only friend is a rat. So, he is going to be a skinny guy, someone who is weak. Why would he be a weak guy if he is muscular? It doesn't make sense!'

(Appendix 1)

The Tale of Despereaux came with a 60-million-dollar budget. Chomet pointed out that he could make it for less if he was given creative freedom. After all, he was also developing *The Illusionist* on the floor upstairs, on a 20-million-dollar[3] budget, which went on to be nominated for an Oscar.

Universal, however, sent a production director to Edinburgh to supervise production. When she insisted on a character more like Gaston, Chomet explained: 'Well listen, I'm not a director for hire, you know. If you don't want me to use my input to actually make a film, I am not a director for hire!' The collaboration ended abruptly the next day, with Universal Studios forcefully taking all the development material from the studio (for more on the incident, see Appendix 1). Universal hired other directors (the second director quit) to complete the film and when it was released, Chomet discovered that Universal had not credited him for his design work:

'They actually took all the material we had, all the development of the film, and they made it somewhere else ... But they kept the main characters' designs! And they kept the design because the design was really good! We did it! ... Happily, I wasn't involved in the making of the film, but they didn't put my name on the credits! I had to go to the press and say these people are using my designs and they are not even crediting me for that! Sadly, this is how the system works'.

(see Appendix 1; see also Cieply and
Solomon, 2008)

Chomet learnt that for many US producers, a director is just someone for hire:

They don't want directors! They want technical directors who are going to direct a film, but they don't want directors who come with their own style. They want 'yes men' to do the direction. They want 'yes men' for actors. They want 'yes, yes ... as long as you pay me'. The creators are nothing to these people. If you want to be yourself, it's very difficult to work with them. They destroy you. It was basically the same with Universal and the Weinsteins.

(Appendix 1)

The Illusionist: creation

When the collaboration with Universal Studios ended, the whole studio worked on *The Illusionist*. On reflection, Chomet had felt instinctively that Tati's was the right movie to be working on. Not only was a fan of Tati's art, he was happy that it was being produced by Pathé, an old, well-regarded French company, dedicated mostly to highly aesthetic films. Chomet also had a lot of respect for Jérôme Seydoux, head of Pathé, and his experience working with him compared to the aforementioned US producers couldn't have been more different. 'Seydoux is a gentleman, and he came to visit us in the studio and he was very happy. He didn't put his nose into anything during the making of the film. He is someone fascinated by drawing and he liked *The Illusionist* and he liked Tati as well.' (Appendix 1)

Animation techniques on *The Illusionist* had evolved from the previous film, though essentially the same methods were used. One issue was that there weren't enough 2D animators around as many of them had gone into 3D animation where there was higher demand for work. Others had left animation altogether. Finally, Chomet's studio managed to gather over eighty artists from all over Europe. The requirements of cinematography were now quite different compared to Chomet's previous film. In making the film, Chomet wanted to stay true to Tati and to his art. So, whilst he already knew his films well, he studied them all again. In doing so, he realized that Tati's cinematography was quite remarkable, almost theatrical, expressing Tati's background in music theatre. Also, his shots were long – some lasted over a minute and a half, which is five times longer than the average animation shot. In Tati's films, the camera stood still in the middle of a room and the actors swung around it. Chomet knew this type of filming would be very difficult and time-consuming in animation: 'Most of the time, you see the characters full, you see their eyes, you see their feet. You can't hide elements of the characters. You see the characters walking around and it is actually the most difficult thing in animation to have a character moving away, because of the perspective. Most of the time it becomes wrong.' (Appendix 1)

Chomet also realized that a traditional storyboard couldn't be applied in this production in the same way as in his previous film, so he made a very precise animatic that took him a year to finish.

> You can't do that in a normal storyboard because there is no editing there. It's all happening in front of your eyes. There were quite a few people working on the storyboard for The Illusionist and it was very precise. If you look at the

storyboard, you have the film right there. I even put in the sound and elements of music, so everything was there and it was working.

(Appendix 1)

Chomet wrote the original soundtrack and Terry Davies orchestrated it. As in all of Chomet's films, music was of utmost importance. It is interesting to remember that when Chomet first read the script on that train journey to Cannes, he had already in mind a musical ending for the film. He knew that he wanted the audience to leave the theatre feeling emotional. Indeed, the film ends with a piano concerto that lasts for eight minutes.

> We lose the sound effects while it plays, so the music becomes the emotional conclusion. So, it was of vital importance to me and for the movie. I edited the picture to that music so it would be carried emotionally. Because there is no dialogue in the film, I used the music as the inner voice of the Tati character and his emotional heart. It wasn't just music I was composing; it was an extra layer of feeling.
>
> (Chomet in Pathé)

The film also includes many effects created in compositing in Digital Fusion and 5 per cent of the drawings were done in South Korea, to minimize production time. Everything went smoothly until a change in producers. This second producer had initially shown little interest in being involved in the project, but French Pathé later assigned him to the film which created major issues for Chomet. The new producer considered the film too long and, although Chomet had made large cuts, he wanted to make it even shorter. So, he commissioned a live-action editor, specializing in fast-paced action movies, to 'cut' the film when it was still unfinished. That editor cut all the segments that contained any emotion, leaving in only the actions of the heroes. The problem, of course, was that it was a poetic, emotional film, not an action film. This editing did not fit with Tati's cinematography, and nor did it work with the themes and style of Chomet's film. Chomet was very disappointed and tried to stop him:

> I said: 'No, you can't do that! It's awful!' He was absolutely speeding everything up! He wanted to have his fast speed film! And I said: 'This is not going to happen. You've got the Tati movies; they are not fast edited. You can't do that! We are going to lose everything!
>
> (for more, see Appendix 1)

Sally Chomet, who was also one of the film's producers, tried to intervene but to no avail. In the end, Jérôme Seydoux stepped in and allowed Chomet to restore the film and re-edit it. Unfortunately, however, some pieces had been lost and were impossible to restore, including a sequence at the rugby stadium in Edinburgh.

> It was a nice scene, where they go to Murrayfield stadium. The girl is with Jacques Tati and they are watching a very funny rugby game and there were all these massive guys and they were really tough on the young lover, and that was the first time she was seeing him. And I believe it was in the original script as well, but because the editor messed up the production, it was not possible [to keep in]. So, that was it. I did all the things I wanted in the end, but there were some beautiful scenes that were cut! He argued that all these little lovely attention scenes were cut because they don't bring anything to the action. But it's not an action movie!
>
> (Chomet, Appendix 1)

The film was restored and *The Illusionist* was eventually released as the director had intended from the start. It proved a great success, was nominated and won many prizes, including the prize for European Animated Feature Film at the European Film Awards. It was also nominated for Best Animated Feature Film of the Year at the Academy Awards. The distribution of *The Illusionist* had a very good start – the best start of all Chomet's films – and it did better at the box office than *The Triplets of Belleville* in England and Scotland, yet surprisingly made only 8,609,949 million US dollars. Despite the film being critically acclaimed as an animation masterpiece, the film was possibly distributed in such a way that word-of-mouth publicity didn't have time to work. Chomet notes that the film had little, if any, publicity and was released at the wrong time of year.

During production of *The Illusionist*, Chomet had taken a short break to shoot *Paris, je t'aime* (2006), a live-action film. This is further evidence of Chomet's talent and flexibility in jumping from one film genre to another, applying different cinematographic techniques to best suit the story that he wants to narrate. For Chomet, live-action is not 'other' or 'contrary to' animation, it is another film technique.

In the marginalia of *The Illusionist* release

At the time the film was released, newspaper reports circulated about a man claiming to be Tati's grandson, who thought that Chomet should have dedicated the film to his mother because, according to him, it was written for her. Chomet has since explained that he dedicated the film to Sophie Tatischeff because she had given him the script. Furthermore, Chomet believes the script describes a father-daughter relationship that Tati addressed to his daughter Sophie.

According to Chomet, when he started work on the storyboard, he received a long, handwritten letter from someone called Richard McDonald, who explained that Tati had an affair with his grandmother during the war and had given birth to a girl. Tati, however, didn't want to have the child because of the war. But the woman kept the child – the mother of McDonald – who, years later, had her own child in Scotland. This man claimed to be Jacques Tati's grandson. Chomet inquired at Tati's estate about the grandson. Whilst they had no knowledge of him, they conceded that with all the details, there might be some truth to the story. So, Chomet invited him to the studio:

> The guy came and I was at my desk, drawing Jacques Tati. We were doing the development at that time, the storyboard and the animatic, when this guy came in. He was not as tall as Jacques Tati, but he was Jacques Tati! I saw him and I said, yes, yes, definitely! He arrived and the way he was moving was very much like Jacques Tati, it was kind of awkward! I was with the animators in the room and we went: 'Scary! Spooky!'
>
> (Appendix 1)

When the film was released, Tati's grandson went to the press, saying that Chomet should have dedicated the film to his mother instead of Sophie Tatischeff, and accused him of doing it deliberately to hurt his mother's feelings. He also accused Chomet of provocation because he had made the film in Scotland. But Chomet argues:

> It's a fiction movie, it's not the story of his life! It was a strange accusation, when I didn't even know he existed. I met this guy when he came to the studio. The animatic was almost finished, the story was made and nobody has ever heard of his family story. I said to him that I don't know his mother. Why would someone force me to put someone's name in the end credits? Also, I'm really not sure the script is for that girl! I think Tati wrote it for his daughter! It's a father and daughter relationship and [Tati] didn't have a relationship with the other girl.
>
> (see more in Appendix 1)

The Triplets prequel

Chomet has often said that he doesn't like to make sequels, so *The Triplets* prequel is something very different. When he made *The Triplets of Belleville*, he also wrote the story of the singers, which differs from the story told in the film. In fact, the film centres more on Madame Souza and Champion than on the singers, leaving their narrative arc unfinished. As mentioned in Chapter 1, Chomet's characters exist in their own worlds outside the film, with their own past and future. So, naturally for him, he wants to develop these characters further: 'I think they are fantastic. I wanted them to carry on their stories. For me, they are the main characters in the *Triplets*.' In the world of *The Triplets of Belleville*, there is another story with the triplets at the centre of the narration:

> Their father was a doctor in a very remote place in North America and he wanted his daughters to become nurses. So, someone suggested he send them to a faraway city called Belleville, which was being constructed at the time, and they should go to a nursing school. They arrive in the city and see a cabaret – as children, they were dancing and singing all the time. They see the cabaret and instead of going to the nursing school, they go to the cabaret and become like those very popular singers of the 20s and 30s. They have to lie to their dad, so they take fake pictures of themselves as nurses … and he believes they are nurses and it carries on and on for years and years, and the story takes place when the daddy is 100 years old – I have done the development and everything … But they want to tell him what they have become because he doesn't even know. He hears one of their songs but he doesn't know it's them singing. And they arrive and that story is happening and a lot of things are happening … It's a very touching story and quite funny, too.
>
> (Appendix 1)

The film *Swing Popa Swing* was planned to be produced by Didier Brunner and his company *Les Armateurs* and had been slated for a 2014 or 2015 release, but Syndicat des Producteurs de Films d'Animation (SPFA) announced in its *newsletter* in March 2014 that production was cancelled. Whilst it is unclear whether the film will ever be released, the existence of the script creates a storyworld, the world of the triplets, in which already two completely different stories take place, with different protagonists that live their adventures in the same universe. It would be also interesting to watch the triplets' story that is not fully told in *The Triplets of Belleville*, which focuses more on Madame Souza's and Champion's adventures. This is a rarity in the animation industry that is better known for sequels featuring the same hero, with more or less the same storyline. However, Chomet's *The Triplets* and *Swing Popa Swing* tell two distinct stories about its different protagonists living in the same universe.

An analysis of *The Triplets of Belleville*

I'd love to be twisted, utterly twisted,
twisted like a triplet from Belleville …

Belleville Rendez-Vous

Introduction

The Triplets of Belleville (*Les Triplettes de Belleville*, Chomet, 2003) is a highly acclaimed international collaboration, mainly financed through respective state funding. It was Sylvain Chomet's first feature film, receiving many nominations and prizes, including Oscars for best animated film and for the song, *Belleville Rendez-Vous* (music by Benoît Charest, lyrics by Sylvain Chomet). The film's screening and success at the Cannes Film Festival in 2003 are proof of recognition of its high artistic value, not only in the context of animation, but in the world of cinema as a whole. The critics were enthusiastic, characterizing the film as 'thrillingly odd', 'quirky', a 'one-of-a-kind', 'wonderfully weird' and 'astonishing'.

Whilst the film was aimed primarily at an adult audience, it also appealed to many children and teenagers. Reflecting on his younger audience, Chomet says: 'We didn't invite them, but they came.' (Appendix 1). The film incorporates many elements reminiscent of the silent-film era and early cartoon-making, with a nod to filmmakers such as Jacques Tati and cartoonists including Albert Dubout. On popular websites, such as Internet Movie Database, the film is classified under the genres: animation, comedy and drama. While this is a useful classification for a broader audience, it is worth noting that animation is not, in fact, a genre: it is a form of cinema that includes all the genres that exist in live-action films. Indeed, Chomet's film straddles comedy and drama. It is a comedy with many underlying dramatic hues, a characteristic of many good comedies. Additionally, it includes elements of the adventure genre and, importantly, although it is not a musical, it is a 'music' film, in which dialogue has been banished and visual and sonic elements function as an integrated whole. *The Triplets of Belleville* can be described as a dialogue-free film and a visual comedy since it contains minimal dialogue. Discussing dialogue and the lack of it in his films, Chomet explains:

> For me, animation is the art of mime, I find that when you can have less dialogue, you can bring the beauty of movement and of the expressions more to the fore. I think there's too much dialogue in films. Above all, especially in Hollywood films, the real trick is to get in lots of quick gags, instead of working on the movements. As far as Walt Disney is concerned you realise that the first films had a lot less 'talking'.
>
> (Chomet in Caruso, 2003)

As Daniel Goldmark notes:

> Chomet's decision to make his film verbally mute doesn't just free up the animation; he is upsetting the way in which we have been trained to interpret animated films – through the dialogue – and, thus, forcing the audience to watch (and listen) all the more carefully.
>
> (2010:143)

More importantly, Chomet's first feature film is a poetic art film, possessing the value of a unique work of art combined with the intrinsic characteristic of cinema: the ability to be seen en masse without losing its value. This is cinema at its best.

Summary

The film tells the story of Madame Souza, her grandson, Champion, a sad and orphaned little boy, and their devoted dog, Bruno. Madame Souza tries and fails to distract her grandson, but nothing seems to lift his spirits until she discovers his love of cycling and buys him a bicycle. Then, over the years, Champion devotes himself to cycling, with his grandmother as his coach. When he is older, Champion trains to take part in the famous Tour de France cycling race. However, in the middle of the race, the French mafia kidnaps him and takes him, along with some other cyclists, to the huge city of Belleville to exploit their cycling prowess on the illegal gambling market. Madame Souza and Bruno must find Champion and save him, which they do with the help of three, elderly, formerly famous singers, the Triplets of Belleville.

Audio-visual systems of meaning

Chomet created a distinctive and effective character design for every single character in the film's storyworld, from the protagonists down to secondary characters, such as the French waiter and the boat that brings Champion to Belleville. The outlines and shapes of Chomet's drawings remain clear and consistent throughout. These hand-drawn elements are incorporated so effectively with CGI technology that the film still manages to preserve the style and aesthetic of a hand-drawn film. And whilst colour is digitally applied to the film, it looks like a hand-painted film, painted with temperas or watercolours. For example, see Figure 4 where Madame Souza follows Champion through the streets in the rain. The frame is a stand-alone watercolour painting, like most of the film's frames. Moreover, the scene is an excellent example of Chomet's use of sound. Madame Souza gives Champion his cycling pace with her whistle to resound in the city's deserted streets.

The animation is rich, detailed, smooth and consistent. Although there are many instances of CGI-animated elements combined with hand-drawn animated characters, such as the hand-animated cyclists pedalling bicycles created in CGI, the result is homogeneous, so that everything appears to be animated using the traditional cel animation technique (see Chapter 3).

Figure 4 Madame Souza trains Champion for the Tour de France. Courtesy of Sylvain Chomet.

Concerning character design, Chomet has developed his distinct style, influenced by his love of the Franco-Belgian comic tradition and his earlier work in comics. His characters are exaggerated and caricaturized. They are imperfect, with their own unique features and peculiarities that reveal certain character traits to arouse the interest of the audience. Madame Souza, for example, is a petite old woman with a clubfoot. This physical characteristic doesn't hold her back – instead, she uses her clubfoot as a weapon in her final victory against the mafia. She is dressed in warm, earthy colours and she wears spectacles that often slip down her face, so she has to keep pushing them back – a small but well-observed detail familiar to anyone who wears glasses. Madame Souza is a resourceful character, who exhibits exceptional strength, determination and physical endurance to help her grandson. She also brings humour to the film through her cacophonous singing and some of her surprising solutions to problems, for example in the scene when, luring Bruno with dog treats, she uses him as a tyre for the truck.

Champion grows from a little boy with a big nose into a tall, skinny adult with a bigger nose and huge eyes that express his melancholia, loneliness and, sometimes, even apathy far better than words could. The muscles in his calves look disproportionately large in relation to the rest of his physique, revealing his hard efforts as a cyclist. Meanwhile, the triplets, Violette, Blanche and Rose, are designed to look happier, smiling more often than the other characters. Whilst the triplets share common physical characteristics, there are also enough differences between them. They are all tall and thin, with very long hair. At their mature age, their colours are also warm, and they wear two types of outfit: everyday clothes and the stage costumes they have preserved from their old, celebrated days of performing even though there's now no longer an orchestra to play for them. It doesn't seem to matter since, even off-stage, the sisters enjoy singing and performing, whatever they are doing. Without the accompaniment of musicians, the inventive triplets make their own musical instruments out of objects around the house, like a vacuum cleaner or a newspaper. In this way, they can be described as 'breathing music'. Additionally, the sisters' names might refer to the three colours of the French flag. Towards the end of the film, when the mafia boss is defeated by Madame Souza and the singers, his car falls into the funnel of a boat. This is followed by an explosion and a shower of fireworks in the sky in the colours of the French flag, possibly signifying that the singers (and their values) have won.

The faithful Bruno is first introduced as a cute puppy, presented by Madame Souza to her young grandson, Champion. When Bruno grows up, he becomes a lovable, overweight dog, boasting a large belly and very thin legs that exaggerate his extra pounds. Bruno is designed mostly with round shapes. His design is hugely caricatured, provoking unconditional sympathy and laughter. His facial characteristics are extremely expressive. He has a big mouth and a big nose that emphasizes his powerful sense of smell, and his eyes also reflect his inner feelings. He is one of the film's most expressive and lovable characters (see Figure 5). Due to a trauma from his days as a puppy, when he was hit by a toy train, trains haunt his dreams and he has developed a habit of barking at any passing train. Through Bruno's black and white dreams, Chomet opens a window to the dog's view of the world, his needs, fears and goals (Figure 6). Bruno is instrumental in the operation to rescue Champion (Figure 9).

The mafia characters have their own design: rectangular and edgy. Dressed in black suits with white shirts, the mafia leaders have short, square bodies, with funny, round noses and little moustaches, creating an overall comic effect. At the restaurant, where the Triplets of Belleville and Madame Souza perform, the mafia boss sits at a table, with his nose barely touching the top of the table. He looks comically insignificant and, yet, this short figure incites fear amongst all the characters except for Bruno, who remains sleeping, dreaming, until he catches the scent of Champion's scarf, which he grabs from the mafia boss and

Figure 5 Bruno accompanies his family at the Tour de France. Courtesy of Sylvain Chomet.

Figure 6 Bruno's nightmare. Courtesy of Sylvain Chomet.

carries on to stage to Madame Souza. In addition, Floquet notes that Chomet's depiction of the mafia draws on a number of French stereotypes:

> ... the receptionist at the French Mafia Wine Center who bears some verisimilitude with José Bové, a left wing anti-globalisation activist. With a beret, moustache and taste for red wine, the French mafia Godfather is a reminder of one famous character by Gotlib, a French cartoon artist of the late XXth century: Super Dupont (a possible translation: Super Smith), some unlikely son of Superman and Mr. Average Frenchman, who would appear in Les Triplettes de Belleville in his drunkard version. Isn't the mafia's moto 'In vino veritas', acknowledging the fact that the French adore nothing but wine?! The hit-men, here again, are the monstrous genetic clones of Men in Black, Inspector Cluzot, and J. M. Folon's flying men.
>
> (2006:9)

The mafia leaders in the film are almost always accompanied by two tall and wide rectangular mafia members, who appear to carry them around. The mafia characters are the only ones that smoke in the film, giving smoking a negative connotation. In contrast, in *The Illusionist*, both positive and negative characters smoke, as this represented the attitude of the era, when smoking was not perceived as a bad habit.

The city of Belleville and its residents are also highly exaggerated with many comic elements. Belleville doesn't simply serve as a background for the narrative; it is a character in its own right. In contrast to its name, which translates as 'beautiful city', Chomet's Belleville is a big, noisy, dirty city with high-rise buildings, crowded roads and overweight inhabitants leading unhealthy lifestyles. From the busy streets and the gigantic hamburger signs, to an obese version of the Statue of Liberty and a giant bottle of wine as a sign over mafia's neighbourhood, the landscape is designed to communicate concerns about modern cities and consumerism. It is noteworthy that though the city is designed to resemble a large North American city, the mafia characters are French, connoting a broader critique of contemporary, urban living, not limited to a specific country or continent.

Animation and movement of the characters are also exaggerated in line with their characteristics. As mentioned earlier, the film heavily relies on animation and mime to communicate the actions, thoughts and feelings of the heroes. As well as their individual design, the characters stand out with their unique ways of movement, which are accompanied with corresponding, distinct sounds.

While Chomet's animation style uses exaggeration, it doesn't follow Disney's twelve principles of animation. More specifically, his film doesn't use any of the prevalent techniques such as squash and stretch or anthropomorphism.

Also, the film's cinematography and camera movement resemble those belonging to live-action films rather than to traditional animation. Chomet uses a wide range of shot types, from close-ups to wide shots in order to narrate his story in the most satisfactory way. The film is not fast edited, giving the audience time to connect with the characters and the world, and not just focus on a series of actions. Chomet's film is full of little movements and details that convey feelings, relationships and meaning, that in many cases are more important than the plot itself. They also create a poetic space for the audience to enjoy and relate to. Moreover, Chomet uses editing to suggest the passing of time and the technological advances that come with it. A powerful example of this is the way that Madame Souza's house changes little by little with the invention of electricity, and then the railway comes to the countryside, bringing in many more people. The train causes Madame Souza's house to bend as it almost passes through it (see Figure 7). Another example of the passage of time is through a series of cuts depicting the change of seasons when Champion is abducted and Madame Souza lives with the singers.

Movement is always accompanied with the appropriate sound and music driving audience attention to what is important, along with adding to the character's personality. A good example is Madame Souza's clubfoot, which

Figure 7 Madame Souza's house – changes over time. Courtesy of Sylvain Chomet.

generates a characteristic sound every time she walks. Daniel Goldmark, in *Sonic Nostalgia and Les Triplettes de Belleville* (2010), provides a detailed analysis on sound and music of the film and how Sylvain Chomet's musicscapes and soundscapes convey place and period. As Goldmark points out, 'the most powerful moments in Triplets have absolutely no music, but instead combine the film's sound design with the many characters' detailed facial expressions, especially those of Bruno, the dog'. He continues by describing a scene in which Champion and Madame Souza return home from a training ride at Parisian suburbs, to underline the importance that Chomet gives to the use of sound during the film:

> Champion's energy is channelled into his ride, muscles training, and he remains mute. At once happy and exhausted, he sits at the dinner-table waiting for his food while alongside Bruno waits expectantly for leftovers. Chomet omits all the background sounds once Madame Souza joins Champion at the table, working on a bicycle wheel while Champion eats his sardines and mashed potatoes. Having fewer random sounds, Chomet argues, gives people more time to look around the room. This scene in particular shows a deft awareness of how the soundtrack can direct the gaze, and likewise affect the viewer's understanding of the dominant themes in the film – in this case, the importance of home and family.
>
> (Goldmark, 2010:146)

Like sound, music also plays a vital role in the film, as it was already mentioned in Chapter 3 and it is used as a major communication system. Every era, every location and every important action is characterized by its music. Chomet notes in his interview that he had a friend in Canada, who is a physicist; he is an absolute expert in Bach and Glenn Gould. There was a scene with the Tour de France race, where he wanted to have music resonating the sound of a wheel, giving the feeling that it's almost difficult to push the pedals of a bicycle. 'And I found this Bach part which is a cycling thing. It worked fantastically! This time we had actually a pianist to play this for us and that was very interesting! Music was very important at that time' (Appendix 1). Parenthetically we should note that the same friend provided him with the equation that appears at the beginning of the film: 'Actually, I said to him "can you put the formula of the universe" and he wrote me the formula of the universe and I put it at the beginning' (Appendix 1). While no equations appear in *The Illusionist*, they re-appear in his live-action *Attila Marcel*.

Colour is also very important. Chomet showed great care in the use of his colour palette and his hues. Whilst creating a balanced whole of high artistic value, he uses colour as a means of signification. Without using flamboyant colour contrasts, he differentiates his palette in order to attribute positive or negative meaning to both the actions of his heroes and the time and locations throughout the film. He creates colour contrasts between countryside versus city, past versus present, older way of living versus contemporary lifestyle. Usually, what has a positive signification, such as the countryside and simpler, older way of living is coloured with warmer, inviting hues, while the contemporary lifestyle in the massive city is depicted with cooler and in many cases darker or greyer hues. The dreams of Bruno are presented in black and white (see Figure 6). Also, as it will be described below, the opening scene that shows the singers in their past glory is painted in sepia.

Figure 8 charts how the film's colour and sound are presented (see Introduction). In Table 4.1, the colour/sound chart is connected to the main sequences and narrative acts that are discussed in more detail later on this chapter. See Chapter 1 for a similar chart on *The Old Lady and the Pigeons* (1997). Comparing the two charts, there is a shift in the colour palette of *The Old Lady* to *The Triplets* with its warmer and 'earthier' green–orange colours. Moreover, a closer look at the colour palette at the centre of the chart shows that *The Old Lady* has a bigger diffusion of colour than *The Triplets*, using a greater range of colours. Yet, although Chomet uses fewer colours in *The Triplets*,

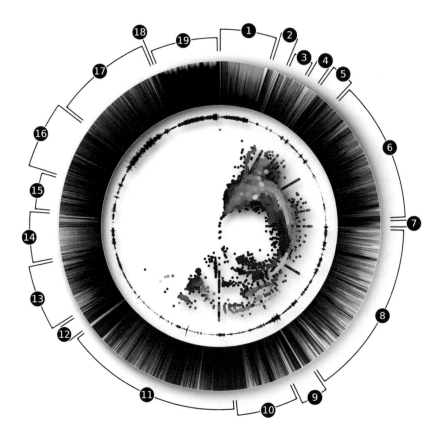

Figure 8 *The Triplets of Belleville* colour and audio chart.

there is a greater number and variety of hues and luminosity. Whilst the green, orange and blue colours are dominant in the colour wheel, the differences in the hue and luminosity communicate even the smallest changes in a very subtle way, something that is also apparent in *The Illusionist*. Moreover, from the wavefront circle, it is clear that while music is important in the film, many of the sequences are based on sounds. The scene described by Goldmark (2010:146) is included in Part 6 of the chart, where Madame Souza and Champion return home from the training and Bruno awaits them. They gather around the table and Madame Souza takes care of everything, taking on the role of trainer, physiotherapist and bike repairer to help Champion (see Figure 9). The corresponding wavefront shows that this is one of the 'quietest' parts of the film

Table 4.1 *The Triplets of Belleville*: the main sequences and narrative actions in relation to the colour and audio chart (Figure 8).

1.	Titles in sepia. Intro sequence: The young triplet's performance.	11.	The triplets meet Madame Souza and take her and Bruno to their home.
2.	At Madame Souza's house. She tries to spike Champion's interest with an old piano.	12.	At mafia's headquarters.
3.	She gifts him Bruno.	13.	At the restaurant where the triplets and Madame Souza perform and mobsters have their dinner. Bruno's dream. He traces Champion's smell.
4.	She finds out what interests him. She buys him a bicycle.	14.	Madame Souza spies on the mafia and finds where Champion is taken.
5.	Passage of time, change of the neighbourhood.	15.	At mafia's illegal races.
6.	Champion grows up and practises hard with Madame Souza always supporting him. She takes the roles of trainer, physiotherapist, bike repairer, dietician, etc.	16.	Champion's rescue.
7.	Bruno's nightmare, passage to Tour de France.	17.	Mafia chases the heroes. They win and escape.
8.	At the Tour de France. Bruno's nightmare, mafia's appearance and Champion's abduction.	18.	Champion is old, back in their home.
9.	Madame Souza and Bruno travel to Belleville.	19.	End titles and post-credits scene.
10.	Madame Souza and Bruno arrive at Belleville, in search of Champion.		

so, as Goldmark notes, the viewer can singly focus on the main themes of the sequence: 'the importance of home and family' and *care*. In general, most of the sequences related to Madame Souza's home (the parts that don't include music) are 'quieter' than the 'louder' parts, such as the mafia's gambling hall and the final 'chase' sequence. Additionally, the chart provides data about the duration and editing of the film, which is apparent from the changes and 'cuts' in colours and wavefront, which will be discussed further in relation to *The Illusionist* (Chapter 5). The narrative analysis below will consider the audio-visual sub-systems presented above in greater depth.

Figure 9 Madame Souza, Champion and Bruno at home, after training. Courtesy of Sylvain Chomet.

Narrative

The opening sequence shows the Triplets of Belleville singing *Belleville rendez-vous* in a crowded theatre. During their performance, many 1930s stars, such as Charles Trenet, Fred Astaire, Josephine Baker and Django Reinhardt, appear on screen. At the same time, well-dressed people arrive at the theatre: big women with tiny men – a tribute to Dubout, who fascinated Chomet as a child. The colour of the sequence is sepia and the style resembles that of early animation. Additionally, the drawing lines are imperceptibly different, so as to distinguish the opening sequence from the rest of the film. The TV programme is interrupted, and, with a camera zoom out, followed by a fade into Madame Souza's house, thus entering the storyworld. The change is also signified by a change in colour of bluish hues, and the start of the next music programme, showing Glenn Gould playing Bach's C minor prelude, a recurrent theme in the film. Chomet shows his protagonists watching Glenn Gould's performance (similarly, later on, the singers watch a Jacques Tati film on TV).

Champion watches television and his grandmother asks him: 'Is that it, then? What have you got to say to Grandma? Is it over?' This is one of the few phrases heard throughout the film. It sets a 'framework' for the narrative. In the first and last scene, the same events are repeated: Champion watches television and his grandmother asks him: 'Is it over?' The second time, Champion has grown old; he is at the same house, coloured in the same hues, and it is implied that he is watching the same film that the audience watches – his own adventure story. This decision to create a sense of mise-en-abyme is indicative of the consciously artistic character of the film. It is a scheme that is also used in *The Illusionist*. It shows a 'movement of life in spirals': the film starts and ends at the same place, though at distinctly different times. It is common for a narrative's heroes to start from one place, then go to another location to fulfil their adventure before returning to the original place. But for Chomet, it seems more than a simple narratological convention, to be further discussed in Chapter 6.

As the narrative of *The Triplets of Belleville* evolves, time passes, and the heroes move from the countryside to the city (for the Tour de France), to Belleville and then back to the countryside, whilst the film's colours change accordingly. The period spent in the house of Madame Souza has a palette ranging from warm green to ochre, whilst the countryside has more orange tones. The passage of time, however, is relentless and, with the advance of technology, the countryside also changes and grows into a suburb of the city. The train passing through almost destroys the house and, thus, becomes a negative symbol of technological progress. It is the same train that haunts Bruno's dreams and that he barks at each time it passes through.

The passage of time is also marked through the increasing number of headstones in the graveyard, depicting both the growing population of the countryside and the ephemerality of life. Figure 7 indicates that sound levels rise with time passing and as the heroes leave the countryside, implying the noisy nature of the cities.

Most of the narrative elements are organized into triads: three singers make up the Belleville Trio; Madame Souza's family has three members including Bruno; the mafia kidnaps three cyclists; and three mobsters constitute each mafia group. This pattern runs through many texts, from ancient myths to medieval literature and fairy tales, and its use in the film links it to a wider body of cultural texts recognizable to audiences. It is also evident in *The Illusionist*.

Narrative programmes

After the opening sequence, the main plot of the film unfolds. An interesting feature of the film is the co-existence of numerous narrative programmes. Most films, regardless of their protagonist, also include a cast of other characters, with their respective stories (*narrative programmes*) and their own goals, helpers, enemies, lessons to learn or obstacles to overcome. Moreover, a single character may have more than one goal or adventure within the course of a film. Heroes might also have multiple helpers and opponents. More importantly, for a character to be a hero, they must have accepted or rejected a 'contract', a mission assigned to them and a goal, which is often an abstract concept, such as a quest for love, care, a wish or sometimes the hero himself (in the sense of internal change or maturation, like in the case of coming of age film themes). Heroes must also overcome obstacles and pass through trials to achieve their goals, which, according to Greimas, is the purpose of a trial (see Greimas, 1984; Lagopoulos and Boklund-Lagopoulou, 2016; Katsaridou, 2019; Lagopoulos and Boklund-Lagopoulou, 2021).

Whilst *The Triplets of Belleville* may appear to have a simple and straightforward plot, it is a complex text with eight main and numerous secondary (or incomplete) narrative programmes deriving from Chomet's rich character development, imbued with rounded personalities, with distinct perspectives, stories and traits that emerge at specific points through the story. *The Triplets of Belleville*'s seven main narrative programmes are: (a) Madame Souza's first narrative programme, (b) Madame Souza's second narrative programme, (c) Champion's permanent narrative programme, (d) Champion's active narrative programme, (e) the mafia's narrative programme, (f) the triplets' permanent narrative programme, (g) the triplets' active narrative programme and (h) Bruno's narrative programme.

(a) and (b) Madame Souza's narrative programmes

Madame Souza has two successive goals that both concern her orphaned grandson. He is her raison d'etre and all her actions are driven by her desire to care for him and ensure his happiness. Yet the sad, little boy seems uninterested in anything the world has to offer. At first, Madame Souza tries to distract him with an old piano, but he doesn't care for it. Then, she gives him a puppy, which, although Champion accepts, doesn't stop him from continuing to sit, distressed, in bed. Eventually, Madame Souza realizes that her grandson loves bicycles. On his bedroom wall is a photograph of his dead parents, smiling down at him from a bicycle. This gives Champion an emotional connection to the bicycle. So, his grandmother gives him a tricycle, thereby achieving her first success, to lift Champion out of his state of melancholic inactivity.

As time passes and Champion grows up, his bicycle rides become more daring as he ventures out of their yard, onto the town's streets. When he decides to train for the prestigious Tour de France cycling race, his grandmother becomes his coach, physiotherapist and bicycle repairer. She acts as a constant helper for Champion. After months of arduous training, Champion earns his place in the race. Madame Souza, on the day of the race, follows her grandson in a first-aid truck with Bruno. She has achieved her goal, even though temporary, until the French mafia kidnaps her grandson.

However, her success is thwarted when she reaches a difficult, mountainous point along the route, where the mafia has scattered nails across the road, bursting her truck tyre, so she can no longer follow Champion. She manages to get the truck moving again when Bruno takes the place of the tyre. Madame Souza's second narrative programme begins at this point in the film, to free Champion from the mafia. This is actually another way to care for Champion, so her two goals are interrelated. The mafia is the main enemy of Madame Souza and Bruno is her major helper; later on, the singers become also her helpers. After a series of trials (detailed below), she finally rescues her grandson.

She searches for Champion, who has been abducted by the mafia. At some point along the route, she spots the mafia's abandoned truck, where she finds Champion's hat. Bruno smells the hat and starts to run. The smell leads him to the sea and to a massive ship, which at that very moment is sailing away. Madame Souza rents a pedalo and, with Bruno beside her, follows the ship to the port of Belleville. Chomet refers to this sea sequence as one of his favourite sequences. Aside from being a beautiful scene, it also connotes the fight against the vast adversities of life. The image of Madame Souza and Bruno on the pedalo, fighting with the storm and the enormous waves and finally winning, is surreal yet uplifting and optimistic; It connotes a win against all odds.

The passage to the city of Belleville is not easy for Madame Souza and Bruno. When they reach the shore, their trials and errors continue. Bruno cannot trace Champion because of Belleville's dirty, pungent air. As Madame Souza has no money, they end up hungry under a bridge in the harbour. Madame Souza starts playing music with an old bicycle wheel and is heard by the three elderly singers, who take her and the dog home and feed them with the frogs they catch. The singers become her major helpers. In time, Madame Souza starts performing with the singers. One night, the mafia arrives at the restaurant where the singers perform. Although Bruno is asleep when the show begins, in his dream, he senses the scent of Champion at the table of the mobsters. The smell is on a scarf that he grabs and takes to Madame Souza. After many adventures, Madame Souza, Bruno and the singers manage to sneak into the mafia's hall where illegal cycling races and betting take place. The room is full of mobsters surrounding a raised platform, where three cyclists pedal in front of a screen. One of the cyclists is Champion.

After a fierce clash with the mafia, Madame Souza, Bruno and the triplets manage to release the platform, climb onto it and help the cyclists escape to the city's streets. The mobster's car chases the cyclists, who are furiously pedalling on the platform, and attempt to kill them. Madame Souza and the singers defend themselves and eventually defeat the mafia. Just as Madame Souza throws the mafia boss's car into the ship's funnels, blue, red and white fireworks – the colours of the French flag – burst across the sky, in a scene that celebrates their victory. They are victorious against the mafia and Madame Souza has fulfilled her purpose: to save her grandson.

(c) and (d) Champion's narrative programmes

Ever since childhood, Champion's chief interest is cycling. As he grows, his objective is to participate in the famous cycling tour. After many years of hard training, he succeeds and takes part in the race. From that point onwards, his active narrative programme ends unsuccessfully and his fate is determined by other characters. He becomes the object of value for the other heroes. First, he is captured by the French mafia that takes advantage of him and other cyclists for its illegal cycling races. Later, Champion is freed by his grandmother and not by his own efforts. Even though he failed in finishing the cycling race and in freeing himself, he continues to do what he loves under any circumstances. So, his permanent goal is achieved and he might be considered as a somewhat successful hero.

(e) The mafia's narrative programme

The mafia is driven by their greed and wish for profit. At first, they are successful when they kidnap the cyclists, including Champion, who stop to rest during the race. But in the end, they are defeated and fail. Interestingly, all the mobsters are men, and this is the film's second male active narrative programme that ends in failure.

(f) and (g) The triplets' narrative programme

The three singers have two narrative programmes, both driven by their love of singing, dancing and playing music. Their two narrative programmes are closely connected and interrelated, as the second narrative programme presupposes the permanent existence of the first. The triplets were once very famous singers. The years have passed and we meet them again under a bridge in the harbour of Belleville. Although they are older, they still possess their spirit and passion for singing. Having heard Madame Souza playing music on a bicycle wheel under the bridge, they go to meet her. They take Madame Souza and her dog to their home even though they themselves live in poverty. Although Madame Souza wants to help them clean up after meals, they do not let her touch certain objects like the fridge, the vacuum cleaner and the newspaper. Since the singers no longer have an orchestra or musical instruments, they use everyday objects – out of necessity or choice – to make music to accompany their performances. The sisters 'adopt' Madame Souza and invite her to play music with them. When Madame Souza tries to save her grandson, they help her. The triplets are consistently successful in their goal – even under threat from the mafia's weapons, they go on singing. They appear to be the film's most successful heroes.

(h) Bruno's narrative programme

As a puppy, Bruno arrives in a box as a gift for Champion, in Madame Souza's house. Ever since the day a toy train ran over his tail, Bruno has had a fear and hostility for trains. He barks at real trains whenever he sees them out of the window.

Figure 10 Bruno and Madame Souza are searching for Champion. Courtesy of Sylvain Chomet.

Bruno grows up without much attention, as Champion is devoted to his bicycle and Madame Souza is busy with Champion. Nevertheless, he is seen as a part of the family. He accompanies Madame Souza and Champion to the Tour de France, and his sense of smell and his dogged devotion are key to locating and rescuing Champion (Figure 9). During the mafia chase through the city, at the end of the film, one of the triplets suggests throwing Bruno off the platform, but Madame Souza hugs him and refuses. At that point, he finally receives the recognition and love he deserves. Bruno is successful too and achieves his objective: Champion is freed and they can return to their home and their old lives.

Notes on the narrative programmes

While Champion is at the centre of every character's story, he himself is not very successful as a hero. He fails to finish the Tour de France; he is captured by the mafia and becomes an object of value that others – the mafia, Madame Souza, the singers, even Bruno – want to acquire. But his 'value' translates differently for the different characters. The mafia wants Champion for illicit financial gain. Madame Souza wants to free him, and help him achieve his goals and be happy. Bruno seems to want Champion and Madame Souza back home, with his everyday routine restored, his food served on time and the trains running to timetable. Finally, the singers appear to want to help Madame Souza in the name of solidarity between artists. It is unclear if they have any interest in either Champion or cycling. It has already been observed that the film's narrative programmes for the men tend to fail, whilst the female characters' programmes are successful. This gives the film a slightly feminist tone.

Another compelling point is that the film narrates the story of Bruno and gives us access to its dreams. In contrast with other contemporary films, like *Finding Nemo* (Stanton and Unkrich, 2003), that use anthropomorphism where the animals behave like humans, Bruno retains the characteristics and behaviour of a dog. So, Chomet offers a delightful insight to the dog's feelings, dreams, memories and adventures.

It is noteworthy to add that the heroes, despite their adventure, do not show significant changes in their characters or in their life conditions once the adventure is over. Madame Souza continues to care for Champion; he continues to look sad, and the triplets continue to sing joyfully. Bruno's status may have altered slightly after Madame Souza's hug and expression of tenderness, but in essence, he is already a member of the family. Overall, the end of their adventure simply restores the heroes to the humdrum of their daily routine. So, the film is less about its characters' personalities changing through adventure, and more about changes through time (and technology) and, significantly, in the relationships that they have created. As Aguilar notes,

> There is a certain melancholy to The Triplets of Belleville because the characters exhibit human flaws and undergo painful situations. Chomet birthed the characters to be fragile, to have meaningful childhoods, lives of their own, and to exist with more purpose than just being funny cartoons … Rose, Violette, and Blanche, the triplets, as well as Madame Souza, her dog Bruno, and her grandson Champion, all come from an intimate place in the director's imagination and were given life via pencil and paper. Their story is not one about gangsters, cyclists, and washed-up stars, but about dreams followed, family sticking together, and the peculiarities that make some stand out from the crowd.
>
> (2018)

At the same time, there is no significant change in society. Mobsters might be defeated with celebrations and fireworks, but no real change is depicted at the massive city of Belleville, which, we may presume, continues to be polluted and inhabited with unhealthy people.

At the end of the film, Champion watches television sitting at the same spot where he sat at the start. Now, he is old, alone in the house of his childhood, and looks as sad and lonely as ever, and is possibly missing his grandmother. We hear Madame Souza ask him the same question she asked him at the start of the film: 'Is it over?' Champion turns his head and, this time, he answers: 'It is finished.' Returning home proves to be more important than the victory against the mafia, probably it is what matters the most. As Goldmark notes:

> Once Champion is rescued and the gangsters defeated, we return to his grandmother's living room one last time. It takes us practically the whole film to get back to this point, a scene from just a few minutes into the film, and to realise that this space – his grandmother's house, at the table where they ate, where Bruno grew fat, where young Champion no doubt watched the Tour on television – was a place of comfort, and was formative for the boy …
>
> (Goldmark, 2010:156)

As things return to normal, 'the past is recovered, the new world is evaded, and the visual nostalgia is reinforced' (Neupert, 2005:41).

Nostalgia is enhanced not only visually but also aurally. The combination of the two conveys to the viewer the inescapable feeling of nostalgia. As Goldmark notes,

'Aural nostalgia plays as strong a role here as does the visual. Charest scores the final sequence – with Champion sitting alone in his grandmother's house, a picture of her and Bruno overlooking the scene – with the same music heard as the film opened when Champion and Madame Souza sat together at the table watching the Triplets and Glenn Gould on television ... and now we have also got 'Grandma's voice added to the mix, another echo of past happiness'

(2010:157–8).

The ending is both poetic and nostalgic, leaving a space for the viewer to feel, think and relate to in their own way. It is also a heavy suggestion on the passing of time and our own temporality in life.

The themes and the isotopies of the film

Throughout the film, there is a clear and intense focus on interpersonal relationships, along with many isotopies related to time, which are closely related to spatial isotopies: the changes of places through time (see Table 4.1). The passage of time is always the bearer of change, either through places, cultural eras or the changing seasons. Alongside the film's message about human temporality, there is also the concurrent theme of ageing and loss. The triplets are seen as young and successful and then, contrastingly, old and poor. Champion grows from boyhood into a man. Although the passing of time is inevitable, in both reality and the world of the film, what makes a difference, according to the film, is the heroes' choices and how they perceive time and confront change. With the natural elapsing of time, this film, refreshingly, does not close with a conventional happily-ever-after ending. Instead, *The Triplets of Belleville* leaves the audience with feelings of loss and nostalgia for another era: possibly, a time when Madame Souza and Bruno were still living – maybe, the time of Champion's lost youth.

The film presents a philosophical view of time, combining how people perceive time with the natural passage of time. More specifically, people perceive time linearly. The present follows the past and precedes the future. On the other hand, natural time is cyclical: seasons follow each other: spring, summer, autumn, winter and spring, and the cycle repeats itself. In the film, human time is combined with natural time, creating the sense of time in spirals. The circularity of time also appears in the daily habits of the heroes, giving their lives a sense of regularity. For example, Bruno knows the train schedules, and whenever a train

Table 4.2 The main isotopies of *The Triplets of Belleville*.

Field	Group of isotopies	Isotopy	Antitheses
Society	Social	Social composition	*Heroes* vs *society* vs *mafia*
		Lifestyle	*Creative lifestyle* vs *consumerism*
			Traditional lifestyle (simpler) vs *new lifestyle* (technologically advanced)
		Social relations	*Family* (biological or chosen) vs *economic interest groups*
		Social values	*Solidarity* vs *profitmaking*
	Economic	Economic	*Poor* (protagonists) vs *middle class* (Belleville residents) vs *wealthy* (mafia)
Interpersonal	Interpersonal relationships	Family	*Absence* (dead parents) vs *presence of family* (grandmother)
		Solidarity	*Solidarity* vs *exploitation*
	Thymic	Care	*Care and friendship* vs *indifference* vs *hostility*
		Loneliness	*Companionship* (young Champion) vs *loneliness* (old Champion)
Culture	Cultural	Cultural behaviour	*Artistic creation* (singers) vs *mechanistic behaviour* (Champion)
			Artistic creation (singers) vs *consumerism* vs *commercialization/exploitation* (mafia)
		Artistic expression	*Artists* (singers) vs *rest of the society*
Place	Spatial	Topological	*City centre* vs *suburbs and harbour* (where the singers live) vs *countryside*
			Countryside vs *transitional space* (sea) vs *city*
Time	Chronological	Time	*Past* vs *present*
			Before vs *after*
			Linear vs *circular time* (nature)
Main themes and axes			*Care* vs *indifference and/or abusiveness*
			Art/creativity vs *consumption and/or exploitation*
			Freedom vs *captivation*

passes by, he runs to the window to bark at it. This routine is integrated into Bruno's daily life, just as cycling is Champion's daily habit. We can conclude that the heroes' everyday life, to which they want to return, is closer to the rhythms of nature. The same theme of the interrelationship between linearity (human) and circularity (nature) of time is also evident in *The Illusionist*.

Time is also a valuable signifier of new discoveries and technological advances that usually are welcomed and adopted. The film examines these discoveries critically and reminisces about a simpler, less advanced, less consumerist and less noisy way of living. Running parallel to the heroes' adventures is the arrival of electricity lines, trains, planes and, gradually, the transformation of rural areas filled with more housing. An essential element of this passage is the changes brought about in the material-technological culture. For example, the film depicts changes in Madame Souza's house. More specifically, the surroundings of her house change over time. In the beginning, the house stands alone in the middle of a field. Gradually, planes appear in the sky; electricity wires are everywhere, and houses go up around them. A cemetery is built on the field on the left of the house and welcomes new tenants daily. Eventually, the urban density becomes suffocating: a bridge with a train line is built so close to Madame Souza's house that it causes the house to lean slightly (Figure 7). Even though this might seem to non-French viewers like the creation of Chomet's imagination, this scene has a reference to the French landscape. Floquet writes: 'The high bridge that pushes Mme Souza's house into a tilt is typical of railway constructions in France during the first half of the 20th century. If you commute by train from Orly airport to Paris, you will actually travel past similar sites' (2006:8).

In the film, time is marked by technological advances – and, subsequently, urbanization – which do not improve the quality of Madame Souza's home life in the countryside. Belleville, which by its nature as a city, is even more technologically advanced, with negative connotations of an impoverished, consumerist way of life that the film's heroes appear to reject as they leave the city. The need for joy and creativity that conflicts with contemporary life is expressed in several ways throughout the film. New technology is also represented by new methods of transport, such as trains, but they haunt Bruno's dream after a traumatic incident when he was a puppy. Champion, too, suffers from a deep childhood trauma after losing his parents. The subject of trauma is a recurrent theme in Chomet's works, such as in his live-action *Attila Marcel*. Nevertheless, the most profound reaction to childhood trauma – and, at the same time, technology – comes from Bruno, who barks at all the trains going by, disturbing his peace (see Figure 11).

Figure 11 Bruno barks at passing trains. Courtesy of Sylvain Chomet.

A closer look at the main isotopies of the film reveals Belleville comprises a society made up of unequal wealth distribution. Madame Souza, Champion and the singers belong to a poorer class, although the triplets were once famous and better off. These poorer characters live outside of the city's centre: in the countryside (Madame Souza) or near the harbour (the triplets). Their homes share similar colours, signifying financial and, crucially, cultural and lifestyle affinities that contrast sharply with the wealthy and obese residents of the metropolis.

Food in the film is a major indicator of poverty or wealth. Madame Souza has no money to buy food and ends up hungry with Bruno under a bridge. The singers live in an old apartment and feed exclusively on frogs, which they fish with dynamite. Frogs as food is a direct reference to the stereotype about French eating habits. Chomet plays with this stereotype, creating a hilarious sequence that can be interpreted in two ways: the singers' lack of money, ironically, enables them to feast on what is considered a delicacy, or sometimes, what has ended up as a delicacy came from necessity. In any case, Madame Souza and Bruno don't share their enthusiasm for eating frogs – Madame Souza, remember, is Portuguese. The condescending French waiter working at the restaurant where the triplets perform is another stereotype, as French cuisine is commonly perceived as 'haute cuisine' (Figure 12).

Figure 12 The French waiter. Courtesy of Sylvain Chomet.

The lack of money is in direct contrast with the mafia's possession of money – they are rich, as shown by the mobsters' lifestyle, such as expensive cars and dining in high-class restaurants. The mafia's wealth comes from abusing people and illegal activities, in contrast to the way the singers and Madame Souza earn their living. Although poor, the singers are presented as self-sufficient and resourceful, finding creative ways to acquire what they need, such as repurposing and reusing household items as musical instruments. In Figure 13, the triplets, with Madame Souza, are playing music at a restaurant using a vacuum cleaner, a refrigerator grill, a newspaper and a bicycle wheel. The same applies to Madame Souza, who, at the beginning of the film, uses her vacuum cleaner to massage Champion's legs. Both she and the singers have a different, resourceful way of life from both the mafia and the majority of the residents of Belleville, who live in a predominantly commercialistic way. According to the above, the singers and Madame Souza, even though poor, follow a *creative lifestyle*, in antithesis to the mafia and the majority of the residents of Belleville who follow a *consumerist* way of living.

It should be noted that *family* as an isotopy concerns interpersonal relations more than a societally defined structure. What bonds the characters to form families is their care for each other, their common interests and their way of life. The triplets treat Madame Souza as a 'fourth sister' because they share

Figure 13 The triplets with Madame Souza play music at the restaurant with home-made instruments. Courtesy of Sylvain Chomet.

the same values and interests. More importantly, Madame Souza, Champion's grandmother, essentially adopts him and raises him. It is interesting that a similar idea of family created 'by love' and not by biological parents also appears in *The Illusionist* and *Attila Marcel*.

Another important isotopy in the field of *interpersonal relationships* is that of *solidarity*. The singers express their solidarity with Madame Souza in many ways: most importantly, by risking their lives to help her find Champion. In contrast, the mafia seems to be driven by profit and not feelings whatsoever. The opposition *solidarity* vs *exploitation* also includes the idea of the *neutral*. For example, no one cares that an old lady and her dog are hungry. The waitress takes their order back the moment she sees that Madame Souza can't pay for it. Although neutral behaviour per se cannot be classified as negative in the obvious way that the mafia's exploitation is negative, in the context of the film, neutrality does bear many negative connotations.

Solidarity is closely related to a third isotopy in the field of *interpersonal relationships*: the *thymic* isotopy and its antithesis, *hostility* vs *indifference* vs *friendship*. If *solidarity* takes into account the actions, the *thymic* isotopy refers to the feelings that drive these actions. The singers feel friendship for Madame Souza while the mafia expresses hostility. The element of *indifference* is manifested as the prevailing mood among the citizens of Belleville and, moreover, is expressed by the indifference of Champion, who expresses neither positive (friendship) nor negative (hostility) emotions throughout the Tour de France.

The concept of *care* is core to the meaning of the film: Madame Souza takes care of her grandson; the singers take care of their instruments, and Bruno takes care of his family. Champion, however, does not seem to reciprocate the care, and he is completely self-absorbed and focused on his cycling.

Freedom and its antithesis, the lack of freedom through *captivation and exploitation,* are also important in the film. The film clearly states the importance of freedom and that exploitation leads to death, as in the case of the abducted cyclists.

The field of culture is heavily represented by the isotopy of *cultural behaviour*, which includes two of the most important antitheses clearly expressed throughout the film: *mechanistic practice* vs *artistic creation* and *commercialization* vs *artistic creation*, which are greatly interconnected.

As already discussed, the singers' artistic creation and the joy they derive from music contrast with the technological progress in Belleville and Champion's mechanical attitude to cycling, which, although he does with a passion, seem to bring him little joy. Art in the film is closely connected with culture and lifestyle. The singers and Madame Souza lead a simpler way of life, removed from technology. Even their means of transport are old-fashioned (and sometimes surreal). Madame Souza travels across the rough sea on a pedalo. While the triplets express artistic creation, the mafia is indifferent to it – their sole aim is profit. Interestingly, though, the mafia's illegal cycling races are a type of spectacle like the sisters' performances.

The film does not give a clear message about cycle races as art forms, since the mechanical, repetitive sounds are antithetical to music, they seem to express oppositional ideas: art as creation and joy vs cycling races as a mechanistic spectacle.

The aforementioned themes are closely connected through space. The space in the film carries a considerable semiotic load. There is a world of difference between the countryside, home to Madame Souza and the big city of Belleville, where the mafia inhabit a rich neighbourhood at the centre, while the poor sisters live in a poor suburb near the harbour (*centre* vs *suburbs*). It becomes clear that in order to escape the mafia, the characters must leave Belleville. So, there is a clear contrast between the *countryside* (the place of daily life) vs *big city* (the place of adventure). Moreover, one of Belleville's landmarks, the obese caricature of the

Statue of Liberty, standing in the city's port, holding an ice-cream cone in one hand and a hamburger in the other, offers a visual commentary on 'imported' cultural lifestyles. On the other hand, the huge bottle of wine and the inscription 'in vivo veritas' outside the mafia's building lead to connotations of 'Frenchness'. Belleville's consumerist lifestyle is interpreted as alien, and at the same time, it has become part of the city's contemporary culture; the city has adapted foreign culture mixed it with French culture, and the outcome is presented critically and negatively. At the end of the film, the mob leader's car falls into the ship's funnel as fireworks explode in the sky in the colours of the French flag, potentially signifying triumph for another way of life. But nothing, in fact, happens in the film to suggest any improvement in the existing social situation.

In conclusion, Belleville's city centre typifies an area populated with skyscrapers, heavy traffic, imposing fast-food billboards, obese residents and the underfed poor. It is far from being a place that promotes artistic creation or any human connections of solidarity and friendship. Rather it is a space where the film locates the action of the mafia. The singers (and the artistic creations) are placed on the outskirts of the city. Artistic freedom is an important and recurring issue in the film, intertwined with notions of personal freedom. The artist must be free and independent; creation must be a choice and a source of joy.

The themes of interpersonal relations and societal and technological change over time are core to the meaning of *The Triplets of Belleville*, and they connect to all other issues and isotopies in the film related to culture, art and society. The passing of time sometimes causes unwanted or even inevitable changes, but one thing that cannot be changed or reduced by time is the care, friendship and love someone has experienced. In the end, Champion is old and alone. He appears sad and nostalgic, remembering his adventures that he watches on TV. Yet, the voice of Madame Souza, who is no longer alive, asks him the same question she asked him when Champion was a child. Her care and love still exist through this short question, revealing a strong relationship immune to the changes of time. In the end, Champion's longing for Madame Souza shows that whilst he appears indifferent for much of the film, he values his grandmother's care and cherishes their relationship. So, by the end of the film, Champion proves himself a successful hero. He has lived a meaningful life and gained his grandmother's love and attention, which accompanies him to old age, filling the void of her physical absence. It is a poetic, bittersweet ending, left for the viewer to interpret according to their own relationships, memories and feelings.

An analysis of *The Illusionist*

Introduction

Sylvain Chomet's second film, *The Illusionist* (L'illusionniste, Chomet, 2010), is quite different from *The Triplets*. It was adapted from a Jacques Tati script and co-produced between France and the UK. Described by critics as 'magical', 'beautiful', 'poetic' and 'touching', the film has, among others, an Annie Awards nomination and an Oscar nomination for best animated film.

Chomet's decision to direct a script intended for a live-action film is a testament to his love of challenge, new ideas and techniques, and his desire to keep moving and developing. Tati's script posed a great risk for Chomet. Production on the film began hot off the heels of *The Triplets'* success, and the audiences that Chomet had won over now expected more of the kind of animated universe that typified *The Triplets*. Meanwhile, Jacques Tati's fans wanted to see their favourite character, Monsieur Hulot, back on the screen. To make things more complicated, the script for *The Illusionist* did not actually feature Monsieur Hulot. It was written for another character that was closer to the real-life Tati. He was a more gentle, serious and melancholic person than his fictional persona, Monsieur Hulot, known and loved all over the world. Tati had worked in music theatre, and although he was made famous by cinema, he witnessed the 'death' of music theatre that led to the destruction of the careers of many of his friends who worked there. So, for Tati, the film script story was closer to his real-life experience. Impressively, Chomet managed to please both his own audience and Tati's fans. Furthermore, he presented another side to Tati in a role that the actor had wanted but never managed to play. The illusionist is Tatischeff (Tati's real name) – not Monsieur Hulot, his most famous hero. The film is very gentle, totally different from the ones where Monsieur Hulot is the protagonist. It takes place over a long period of time, across several locations that include a good deal of travelling, which is unusual for Tati's films. Chomet didn't make any major changes to the original script (discussed in more detail below) and closely studied not only Tati and his films but also the details of the era to convey a faithful adaptation of the story. The film's genre is drama, comedy and family. As with *The Triplets*, there are reservations about the categorization of animation as a genre. It should be added that it includes comic instances, and while it is not a musical, it is a film highly related to music.

Summary

The film tells the story of a French illusionist who, in 1959 – on the cusp of a changing era – is forced to leave France and travel along with his rabbit to find work in the declining world of music theatre. He travels to London but is unable to compete against the sweeping tide of modern entertainment, so he travels farther away and ends up on the remote Scottish island of Iona, where he performs at a local pub. During his stay, he meets a young girl, Alice, who still believes in his magic. She follows him to Edinburgh, and they develop a father-daughter relationship. Despite his meagre finances and difficulty finding work, the illusionist does all he can to support Alice. Meanwhile, as musical theatre declines, Alice grows older and falls in love with a young man. The illusionist decides she no longer needs him. He leaves her a note, releases his rabbit into the wild and seeks out a new journey, away from his art as an illusionist, but most likely a journey that takes him closer to his own daughter, whose photo he always carries with him.

Audio-visual systems of meaning

The film includes dialogue between characters speaking in French, English and Gaelic. The words serve mainly as sound enhancers to the characters' gestural communication rather than conveying important information. The illusionist and Alice don't speak the same language. The natural language 'babel' presented in the film also signifies the communication gap between characters of different cultural backgrounds that are bridged through gestures and actions. This use of dialogue is in line with Tati's own cinematography. Laurent Kircher notes:

> What distinguishes Tati's films is the way he uses sound to amplify or contradict the images we see on the screen, adding another layer of detail which both adds to the charm and structural complexity. Most tellingly, dialogue is used not to

convey information to the audience, but rather as if it was just like any other form of background noise. It is this curious aural mosaic of background sound, music and image that defines Tati's uniqueness and that was something we had to get right, too … But the fact there's no dialogue makes the audience try to understand the characters even more. Because it's not laid out for them, they have to invest further and that's the true value of this type of animation.

(Kircher, *The Illusionist*: 9)

Generally, Chomet remained true to the script, with only a few changes. Notably, he relocated the original setting, Prague, to Edinburgh. After visiting modern-day Prague, Chomet found he was unable to locate in it the spirit of the old city that appears in the script. Around that time, Chomet visited Edinburgh, which he felt best captured the atmosphere of Tati's script.

For me, it was easier to make this a bit more personal – a bit more real – by changing the location from Prague to Edinburgh because I thought there were a lot of elements in the scenery in Scotland which were really quite close to the story, especially the change of light and mystery. Scotland is a place of mystery, of magical legends. At the same time, I don't like to invent places, you know. I prefer to sketch what I'm watching and I was in Scotland at that time, so I was inside the backgrounds. And Edinburgh is a very important character.

(Chomet in Desowitz, 2010)

Indeed, the ever-changing Northern lights – perfectly recreated by Danish art director Bjarne Hansen – along with the city's constant weather shifts create a feeling of perpetual change, contributing to the magical atmosphere of the film. Another of Chomet's changes to the script is the 'stew scene' (see Figure 14), where the illusionist is afraid that Alice has cooked his rabbit. Yet the illusionist sits at the table, not eating and not knowing how to behave. Finally, the rabbit appears, carrying in its mouth the string of sausages that the illusionist had earlier bought and hidden behind the sofa. Relieved, the illusionist can enjoy his meal. Though this scene was not in Tati's original script, it is reminiscent of the humour in Tati's films. Animation director Paul Dutton notes: 'The stew scene showcases one of the purest Tati moments, although this is one of Sylvain's own creations' (Dutton in *The Illusionist*, Sony Pictures Classics).

Adapting a script written for live-action cinema into an animation film provides challenges concerning cinematography. Tati's cinematography was essentially theatrical; he didn't use close-ups or camera movements, and he used wide shots. As Chomet notes, Tati hated close-ups, and there aren't any in his films. The characters approach the camera or move away from it as if they are on stage. Following Tati's cinematography would be challenging yet, uniquely,

Figure 14 The 'stew scene'. Courtesy of Sylvain Chomet.

Chomet adapts it to animation. A further layer of difficulty is that the film is very slow-paced, with slow editing and unusually long shots for an animation film. Chomet notes that *The Illusionist* has roughly one-third of the shots in *The Triplets*. The animation in this film is focused more on body language and subtle gestures and is less about facial expressions since, true to Tati's style of filmmaking, there are no close-ups.

The film seems simpler than *The Triplets*, but as Chomet notes: 'Nothing is more complicated than trying to do things very simply, and to make them look simple' (Chomet in *Electric Sheep*, 2010). Whilst adhering to Tati's cinematography, Chomet's camera work brings its own artistic merit to the film. For example, in the final sequence, after the illusionist leaves his rabbit on the hill, Chomet starts with a medium wide shot and then slowly pulls the camera back to an extreme aerial wide shot rotating around the city.

The film's animation techniques can be likened to *The Triplets* (see Chapter 3). Both films use 2D, hand-drawn animation, complemented with CGI. The aesthetic result is unique: in addition to a harmonious and poetic whole, every frame is a stand-alone painting. Its backgrounds and character designs are realistic. The character of the illusionist, Tatischeff, looks like Jacques Tati and is recognizable from the first moment he appears. Tall, thin and clumsy – like Tati – but also a more complex character than fans might have known him to be. Chomet notes that when working on his hero design, he based it on the real Jacques Tati. He drew him from family photographs from that period. So, there is no pipe, no overcoat, as in the case of Monsieur Hulot.

Tati was an elegant man with massive hands and white hair, always smoking cigarettes instead of Monsieur Hulot's pipe.

The illusionist's body movements are also very similar to Tati's in real life. In fact, in the film, Chomet distinguishes between the 'off-stage' illusionist and the 'performing' illusionist. Chomet, in order to make the distinction more clear, put one lead animator, Laurent Kircher, in charge of handling the character when he is engaged in his daily activities, and made another animator, Thierry Torres Rubio, responsible for animating him when he is on stage, where he resembles more Monsieur Hulot than real-life Tatischeff.

Moreover, Chomet differentiates between the on-stage and off-stage versions of the illusionist through the colours and styles of clothing. On stage, he wears a red suit with orange socks that match the band around his hat. In his everyday life, he wears clothes ranging from green to ochre. But when he is forced to perform in situations that make him uncomfortable – as in the shop window – he appears in a pink suit rather than his usual red one.

In one interesting scene, Tatischeff goes to a cinema called CAMEO (a cinema that also exists in reality. The CAMEO is one of the oldest cinemas in Scotland) where, up on the big screen, he sees live-action footage of Tati in the role of Monsieur Hulot. They stare at one another as if they are looking in a mirror and ask the other: 'Do you want to stay?' But they both reply: 'No, no, no', and then they leave. Chomet also incorporates live-action in *The Triplets*, but in this scene in *The Illusionist*, the mirrored relationship between the two 'Tatis' confirms their shared identities, despite them occupying parallel universes. Monsieur Hulot lives in a world created by Tati, and Tatischeff exists in Chomet's universe. It is ironic that the most authentic depiction of the 'real' Tati appears in a film directed by another director.

But it isn't just Tatischeff that Chomet depicts truthfully. His entire cast of characters in *The Illusionist* are rooted in accuracy and 'realism'. Alice, the young Scottish girl, is, according to Chomet, designed to be a Scottish girl-next-door-type and not a stereotype like the Scottish protagonist in *Brave* (Andrews and Chapman, 2012). Chomet observed that common perceptions about the appearance of the average Scottish girl were narrow. So, he created Alice, imbuing her with the most common characteristics he saw in Scottish women. Alice's appearance alters as she grows older and is connoted by changes in her clothes and hairstyles. As a child, she is poor, which is reflected in her clothing. Her shoes are battered, so the illusionist replaces them with a pair of new red shoes. The red sharply contrasts with her tired-looking clothes painted in brown-green hues (Figure 14). Gradually, her clothes are replaced with new, more fashionable items.

By the end of the film, when she is an adult, her clothes are brightly coloured: she wears a white coat, white high heels and a light blue dress (Figure 14). Her appearance is reminiscent of fairy tales and seems to reference Disney's *Alice in Wonderland* (Geronimi et al., 1951), who dresses in similar colours.

Young Alice in *The Illusionist* is eager to grow up and dress in the style of a well-groomed, middle-class woman. In one scene, she tries on new white high heels, but doesn't know how to walk in them. She studies the ladies at the theatre who walk gracefully in their heels, and she tries to imitate them but without much success. It isn't until she is older that she is able to stride confidently in her heels. Towards the end of the film, Alice looks like a shop window mannequin, and a young girl, dressed like Alice from her first days in Edinburgh, looks up at Alice in the same way that she used to admire all the well-dressed women (Figure 15). This is another example of the 'spiral'

Figure 15 Alice changes as she grows up. Courtesy of Sylvain Chomet.

movement – an event occurring in the same place, at a different time – that is often evident in Chomet's films. As Alice grows up, a new girl takes her place, and she too wants to be grown up. These unending and irrevocable 'spirals' of change that time brings to people's lives and to every object in existence are discussed in more detail below (see also Figure 7).

A key character that accompanies the magician both on stage and in the course of his daily life is his rabbit. Actually, in the original script, the rabbit was a chicken, but Sylvain Chomet didn't think that would work, so he replaced it with a white rabbit. The illusionist pulls the rabbit out of his hat, which the rabbit doesn't always like and has a tendency to bite back. But generally, the rabbit and the illusionist enjoy a close relationship. In one of the most emotionally powerful scenes, the illusionist releases the rabbit into the countryside, where other rabbits live, so it can live free in its natural environment. But the rabbit doesn't run: it stands and sadly watches Tatischeff walk away. The rabbit's lowered ears condense all the sadness of their parting in just one movement, demonstrating the power of animation at its purest (Figure 16).

There is also a significant group of characters, vaudevillians, who reside in the same hotel as the illusionist. The clown is skinny and profoundly desperate from the lack of work and poverty. Usually, he wears a mix of everyday clothes with elements of his clown outfit and is often in clown make-up or a clown's nose. The ventriloquist is dressed in the same costume as his doll that he carries around with him everywhere. The pair are so bonded that, at the end

Figure 16 The rabbit watches Tatischeff walking away. Courtesy of Sylvain Chomet.

of the film, when the doll is for sale in a shop window and has to be given away since nobody wants to buy it, it denotes as much about the devaluation of the ventriloquist himself.

> Three acrobats also live in the same hotel as the illusionist. They are dressed in white, blue and red (the colours of the French flag) and adapt more easily to the new 'Billy Boy and the Britoons' lifestyle. By the end, though, they pursue other jobs that have nothing to do with the theatre. According to Animation Director Paul Dutton, these characters are all 'like the illusionist, out of their time. That's one of the bittersweet threads in the story: a bunch of vaudevillians in relentless pursuit of an ever-smaller audience. When Alice comes into the illusionist's life, he's just so grateful he is able to entertain this devoted audience of one.'
>
> (Dutton, *The Illusionist*, 10)

In contrast to the illusionist, who manages to separate his on-stage and off-stage identities, the other vaudevillian characters are highly defined by their respective professions: they wear their theatrical identity all day, every day – even when the acrobats start different, non-theatrical jobs, they still behave like acrobats. The illusionist's dual identities might signify his ability to separate his personal life from his professional life, which ultimately allows him to move on. He is also different to the other performers because of his relationship with Alice, who gives him something to return to. So, he is not lonely like the clown or the ventriloquist.

Figure 17 Images of Edinburgh. Courtesy of Sylvain Chomet.

Finally, another key protagonist in the film is the time-specific location of Edinburgh and Scotland, in 1959. The film is bursting with depictions of old Edinburgh, from its buildings and roads, to the railway through Scotland. Many shots resemble city postcards from a bygone era (Figure 17). As Gritten notes:

> The film's strength lies in its visual beauty. Every frame looks like a delicate watercolour. Chomet has taken great pains to capture Edinburgh's unique geography, architecture and its distinctive light. Its hills, buildings, alleyways, corner shops, vistas and buses look exactly as they did in 1959.
>
> (2010)

The colour and sound chart (Figure 18) are accompanied by Table 5.1, which relates the chart to the film's main narrative sequences and actions (see Introduction and Chapter 4). We may notice in Figure 16 that Edinburgh's dominant colours are warm, with green and brown hues. In general, these are the dominant hues of the film. In contrast with Edinburgh's urban area, on the remote Isle of Iona, the technological and cultural changes arrive with a big delay.

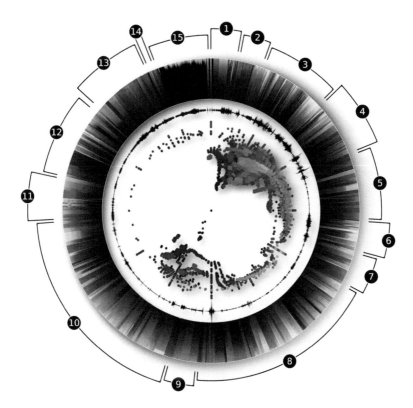

Figure 18 *The Illusionist* colour and audio chart.

Table 5.1 *The Illusionist*: the main narrative actions in relation to the colour and audio chart (Figure 18).

1.	Titles in sepia. Intro sequence: The Illusionist performs at a theatre.	9.	Things are getting worse and the illusionist works nightshifts at a garage. He gets fired.
2.	The film starts. The illusionist's performance continues in colour. The audience is cold and he loses his job.	10.	The life of the illusionist (and the vaudevillians) gets harder as it becomes almost impossible to find work. Tatischeff has to do humiliating jobs.
3.	The illusionist moves to England. His problems with finding work continue.	11.	Alice falls in love with a young man and the illusionist sees them together.
4.	He travels to the Isle of Iona.	12.	While Alice and the young man enjoy their date, Tatischeff prepares to leave.
5.	He performs at the local pub. He meets Alice.	13.	He releases his beloved rabbit and leaves on a train. Meanwhile Alice finds out that he has left. At the train a scene with a young boy depicts that Tatischeff has changed.
6.	He travels to Edinburgh. Alice follows him and she reveals herself on the boat. Their father-daughter relation begins.	14.	Alice turns off the lights of their room and little by little all the lights of the city turn off.
7.	They arrive at Edinburgh. They live at a vaudevillians' hotel and the illusionist finds work in a theatre.	15.	End titles. We see the picture of Sophie Tatischeff, which is the picture he had always with him. He returns back home to his daughter.
8.	We watch their everyday life, while the illusionist struggles to find work and to buy everything that Alice wants.		

There, the dominant colours and sounds are those of nature. As it is apparent from the chart, the colours create a harmonic whole, and it has fewer colours and contrasts than in *The Triplets*, with a constant change of colour hues, connoting the subtle but continuous changes. In Figure 14, the 'stew scene', warm, orange colours depict the warm relationship between the illusionist, his rabbit and Alice, signifying the importance of family (discussed further later in this chapter). There are few black or dark colours. Most of the cooler colours, such as shades of blue, are related either to the environment, like when the illusionist travels to Iona, or to the time of day. For example, there are lights with warm colours and blue/grey details in night scenes. The gentle colour changes are in line with the film's poetic narrative, which is based on slow changes over time and not on fast action scenes. Although there is a lot of music and sound in the film (see wavelength circle chart), for most of it, the level is not very loud and in keeping with the poetic mood of the images. Also, the film's gentle sounds contrast with the loud singing of The Billy Boy and the Britoons pop group and other loud sounds signifying the arrival of a new era. Moreover, the change of colours and wavefront makes it apparent that the scenes are long and the editing is slow.

The film's sound complements the realism of its visual elements. Edinburgh has its own sounds, from cars to people and the constant buzz of a modern city. In contrast, the remote Isle of Iona is dominated by the sounds of seagulls. In many parts of the film, there is no music at all and the emphasis is placed on sound as the carrier of meaning. For example, the sound of Alice's old shoes as she walks on the wooden floor reveals that the sole has come off, making it difficult to walk. Later, walking about in her new shoes, the sound they make is clear and steady, marking her new confidence. In another scene, when Alice turns on a tap in the hotel they share with the vaudevillians, the sound denotes the building's decrepit and poorly maintained plumbing, which sets up the comedy arising from Alice and the clown unwittingly stopping the other's water supply every time they turn on their own tap.

Once again, music plays a vital role alongside sound in the film. Just as Chomet composed the music for *The Triplets*, he also wrote the original soundtrack for *The Illusionist*.

> I composed on a computer keyboard, and gave the printed score to Terry Davies to clean it up and orchestrate … The Billy Boy and the Britoons songs were recreations of the 50s era and I wanted to keep my score in the same vein. I also wrote the theme music for the illusionist's stage act, the one he enters to and has playing whilst performing. That was turned into a song for the end credits where an assortment of imitators in the style of Charles Trenet, Serge Gainsbourg, Edith Piaf and Jacques Brel sing what is a very funny medley. The song is very evocative of the music Tati used in his own films, heavy on piano and embellished by vibraphone to give it that circus flavour. That was the only piece of music I made into a real Tati homage.
>
> (Chomet, *The Illusionist*: 13)

One of the most striking scenes where the music is especially powerful comes at the end of the film, when the sound effects are muted for an eight-minute piano concerto.

> 'So, the music becomes the emotional conclusion ... I edited the picture to that music so it would be carried emotionally. Because there is no dialogue in the film, I used the music as the inner voice of the illusionist's character and his emotional heart. It wasn't just music I was composing – it was an extra layer of feeling' (Chomet, *The Illusionist*).

Narrative

The story of *The Illusionist* flows effortlessly, making it easy for the viewer to follow. The film's slow pace allows time to draw the audience's attention to every detail. For example, a precise date in the narrative is indicated on a poster declaring: 'Nixon-Khrushchev have war of words'. On 24 July 1959, Richard Nixon and Nikita Khrushchev had the famous 'kitchen debate', one of the most famous episodes of the Cold War.[1]

The film opens in sepia hues. There is a theatre stage accompanied by the sound of curtains that won't open because of a technical problem. Then the illusionist appears and the music begins, and he starts performing to the sound of people clapping their hands. Clumsily, he tries to pull a rabbit out of his hat, and the rabbit bites his finger. At the end of his show, the few spectators in the audience are unmoved and barely clap for him. This is followed by a shot of pigeons flying past, to the same theme music, signifying both an era flying away and the magician's own movement from theatre to theatre and, finally, his migration.

The opening titles show a series of theatres: Music Hall de Paris, Mogador music hall, Olympia music hall, Bobino, Caveau de la Huchette (Huchette cellar), Lido and, finally, the Carrousel du Rire. As the camera approaches, the scene turns from sepia to colour. The marquee displays the title: *The Illusionist*. The illusionist's name, Tatischeff – the real name of Jacques Tati – is written on a poster. He is on stage, in his red suit, acting for a very small and unenthusiastic audience. His rabbit escapes and bites a musician. The illusionist tries to catch the rabbit, while a singer dressed in a sexy black dress, holding a long cigarette pipe takes his place on stage. The audience applauds the singer with excitement.

Inside the illusionist's dressing room, the paint peels off the walls and the electric plugs have worn out. He looks at a photo, then picks up the rabbit and puts it in its cage. The boss knocks on the door. He is smoking and blows the smoke into the illusionist's face. He drops the cigarette on the floor and stubs it out. From his gestures, it is clear that the magician is fired. Then the adventures of the illusionist begin.

Narrative programmes

The film includes the illusionist's three narrative programmes, which are closely interrelated: the programme of Alice, the story of the rabbit, along with the stories of many other heroes, such as the vaudevillians living at the hotel, consisting mainly of the stories of the clown, the ventriloquist and the acrobats.

(a), (b) and (c) Tatischeff's narrative programmes

The illusionist's first objective is to find work and earn his living, a task that becomes increasingly difficult with the changes of modernity (*initial state*). He has to leave his home country and travel abroad to find work (*acceptance of the mission*), but his audiences have turned their attention to modern entertainment and no longer pay attention to his outdated magic tricks (*failure to achieve his goal*). The locations where he performs are gradually downgraded to less and less prestigious ones (Figure 18). At a fair where he tries his best, only a Scotsman, who is drunk, pays him any attention and invites him to a remote place, the Isle of Iona (*helper*). After a long and beautiful journey, the illusionist arrives on Iona at the same time as electricity comes to the island. Yet, it is a very remote place, far away from the new trends. The illusionist is invited to perform to mark the arrival of electricity (Figure 18). He performs, and the audience is very receptive (*first success*). It is worth noting that wherever the illusionist goes, he carries with him a photograph that he always places in the mirror of his dressing room. Later, it becomes apparent that the young girl in the picture is his daughter, whom he is probably separated from in order to look for work. So, his other major goal, parallel to his first goal to earn a living, is to return to his daughter.

At a pub on the Isle of Iona, a young girl, Alice, who cleans the pub and the guests' rooms, is extremely impressed by his magic tricks. While he is in his room, Alice spills a bucket of water with a bar of soap in it. He picks the soap up from the floor and 'magically' gives Alice a new bar of soap in a box. The next day, he finds out that Alice has washed his shirt. He has noticed by the state of her shoes that she is poor and, out of the money for his performance, buys her a pair of red shoes (*magic object*). At this stage, although he cares for her well-being, he hasn't yet 'adopted' her. He leaves the island to go to Edinburgh. At the ship, she appears suddenly and sits opposite him. When the ticket collector appears, the young girl asks him to magic her a ticket, and he doesn't let her down. From then on, he acquires the third goal, alongside his other two: to care for Alice. Moreover, Alice is mesmerized by his magic, and with her childish naivety, she is impressed with his tricks, providing him with a devoted audience of one, at a time when he most needs it. She also takes care of him and eases his loneliness. Consequently, Alice acts like a *helper* to Tatischeff.

They arrive in Edinburgh and find a place to stay in a hotel, a 'house' for vaudevillians. They help him and Alice and form an atypical, albeit temporary, extended 'family' for the new arrivals. He searches for theatre work whilst caring for Alice, who, in turn, cares for him, quietly transforming the ruin where they live into a home.

The illusionist doesn't really try to dispel Alice's belief in his magical powers. The one time he tries, outside a fish-and-chip restaurant, he fails. She didn't seem to understand him, but it was not only a matter of the different languages they spoke or the loud sounds that interrupted their conversation. It was more a matter of role: for her, the illusionist is a father figure, which might give him near magical qualities in her eyes. Once he accepts this paternal role, he doesn't want to dispel her childhood illusions, making her grow up too quickly.

As time passes, it becomes increasingly difficult for him to find work in the theatre, and he has to do various odd jobs, like working night shifts at a garage. Yet, at the same time, Alice wants things – shoes, a coat, an expensive dress – which he tries to deliver whilst protecting her from his problems and the cruelties of life. He keeps her away from the theatres and pushes her away when she tries to come before a shop window, where he has to do a humiliating job. As her 'father', he is willing to sacrifice everything for her. There is a beautiful scene where she stands in the middle of a busy road, in danger of being run over. He throws himself in front of her to protect her and stop the traffic and raises his umbrella in the air in a quixotic manner, risking his own life. The illusionist succeeds in providing Alice with all she needs to grow up, both materially and emotionally.

Meanwhile, his work situation gets more desperate and degrading. At one point, he is forced to sell his magician's paraphernalia. When the acrobats find work for an advertising company, they give him a card, and he too gets a job, but it is only a temporary success. This is a morning job, and he manages to wake up only with the help of his rabbit. He ends up in a humiliating situation, performing in a shop window and at a liquor store. He decides that he will not do this again (Figure 19).

When he finds out that Alice has fallen in love with a young man, the illusionist sees she has grown up and no longer needs him. It is time for him to move on and let her live her own life. He leaves her a note 'Magicians do not exist' and frees his faithful companion in life and on stage, the rabbit, and takes the train. (He has achieved his third goal, to raise Alice.)

Figure 19 The illusionist performs in less and less prestigious places. Courtesy of Sylvain Chomet.

On the train, a young girl, sitting with her mother opposite him, drops her pencil. The illusionist picks it up, and even though he could magically change it for a new pencil, he hands her the original, used one, she has dropped. The age of magicians has passed, and the illusionist has realized it. At that moment, he makes a defining decision that reveals that, like Alice, he too has matured and changed. His first narrative programme ends on a partial success. He failed to find work in theatre, but he matured and moved on.

He looks at the photo that he always carries with him. It is seen in the end titles as a photo of Sophie Tatischeff, Jacques Tati's daughter in real life. The scene implies that the illusionist, Tatischeff, is returning to his daughter (he reaches his second goal successfully).

Despite the sadness of the end of music theatre and that he will no longer be an illusionist, the film's ending is optimistic. The changing of the era is an unbeatable enemy. Realizing the inevitability of change, he might move on to do something else – just as Tati himself did, reinventing himself in the film industry. Ultimately, the illusionist is a successful hero: he raises Alice, he matures and, finally, he returns to his daughter – maybe not richer, but definitely wiser.

(d) Narrative programme of Alice

Alice is a young girl who lives in Iona and works at the village's pub. She is profoundly poor, most likely an orphan (*initial state*). Her goal is to have a parent to take care of her and to have all the things that she can't have. Her narrative programme is mainly a coming-of-age story.

She meets the illusionist on the same day that electricity arrives in their village, and she is impressed by him. She does everything in her power to take care of him: she cleans his clothes; lights a fire in the fireplace in his room. When he 'magically' presents her with a new pair of red shoes (*magical item*), she decides that she wants to live with him and secretly follows him to Edinburgh. As the magician accepts her, a father-daughter bond grows between them. In parallel, she wants to look like the girls from the city, and she wants new clothes like those that she sees in shop windows. She keeps asking the illusionist for a new dress, new coat and shoes. She doesn't seem to realize how poor the illusionist is, and he does his best to keep it from her. She believes he really does possess magical powers and she relies on him for everything.

Nevertheless, she starts to realize the reality of their situation when she sees the illusionist performing in a shop window. Even then, she tries to go to the window and greet him. For her, he is still her father, so nothing has changed. The real change comes after she meets and falls in love with a young man. As the illusionist leaves her life, the magic of her childhood is over, and meets her goal successfully. Another stage in her life, with its own magic, begins in the arms of a young man. The camera (from above) shows the couple walking in the rain, covered with her white raincoat, whilst other people walk in the opposite direction, under black umbrellas.

(e) The rabbit's narrative programme

The little white rabbit, often mentioned in the movie reviews, has its own story. It appears – often unwillingly – with the illusionist in his shows and also has a relationship with him off-stage. It is a character that occupies both the illusionist's theatrical world and his personal life. The rabbit is a music theatre performer, partner and the illusionist's closest friend.

The rabbit is always there, waiting for him to come back, sleeping on his belly, biting his finger when forced to perform. But there is a genuine connection and love between the illusionist and his rabbit. The rabbit cares for him and helps him. In one scene, the rabbit makes sure that the illusionist wakes up or he won't get to work. The rabbit is a member of the illusionist's small family.

In the end, the magician frees his rabbit into the countryside to be with other rabbits. The rabbit is sad. Its ears flop as he watches the illusionist leave. But it soon discovers another world, its natural world, occupied by other rabbits hopping around. The rabbit's first goal (to help the illusionist) is met successfully, and now it embarks on another adventure on its own.

(f) The clown's narrative programme

The clown meets the illusionist at a set of traffic lights and helps him by pointing him in the direction of the Royal Theatre and taking him and Alice to a place to stay, the vaudevillians' hotel. He is poor, alone, desperate and hungry. His initial state only gets worse as he can't find work and goes hungry. His goal is to survive and to continue being a clown.

In one scene, he drinks alone in his room, listening to a happy tune, which refers to his performance as a clown. As time elapses, his situation worsens. At one point, he is ready to commit suicide when Alice knocks on his door, bringing him a plate of warm food. The clown eats it greedily. This is only a fleeting success as, although Alice has saved him with a hot meal, his situation continues to be dire. Besides hunger, he must face a cruel society that might be a worse enemy than hunger. Towards the end of the film, three youths beat him, kick him and leave him wounded on the street as two police motorcycles approach.

(g) The ventriloquist's narrative programme

A resident of the vaudevillians' hotel, he lives alone with his puppet, which he carries with him everywhere. The puppet is his only companion, and, at one point, he is so poor that he is forced to sell it – but nobody wants it even when it is free (Figure 20). He has a good relationship with Alice and gives her the ingredients and a recipe book to cook a stew. When Alice brings him a plate of the stew, he sits down to eat it at the table with his puppet. Unfortunately, things don't go well for him either. Later, when Alice meets him in a pub and greets him, he faints and falls down drunk on the floor. The final time he meets the illusionist, the ventriloquist is living as a beggar. The illusionist sees him asleep on the ground and gives him some money without waking him. A disabled dog approaches him – maybe his new companion in misery (Figure 20).

(h) The acrobats' narrative programme

The three acrobats look like they are triplets or brothers. They also live in the same hotel as the other performers. However, unlike the others, they appear to maintain their good spirits. They live and train together, so they do not suffer from loneliness. They are the only ones who adapt to the modern way of life. By changing their style, they find work at an advertising company. Nevertheless, they do not forget their fellow entertainers and hand a business card to Tatischeff to help him find work.

Notes on the narrative programmes

Interestingly in the film, the adversary of any one character is not another character. Their common enemy is time and the changing of an era, heralding new ways of living and entertainment. Meanwhile, the public follows the changes en masse and become exponents of the new ways of life, whilst devaluing and maltreating those they once applauded. Entrepreneurs also treat them harshly and often steal their money or pay them poorly. These circumstances inevitably drive music theatre professionals to the margins of society, into poverty and,

Figure 20 The ventriloquist sells his doll and becomes a beggar. Courtesy of Sylvain Chomet.

eventually, to extinction. Only characters – like the acrobats and Tatischeff – able to adapt to the new reality manage to survive.

Despite the illusionist's trials and tribulations seeking work in the new era, there are always those willing to help him, sometimes when he has not asked for it. From the drunken Scottish man at the fair, to the clown and the acrobats, there is always someone around to invite him to a celebration, hand him a lead to a job or take him to a theatre. Most of the time, this help comes from the other artists as an act of solidarity. At the same time, there is always someone (usually a boss) to underpay him or, even worse, steal from him.

One difference between the illusionist and his fellow artists is that his identity is not exclusively bound up with his profession. He has a personality and interests beyond his work. This helps him realize and accept the fact that the age of theatrical magicians is over. Also, he is not a solitary character. Both Alice and his daughter in the photo give his life meaning and purpose.

The film is remarkably complex on the surface and also at a deeper level. One of Chomet's characteristics is that he makes complex films appear simple. Even though the film narrates many dramatic and tragic stories, it ends on a hopeful and uplifting note, with Tatischeff on the train, looking at the photograph that has accompanied him throughout the film. A wide shot follows, and the camera zooms out of the train that is about to take him away towards new places and new adventures.

Then the city's lights gradually turn off – the stand where the ventriloquist's doll sits goes dark, and the lights of Royal Music Hall switch off. While the film fades to black, a little firefly appears and dashes away. Chomet does not leave his viewers without light and hope, not even for one second. In the next frame, Sophie Tatischeff's photo appears with the end titles.

The themes and isotopies of the film

This film discusses the passage of time and the irrevocable changes it brings both as a societal change and as a personal one. The coming-of-age theme is common in many animation films, for example, *Spirited Away* (*Sen to Chihiro no Kamikakushi*, Miyazaki, 2001) and *Finding Nemo* (Stanton, 2003), and it also appears in *The Illusionist*. The difference is that in *The Illusionist*, the passage from one life stage to another, through trials and increasing maturity, is not limited to the growth of Alice but also extends to most of the film's characters. More importantly, the central focus is on the 'father's' journey and the trials he has to overcome to raise his 'daughter' Alice before he finally lets her go. Additionally, as the old era retreats, a new one is born; everyone is challenged to pass a trial, accept change and adapt to the new situation. Heroes have either to adjust to the new times or disappear.

One of the recurrent themes in the film is *interpersonal relationships*. As in *The Triplets*, there is a strong *family* isotopy, presented in the forms of biological family and adopted family. The vaudevillians act as an extended family to Alice and the illusionist. The isotopy of *solidarity* contrasts the attitude of broader society, where *cruelty* is displayed against the weakest. In the film, cruelty is expressed as indifference, exploitation of the vaudevillians by penny-pinching

Table 5.2 The main isotopies of *The Illusionist*.

Field	Group of isotopies	Isotopy	Antitheses
Society	Social	Social composition	*Vaudevillians* vs (general) *Society*
			Old time professions vs *new professions*
		Lifestyle	*Old or traditional* vs *new or modern lifestyle Melodic* vs *unmelodic* (loud)
		Social relations	*Family* (biological or chosen) vs *professional groups*
		Social values	*Traditional* vs *modern values*
	Economic	Economic	*Poor* (protagonists) vs *middle class* (Edinburgh residents) vs *wealthy* (modern artists/bosses)
Interpersonal	Interpersonal relationships	Family	*Biological* vs *'adopted' family* vs *extended family*
		Solidarity	*Solidarity* vs *exploitation* vs *cruelty*
	Thymic	Care	*Care and friendship* vs *indifference* vs *hostility*
		Loneliness	*Companionship* vs *loneliness*
Culture	Cultural	Cultural behaviour	*Solidarity* vs *indifference* vs *brutality*
			Melodic vs *loud* (unmelodic)
			Traditional vs *old* vs *new*
			Magic vs *illusion* vs *reality*
		Artistic expression	*Old* vs *new*
			Music theatre professions vs *pop groups*
Place	Spatial	Topological	*Countryside* vs *'the in-between space'* (travelling) vs *city*
Time	Chronological	Time	*Past* vs *present*
			Before vs *after*
			Linear vs *circular time* (nature)
Main themes and axes			*Care* vs *indifference and/or abusiveness*
			Change and survive (succeed) vs *inability or refusal to change and self-destruction*
			Solidarity vs *cruelty*
			Magic vs *illusion* vs *reality*

bosses and, in its most extreme manifestation, as an act of violence. For example, as mentioned above, the clown is beaten to the ground by three children and left alone on the street. In an interesting detail, these three children depict three of the film's animators in a cameo appearance.

Friendship is expressed in its purest form in the relationship between the illusionist and his rabbit. The thymic (sentiment) isotopies are isomorphic to these of friendship, family and solidarity. There is also a strong and prevalent feeling of loneliness, expressed mainly in the group of unemployed artists. Ironically, these characters, who once enjoyed big audiences, are now reduced to scarce and often non-existent spectators. Instead, the performers pass their days alone, often in despair, in their rundown hotel rooms. Loneliness and desperation are expressed mainly by the older generation, while younger characters such as Alice and the acrobats follow the flow of changes. There is also a prevalent economic isotopy, connecting the old-era entertainers with poverty, and the new artists, like The Billy Boy and the Britoons band, with financial success.

The overarching theme that connects all of the above is that of *change* – social, cultural and personal – which, in turn, is related to time and, most specifically, to the developments in history and technology that made the music theatre obsolete. In *The Illusionist*, the music theatre era is a magical time, more innocent and melodic compared to modern forms of amusement and technology, when people do not have the belief or patience to enjoy a magic trick. For example, at the beginning of the film, a little boy and his grandmother watch the illusionist magically fill an empty glass with wine. The grandson points out to his grandmother that it is just a trick. Of course, she knows it is a trick, but she can still enjoy it – unlike her grandson.

Alice, in contrast, comes from a distant, isolated place that has only just got electricity, so she still has faith in magic. The era that is about to end also has its own *social values*, witnessed on the Isle of Iona where at the celebration for the coming of electricity, the pub owner stops everyone, brings in the village's eldest man, and together they welcome the electricity. Moreover, despite their poverty, the vaudevillians do not steal or act immorally or illegally. They sell their work instruments, starve, and become drunks or beggars but never steal. In contrast to their behaviour, theatre owners underpay their workers, essentially stealing from them.

Whilst in *The Triplets*, change in the form of transition to modernity has already happened, in *The Illusionist*, the story takes place on the cusp of a new era, when everything is changing rapidly. The illusionist belongs to the dying breed of music theatre artists who are being quickly replaced by new forms of entertainment. While artists of the previous era suffer, trying to survive in the new world, the rest of society welcomes the changes and savours them.

Change not only manifests in relation to time but also to place. During the film, the illusionist travels to different places on different forms of transport (trains, ships, cars). This travelling presents a constant change of scenery. The illusionist initially lives in France, then travels to London and then to the Isle of Iona (see Figure 21) before settling for a while in Edinburgh. Finally, he takes the train back to France, where his journey started. This spiral narration is also present in Chomet's previous film. The same pattern appears when a poorly dressed girl looks at the now well-dressed Alice in the same way she once admired elegant women upon her arrival in Edinburgh (Figure 15). According to the film, personal change leads to another state of *maturity*, whilst the inability or refusal to change leads to self-destruction.

Freedom is a crucial theme related to both change and maturity. Alice has to grow up for the illusionist to leave her to live her own life, and at the same time, he has to mature and acknowledge that she does not need him anymore. He also frees his rabbit from captivity.

The antithesis *of magic* vs *illusion* vs *reality* creates a net in which all the other codes connect. In addition, it plays with the real-life references from Tati and Chomet's experiences. The film is per se a dazzling illusion, a never-ending

Figure 21 The illusionist travels to Isle of Iona. Courtesy of Sylvain Chomet.

mise-en-abyme, where the illusionist, real-life Tatischeff, Monsieur Hulot and Chomet's own experiences, along with his own perception of Tati, meet and reflect each other, like in an old circus' mirror room. We will all inevitably grow up; yet, the film invites us to suspend our disbelief and enjoy its magic, while at the same time it grounds us in the reality of a long-gone time of innocence.

6

Conclusions

In the previous chapters, we presented a comprehensive approach to Chomet's animation works, focusing on his animation feature films. We referred to the author, his studies, influences, collaborations and previous works, and the context and circumstances under which the films were created. We briefly reviewed pertinent issues of animation theory and history. We discussed aspects of the films' production, funding and distribution. Finally, we presented the analysis of the two films, and we reached conclusions concerning their narrative and meaning. As mentioned before, our film analysis methodology is grounded on Algirdas Julien Greimas' theory (see Introduction; for a more in-depth study, see Lagopoulos and Boklund-Lagopoulou, 2016; Katsaridou, 2019; Lagopoulos and Boklund-Lagopoulou, 2021). Moreover, our analysis focuses on the synergy of all the sub-systems (both visual and auditory) as they convey a very different message if isolated. From all the above, it becomes apparent that the films, apart from their undeniable high intrinsic artistic value, are also significant for animation history and evolution.

As animation films are cultural products, they are essential carriers of European culture abroad. It follows that since culture and society are interlinked and inseparable, Chomet's choice to produce animation films that express different ideologies from the dominant paradigm has a social impact. It is not our claim that Chomet's films alone might change how animation films are perceived or what they communicate. Still, in the previous chapters, it becomes evident that he created a rift in animation (and storytelling) and proved that a 'different' animation is possible. Furthermore, he evinced that the production of animation films that differ from the dominant paradigm is economically feasible as well.

Additionally, it became apparent that Sylvain Chomet is multifaceted and continuously evolving regarding his art and production methods and techniques (see Appendix 1).

Below we will focus on the conclusions derived from examining both films' analyses.

In both *The Triplets* and *The Illusionist*, the technique is more or less the same, that is, 2D hand-drawn animation with integrated CG animation (see Chapter 3). Some of the artists have worked in both films, providing continuity concerning artistic input in the productions. However, the films were produced by different companies in different countries under different circumstances. Both films display a high level of artistic excellence and care for detail and quality.

Nevertheless, the two films are pretty different, with their first dissimilarity in their scripts' origin. As already mentioned, *The Triplets'* script is based upon Chomet's original script, while *The Illusionist* is an adaptation of a script written by Jacques Tati.

Concerning *The Illusionist's* adaptation, Chomet chose to be faithful to Tati, not only as far as the script is concerned, but also to his cinematography. One should acknowledge the care with which Chomet approached Tati as an artist and as a person. He also researched the era when the music theatre was in decline. Chomet's choice to make this film can be considered a gesture of great respect for Tati. His choice to make a 'faithful' adaptation inevitably differentiated this film from his previous one and, as discussed in Chapter 5, brought about many challenges during its making.

Although both films look at serious issues, *The Triplets* approaches them in a more comic manner than *The Illusionist*, which tends to be more melancholic and dramatic. Nevertheless, both films use comical scenes to communicate grave issues, along with a sense of melancholy mixed with an underlying optimism, a combination characteristic of Chomet's films. They are both poetic, as well. All of their elements carry the quality of a poem, from the colours, to the music and the sounds to the rhythm and the storytelling. We may say that Chomet, in essence, composes audio-visual poems.

A good example is the last scene of *The Illusionist*, where the train leaves, the camera zooms out from the train, and we watch the city's lights go out one by one, as the music provides the audience with a sentimental closure. Beyond their meaning, Chomet's films evoke emotions and create experiences. Chomet expresses himself in this unique way by any means (we also encounter it in his live-action film, *Attila Marcel*), whether he has written the script himself or it is an adaptation of someone else's text. We may say that 'poetry' is intertwined with Chomet's mode of expression.

Comparing character design, they are all unique, with distinctive personalities and traits. The characters in *The Triplets* are slightly more exaggerated than in *The Illusionist*. In the first film, there is more facial animation and exaggerated expressions; Bruno in Figures 5 and 10 is a great example. In contrast, *The Illusionist* is based more on the figure's animation, and it is full of little, delicate body movements that gently communicate the feelings of its characters. This choice is interlinked with the differences in the stories and the cinematography – however, Chomet's artistic signature is evident in both films.

Concerning the cinematography, all kinds of shots are used in *The Triplets*, like close-ups and medium and wide shots. In *The Illusionist*, however, Chomet adapted Tati's 'theatrical' cinematography, and, as a result, the shots are mainly wide with an absence of close-ups. Moreover, *The Illusionist* is characterized by long shots and slow editing. *The Triplets* have much faster editing, especially in its 'action' scenes, for example, the sequence where the mafia cars are chasing the bikers' platform in the streets of Belleville. There is much action taking place in *The Illusionist*, too, but it is action concerning internal characters' feelings and depicting changes over a long period of time – not in the form of fast-edited shots.

Following this, it is evident that Chomet does not adjust the stories he wants to tell to a particular mode. He does not 'force' the film to fit one manière; on the contrary, he 'listens' to the story's needs and narrates it in the best-suited way, even if this is more challenging for him. As previously discussed, his artistic practice indicates that he is open to change; better still, he seeks change and variation. At the same time, he has developed his artistic, idiosyncratic style that the audience can instantly recognize. His films are different from one another, each constituting a unique experience for the viewer. However, the audience can tell that it is Chomet speaking to them from the first few moments of the film – a characteristic that great directors share. For example, although Chomet follows Tati's cinematography in *The Illusionist*, the viewer can immediately recognize that it is a film created by Chomet.

Regarding the story, both films are multi-layered and rich in narrative programmes; they narrate the adventures of many heroes besides the protagonists'. Specifically, both *The Triplets* and *The Illusionist* have seven fully developed and interconnected narrative programmes and many more partially developed programmes.

Each character assumes multiple roles. For example, Madame Souza is the hero of her own adventure, but she is also Champion's helper and the mafia's enemy. Interestingly, while the films' heroes seem alone and lonely sometimes,

Chomet surrounds them with many helpers. Even in a hero's darkest hour, there is always someone to make at least one little gesture of friendship or solidarity.

Chomet practically proves that he is sincerely interested in his characters. He gives them a past, a present, a future, desires, traits and flaws. Remember, when he was a child, the characters he created were his friends, who appeared real to him (see Chapter 1 and Appendix 1). He finds a way to share all these interconnected stories with the viewer whilst simultaneously creating a sense of 'simplicity' on the surface. We believe that here lies one of his most essential storytelling skills: he can narrate the most complicated, serious and sometimes 'existential' story with the smoothness of a bedtime story and the gentleness of a poem. However, Chomet is not the 'happily ever after' writer or director.

Nevertheless, he will never let viewers exit the theatre without hope, relief and the sense that they had a meaningful and beautiful experience. It might be in any form: a song, a gesture or even a firefly lighting the darkness. He also ensures that the viewer will experience some spontaneous moments of laughter, such as in the 'stew scene', or when Bruno takes the place of a tyre. He has the charisma to see the comic elements in a tragedy and vice versa.

Both films have more than one theme. However, they have recurrent subjects that they discuss, such as interpersonal relationships, loss, care, and social and personal change (later to appear in the film *Attila Marcel*), indicating that he is deeply concerned about these issues.

Moreover, his heroes are unique and exciting. They are not always successful or perfect; they are multifaceted and create deep relationships and strong bonding with each other, even if they are just a dog or a rabbit. The illusionist's rabbit was his partner both in his personal and in his professional life. It is also interesting that neither young Champion in *The Triplets of Belleville* nor young Alice in *The Illusionist* is the protagonist. The real protagonists are Madame Souza and Tatischeff, who are both either old (Madame Souza) or middle-aged (Tatischeff), putting older characters at the centre of the narrative is in line with his choice to make animation interesting for an adult audience. He strays from the dominant age and design stereotypes prevalent in animation. As discussed in Chapter 2, he does not 'hide' his characters' age, gender, disability, origin or race. Nor does he try to evoke approval by creating 'round' or cute characters. Madame Souza, for example, is an old lady from Portugal who has a clubfoot, and Champion has too big calves thanks to his cycling training. Even in the case of Alice, Chomet did not design just a girl; he tried to combine the most common characteristics of the girls he saw in Scotland. In other words, instead of trying to approach a deceptive, universally approved type, he gives his characters a particular cultural identity.

Chomet's films are usually identified as French. Indeed, there is a prevalent 'Frenchness' in combination with English and other traits as a result of both his cultural background and his work on French comic books (for more about French cultural intertexts, see Floquet, 2006). We should also acknowledge that he learned animation in London, where he adopted the principles of excellence and collaboration that characterize all his practice, as mentioned in Chapter 1.

As mentioned above, Chomet does not try to make 'odourless' films to appeal to 'universal' culture. Instead, he makes films with cultural identity, and at the same time, he invites a worldwide audience by leaving the films open to different interpretations. As he states, he likes people to interpret and connect to his films based on their own experiences and cultures. He notes, 'I'd like them to make it their own and match it to their own memories. One gentleman came and told me that the film had moved him because Madame Souza reminded him of his own Greek grandmother. I liked that' (Chomet on Foley). This statement is in line with our position that a 'universal' culture, where everybody understands the films in the same way, is elusive. Trying to produce such films, as in the case of many mainstream films, may strip the films of their meaning rather than communicate it to everyone (see Chapter 2). At the end of the day, this results in no cultural products at all.

Additionally, as discussed below, his heroes' age reflects Chomet's stance against age-related prejudice. The same stance applies to other prejudices, like disability and beauty stereotypes.

Another engaging issue is the use of visual or auditory contrasts between the sub-systems of the films to evoke feelings and transfer their meaning. For example, the time and place where each film takes place have a distinctive colour or music. Of course, each narration is based on change since we have no story without an action that changes the previous situation. However, the films under discussion contain the notion of change at their core. We may argue that change is a 'background' hero in both films. Change is the trigger of films' prevalent feeling of nostalgia. The constant comparison of the previous era with the new creates the feeling of nostalgia that many scholars have pointed out. It is a strong and personal feeling that invites viewers to turn to their past and personal reminiscences.

It is not only the situation of the heroes that changes; we witness essential historical and social changes simultaneously. Time changes alter space, both the physical and the social. These changes usually are not connected with positive connotations. More specifically, it seems that, for Chomet, the notion of 'progress' did not always signify something positive and does not result in a better society and quality of life – at least not always. In *The Triplets*, changes and progress are linked to an urban, over-consuming, unhealthy lifestyle. In *The Illusionist*, the harmonious natural sounds on the Isle of Iona and the melodious music of the previous way of life give way to the sounds of cars and the buzz of the city accompanied by the loud, unmelodic music of The Billy Boy and the Britoons band. Although change is dominant in both films, in *The Illusionist*, it decisively affects the fates of the film's heroes and becomes a survival factor.

As mentioned above, although the films differ significantly in the stories they narrate, they have similar themes and shared concerns in their deep structure. As we see in Tables 4.2 and 5.2, both films discuss issues related to the fields of society, interpersonal relations, culture, place and time. Additionally, they share the same isotopies; in some cases, they share the exact oppositions. For example, the isotopy of *care* is expressed by the same opposition in both films: *care and friendship* vs *indifference* vs *hostility*.

Moreover, isotopies of space and time dominate both movies. In both films, the countryside and nature have positive connotations, while the massive city of Belleville has negative ones. However, in *The Illusionist*, Edinburgh is depicted as a beautiful city at a time when the protagonists experience difficulties. The city is surrounded by greenery and nature; its buildings are excellent examples of architecture. The typical, unsteady weather of the city and the constant changes of light intensify the feelings of perpetual change.

The past eras (in both films) are isomorphic with the positive axes of lifestyle, care, friendship, solidarity and creativity. Nevertheless, the lifestyle connected to the past is also related to economic hardships, poverty, hunger, wretchedness and, in some cases, annihilation. The natural passing of time is not seen as either good or bad. It just happens, reminding the viewer of the cyclicity of nature's time, in contrast to the human's linear perception of time, moving from past to future. Furthermore, as time is related to age, in the films, age is not perceived as a flaw but rather as a result of the natural passing of time. It is not the older age that made the triplets poor. It seems that they can create art and enjoy life at any age. The same is true for *The Illusionist*, where the music theatre artists cannot find a job, not because of their age but because of the changes in the entertainment business. Linear time and the notions of 'new' and 'progressive' produce all these adversaries to the heroes.

On the other hand, the acrobats, who seem younger than the rest of the vaudevillians, quickly adjust to the changes, but this is possibly not because of their skills due to their age; it is because they are more connected culturally to the forthcoming era. We can suppose that their resemblance to the members of the pop group The Billy Boy and the Britoons is not accidental.

Interestingly, although this is not one of his films' dominant themes, Chomet expresses a relieving anti-discriminative view concerning age. In our times, ageism manifests as 'natural' and self-explanatory. Contrary to many mainstream films, maintaining and reproducing an ideology that leads to the marginalization of older ages, Chomet freely begs to differ, creating a rift of doubt in the prevalent ageism narrative. The visibility of all ages is only an example of how the films differ from the unfounded but dominant stereotypes that are constantly recycled in animation films. It is refreshing that Chomet does not even argue against the inequalities and discrimination because, in his films, there are no such discriminations of race, age, disability or gender. Prevailing prejudices, ideologies and mythologies do not constrain Chomet. Considering that the films were created many years ago and that presently the EU is still developing policies against the vast issue of prevalent ageism, in addition to promoting an inclusive society, we may conclude that Chomet is a revolutionary artist ahead of his era. This demonstrates the importance of auteur animation concerning what animation may express – more specifically, animation films that are produced to be screened to a broad audience and are not limited to a specialized one at festivals.

Moreover, family is a crucial isotopy, appearing in both films. It is a social structure that, most of the time, is not based on the normative nuclear family but on the heroes' decision to form one or become part of a family. In both films, there is a single-parent family with an adopted child. In *The Triplets*, Madame Souza undertakes to raise her orphaned grandson taking the place of his mother, and in *The Illusionist*, Tatischeff raises Alice, taking the role of her father. It appears that he also has a biological daughter, to whom, we may presume, he returns after leaving Edinburgh, but this is another adventure which starts when the film ends. Both families are complete with a domestic animal, not a pet, but an active family member. In both films, groups have formed that function as extended families (e.g. the singers with Madame Souza and Bruno, and the vaudevillians living at the same hotel). These groups' formation is based on shared interests and, most importantly, on the notion of care. The heroes care about others, leading to friendships and acts of solidarity. These positive values exist in both films, and they are the driving force that propels the heroes to act and the plot to unfold.

Most emotional (thymic) isotopies associated with the heroes are positive. However, some heroes, such as Champion and the vaudevillians, experience loneliness. The feeling of loneliness brings forward issues of loss and the need for companionship. It is also related to the creator's life. As Chomet notes, he prefers to work in a studio than alone. He stated that he is social; he loves animation but does not wish to be alone doing only his work. Friendship, collaboration, companionship, family and memories of love and care are all concepts that counteract loneliness in the films and, we may presume, in the director's life.

In general, society in both films is made up of unequal wealth distribution. The artists, the most creative and those who care for others, belong to the lower-income class. The films comment on new ways of life, related to indifference for the others and, occasionally, exploitation (e.g. the mafia in *The Triplets*) and cruelty (e.g. the children that beat the clown in *The Illusionist*).

In addition, Chomet discusses artistic creation. Culture is expressed through the high value of artistic creation in opposition to mechanical reproduction and degradation of quality. Culture and society are intertwined in his films. Importantly, artistic creation has never ceased to exist in *The Triplets* due to the lack of material resources. Even though they are poor, the singers are resourceful and find ways to produce music with whatever they have, like a newspaper or a vacuum cleaner. In *The Illusionist*, however, the picture is gloomier. The artists are poor, and they starve. They have the means to make art but do not have a place to perform. The audience is no longer interested in their art, which they consider obsolete. Instead, it craves for new, technologically advanced entertainment.

Whilst the films do not make any explicit references to animation itself, we would like to point out that they were produced at a time when the 'new hype' of 3D animation prevailed, supported by the popular narratives of 'progression' to a 'new' and consequently 'better' animation. The period was difficult for directors and producers who dared to pioneer and defend a different style or mode of production from the dominant one. For example, Chomet and Brunner had to go through lengthy and very time-consuming processes to make *The Old Lady* and *The Triplets* come to life, not to mention that Chomet had to fight to secure that *The Illusionist* would not become a fast-paced film. Whilst parallelisms like that are highly hypothetical, the solid context begs for a comparison between the artists' situation in the films and the general struggle that the 2D animators endured to survive during that era. As mentioned in Chapter 2, the audience's enthusiasm towards practically all 3D films just because 3D is technologically new is gradually receding. Meanwhile, many 2D artists had been forced to abandon hand-drawn animation and find other ways to earn a living. That had severe consequences for animation in general. A good example comes from Chomet, who encountered many difficulties finding skilled animators for the production of *The Illusionist*.

The subject of freedom is significant in both films, either artistic or human freedom in general. It might be the freedom deriving from Alice's coming of age or from maturing and 'leaving behind' old ways and beliefs. It is also expressed in *The Triplets*, in Champion's story, in the antithesis of *freedom* vs *captivation/ control* and the singers' lifestyle. Concerning artistic freedom, it seems to flourish away from the centre of the cities, at least in *The Triplets*.

The artists and creative people, in general, have to leave the centre of the consumerist lifestyle to live and create. The antithesis of *freedom* vs *control* drives another parallelism in terms of auteur film animation vs industrialized animation related to available funding and resources. Europe has long decided to move towards an upgrade of its position in the production of animation films and, more particularly, the production of a distinctively 'European' animation. We have witnessed a remarkable increase in European animation production in recent years.

Nevertheless, films, as mentioned above, are also powerful cultural products apart from being a profitable industry. Consequently, the European animation production's quality and uniqueness should be safeguarded and not be defined by the import and imitation of popular techniques, stereotypes or ideologies. Since the eve of animation, Europe has been related to art, auteur films and diversity. We believe these characteristics should be preserved for a long-term flourishing, profitable European animation to be achieved. Japan's example, mentioned in Chapter 2, proves our point. Japanese anime is one of the most important contemporary cultural products that Japan exports and carries an inherent 'Japaneseness'. Films like the ones by Hayao Miyazaki are pretty different from what the US industry produces. In our opinion, it would be both exciting and profitable if different animation films from different countries could be available and easily accessible to the general public.

Even though Chomet is not the only European animator or director to use adult heroes, he is, to our knowledge, the first in contemporary European animation history who dared to make a feature film with adult protagonists and received universal appraisal and success. In the United States, Pixar has also shown an interest in attracting adult audiences to its films, such as *WALL·E* (Stanton, 2008) and *Up* (Docter, 2009) – two films whose protagonists are not children. However, there is a radical difference in these films' approaches. More specifically, there is a difference between creating films for teenagers and adults that can be viewed by children and making films for children that adults can also view. As David A. Price notes, 'Pixar films reach whole audiences because they know how to make characters that are appealing to children and then give them adult problems' (Price, 2009). This practice involves a degree of censorship, both in the design of the characters and in the presentation of their stories, which must be in line with the 'universal' perception of what is appropriate for children.

On the contrary, Chomet does not create his characters focusing on children. Nor does he ignore them. He creates interesting characters and stories, period. Even though his films do not contain violent or sexual scenes, some issues resulted in a PG rating. For example, some of his characters smoke, either because smoking connotes the 'bad' guys in *The Triplets* or because they live in an era where smoking was a socially accepted habit. Back then, it was not perceived as a bad habit at all.

Chomet's characters are different, funny and sometimes even a little crazy. They are constantly engaging because they are original and designed to serve the narrative, not to recreate a worn-out model of 'correct behaviour' or succumb to conservative perceptions of what may or may not be presented in an animation film. They are refreshingly unusual.

In conclusion, the films under discussion are unique works of art and quite rightfully got their place in the international history of animation as well as in the hearts of their audience. Through these films, Chomet unfolded his virtuosity as an artist, director and storyteller. He also helped the evolution of French and European animation in general and communicated high-importance social values. He defended and reintroduced the role of the auteur director and the artist's choices at a time when the big studios pushed auteurs out of the picture. He supported the films as art and cultural products, which can be profitable as such, against the prevalent focus on the commodification of films only for profit. He opposed the century-long prevalent view that animation is only for children by producing animation films mainly for adults and teenagers. The success of Chomet's films proved that adults love animation too.

Chomet also demonstrated that after the 'hype' of 3D as the manifestation of technological advances, it all comes down to the quality of a film, in whatever technique it is produced, and additionally, that different styles and methods of production might as well benefit from the new means that technology offers. Technology is not necessarily related only to one style; advancement should not be limited to mimicking 'realism' and live-action.

Moreover, he opposed the 'purists' of the 'traditional' style, which looked at any change in the production methods as a kind of betrayal by welcoming and incorporating technological tools into his production. At the same time, he opposed the ones who considered this 'traditional' animation old-fashioned because of the very same technological advancements.

As mentioned above, as more and more animators move to work in what might be called 'realistic' animation for the needs of the live-action industry, a merge of the forms emerges, not for the benefit of animation form. It tends, in many cases, to become merely a tool to live-action films' production line. Chomet's animation belongs to a small group of directors who stand the ground of animation as a form, preventing it from being a substitute or imitation of live-action. He retains the poetry and the distinctive way that animation communicates.

Moreover, he expresses a different paradigm and ideology to those that mainstream films reproduce. He is free from conventions replicated for a hundred years by the show business industry and from stereotypes related to race, beauty, age, disability or gender, as discussed above.

His films make us move away from the 'fast food' culture, in which one film is similar to the other. As Chomet himself says, mainstream films ease the audiences because they know the taste, what will happen and how it will end. It is like eating the same hamburger again and again. It always has the same taste. However, this is not art or experience, both of which have the characteristic of uniqueness. They also entail a sense of risk for both the audience and the artist because the audience will see something new, and the artist will present something new. It is a risk worth taking when communicating through any form of art. Chomet and the audience have taken this risk successfully, thus creating a bond of trust and communication.

Chomet cares about his viewers, people and society. He foremost cares about animation. His films have forwardness and sincerity derived from the fact that Chomet puts pieces of himself and his experience in his films, pieces that he does not try to present 'realistically' but directly and sincerely from his poetic angle. This directness and sincerity pervade his films. On the production level, this is expressed by his dedication to achieving the highest degree of excellence, sometimes with limited means.

Contemporary animation needs creators like Chomet, who pave the way to something new, alternative, different and unique. Since the beginning of its history, animation has been perceived as the 'art of illusion'. If the illusion is lost, if surprise and magic transform into a more or less successful imitation of reality and a repetition of the same old themes and stories, somewhat changed but always the same, then what has animation become?

Chomet's animation films continue to invite the audience to have a unique experience in a unique universe created for them, where heroes reside and live their lives and adventures. He does not hide the constructiveness of his films behind mainstream tricks of realistic depiction. The hand-drawn lines and the watercolour style let the audience know from the beginning that this is not 'real'; it is an illusion that someone prepared with the most outstanding care for them. The audience suspends their disbelief and lives for two hours in this unique universe, connecting sentimentally with the hand-drawn heroes and empathizing with their hardships and adventures. When the film is over, they leave the theatre feeling that they had a meaningful experience. This is animation at its best. It is proof that animation magic still exists.

Beyond *The Illusionist*

After *The Illusionist*, Chomet's next feature film was the live-action film *Attila Marcel* (2013). The first idea, the title *Attila Marcel*, arose during *The Triplets of Belleville's* production (see Chapter 3). It took many years for the story to mature and become the homonymous film. Claudie Ossard produced it for *Eurowide Film Production*, who, among many other well-known films, also produced *Amélie* (Jeunet, 2001). Pathé handled the film's distribution in France and its international sales. *Attila Marcel* was made on a budget of 6.7 million euros.

The film focuses on the story of Paul (Guillaume Gouix), a young man raised by his two eccentric aunts (Bernadette Lafont and Hélène Vincent) in Paris since the death of his parents when he was a child. At the age of thirty-three, he still does not speak due to a trauma in his childhood, which caused him the loss of memory and speech. His aunts dream of seeing him become a virtuoso pianist, but even though he practises dutifully, he remains sad until Madame Proust (Anne Le Ny), his upstairs neighbour, gives him a herbal remedy that unlocks repressed memories from his childhood. He discovers what really happened to his parents. It opens with a quotation from Marcel Proust, which resumes the film's theme: 'We are able to find everything in our memory, which is like a dispensary or chemical laboratory in which chance steers our hand sometimes to a soothing drug and sometimes to a dangerous poison.'

The film belongs to the 'Chometian' universe. Different though it may be from his other films, it bears many common characteristics. Amber Wilkinson notes: 'While the influence of Proust may be clear, *Attila Marcel* is also uniquely Sylvain Chomet. With its put-upon young prodigy and its twin-set of aunts, the film recalls *Les Triplettes De Belleville*, while Guillaume Gouix's doe-eyed and Tatiesque performance recalls the delicate (and silent) melancholy of *The Illusionist*' (Wilkinson, 2014).

The film invites the viewers to think about serious issues, like childhood trauma, domestic violence and repressed memories, while simultaneously providing relief through its comic elements and music that evokes feelings and changes the mood. As it is valid for all his films, music plays a vital role in *Attila Marcel*. Chomet notes:

> I really wanted to do a film which was about music but not to be obviously to be a film where everyone suddenly bursts into song – although there's a couple of scenes like that. But the music is the central theme of the film. That's what makes all the memories come back. So, I had all that and then I met producer Claudie Ossard on Paris, je t'aime and I had already a lot of music written – most of them I wrote in North Berwick [in East Lothian], so I was looking out the window at sea and it all came. Then I discovered the ukulele. I discovered ukulele in Scotland, which is very funny.
>
> (Chomet in Wilkinson)

We may trace Chomet's experiences, feelings or memories in his films, and *Attila Marcel* is no exception. In a question that Wilkinson asked him about the prevalence of the idea of memory in the film, he confirms the aforementioned trait:

> Yes, it interests me a lot. I was a child around that period, in the early Eighties, I would be in my 20s but the Seventies was a really strong period for me, so I've got a lot of memories about that. I would say that my family would be a lot more like the Attila Marcel family than the aunts. I have a friend whose background is aristocratic and I was invited for a week to spend some time with him and his family in a castle. And I was really shocked and I was observing, while I stayed there, how they communicate or they don't communicate but they're all very polite, very clever people – a lot of culture but they don't say much about feelings, they hide a lot of things. And it's very much what I tried to do with Paul and his family.
>
> (Chomet in Wilkinson)

Concerning its themes, in this film, as in his previous animation movies, coming of age, maturity, care, time and past have a strong presence, even though they are expressed differently in each film. Family and friendship themes have already been present in his films from *The Triplets of Belleville*. In *Attila Marcel*, as in *The Triplets of Belleville*, the hero lost his parents and is raised by relatives. The orphaned child is a subject we also meet in *The Illusionist*, yet differently. Every film has something new and unique to add to the common themes, distinctive points of view and layers of understanding. Therefore, a theme continuity puts

Attila Marcel in the same universe and establishes a dialogue between the films, whether they are animation or live-action.

Chomet brought many elements from his animation films to his live-action, the same way he did the opposite. He used live-action elements in animation, such as in *The Illusionist*'s cinematography. The way he perceives cinema and creates his films is one more reason that makes Chomet's art exceptional. He sees cinema as a whole, selecting the form that best serves the story he wants to tell while maintaining his style. As a result, he treats animation and live-action cinema as equal but always distinctive forms of cinema. Furthermore, he indicates that all forms of cinema can converse, and there can be 'loans' from one form to the other while, at the same time, preserving their identity and autonomy. Chomet expresses his idiosyncratic artistic language (parole) with animation and live-action, leading to an upgrade and enrichment of both cinematic forms (see Figure 22).

Breaking barriers between forms is sometimes tricky, as specific notions about what is acceptable or not for each form is established, especially in the minds of the experts and the institutions, which inevitably influences the general public's perception. Let us look at an example from *Attila Marcel*. Chomet was already recognized as one of the most important French contemporary animation directors when the film was made. In this context, some critics felt that Chomet 'betrays' animation by moving to 'the opposite' form, while others from live-action expressed a particular curiosity or even scepticism. Interestingly, some film critics stress the director's background in animation. Their critique includes many comparisons between the forms and expresses a rigid perception of what 'should' or 'should not' be present in a live-action film.

Most critics highly praised it, while others criticized it, mainly because of the narrative devices they considered 'appropriate' for animation, but not for live-action. In our opinion, these ideologies reproduce old-fashioned stereotypes that lead to a limited and short-sighted view of the cinema as an art form.[1]

Intriguingly, the film was very successful in South Korea, where Chomet's animation films had not been screened, so the audience watched it without any of the bias mentioned above. It was only after *Attila Marcel* that his animation films were screened in South Korea and were also very successful.

Another thought-provoking issue concerning *Attila Marcel* is that it is a transmedia project. Sideburnn launched a free application in partnership with Eurowide Film Production and Pathé Distribution. The application '... allows

Figure 22 Sylvain Chomet at the shooting of *Attila Marcel*. Courtesy of Sylvain Chomet.

users to take a behind-the-scenes look at the film, including mini-games that pay homage to the Point'n Click genre of the 1990s … To unlock the bonuses, you have to explore the film sets, created by Carlos Ponti, in search of hidden objects and complete several challenges' (AlloCiné, 2013). This application adds to our position that Chomet creates storyworlds in which many different heroes may exist, and their adventures can be presented in various media.

Moreover, it is noteworthy that the application follows the old point-and-click genre, mainly used for adventure or detective games of the 1990s, as it is in line with the reminiscence of the past that the film invokes. While *Attila Marcel's* analysis is not per se in the book's scope, we believe it is a film that deserves its own attention and analysis and shares very strong filmic discourse components with Chomet's previous animation films.

It should be noted that *Attila Marcel* was neither the first nor the only time that Chomet directed a live-action movie. As mentioned in Chapter 3, he co-directed the film *Paris, je t'aime* (2006) (segment *Tour Eiffel*). Later, in 2016, he wrote, composed the music for and directed the film *Merci Monsieur Imada*, produced by the French Artistic Association Adami. The film is a comedy that takes place during the shooting of a film, with a nasty director torturing his actors. At the end of the film, the iconic actor Bernard Menez made a guest star appearance. The film had a great reception at the Cannes film festival. Chomet describes it:

> We went to Cannes, and the audience in Cannes can be really good and very responsive, or very cold. My film was the third one, and I was with the other people in a big theatre, and during the two first films the atmosphere was really tepid, people were very cold. That was really harsh, and I wanted to leave because I knew my film was coming in, and I didn't know if it was going to work. And when it did, it was really the first time people started to laugh straight away and never stopped for 15 minutes! That was mad! Everything I thought was working. I remember that was really a great feeling!
>
> (Appendix 1)

A few years after *Attila Marcel*, Sylvain Chomet planned to direct *Swing Popa Swing*, the prequel to *The Triplets of Belleville*, discussed in Chapter 3 (see also Appendix 1), which was to be produced by *Les Armateurs* and Didier Brunner. To our knowledge, the production was cancelled due to financial issues. Securing funding for a film that is not considered 'mainstream', like Chomet's films, was always a huge challenge, despite all of his success and *The Triplets'* devoted audience. As it is written in Chapter 2, this is a huge issue, not only for Chomet but for contemporary animation as a whole. While in recent years, some brilliant animation films have been produced, especially with France's contribution, in many cases, their creators had to overcome immense obstacles and endure long struggles to secure their funding for production and distribution. Didier Brunner noted in a 2016 interview at Cineuropa concerning European animation:

> There is another threat to finding funding for these films: the reluctance of television channels to broadcast them. France Télévisions invests in two or three animated films per year, and mainly those targeted at children … Canal+ has also adopted a cautious outlook when it comes to animated films. They feel as though it would be difficult to implement them into their channels, while requiring lots of investment.

Since then, the situation has become even worse in terms of producing auteur films, especially for adults. Even though French animation production is flourishing and has almost tripled in quantity, most of its production is again focused on TV series and some great animation films that mainly target children's audiences.

In 2014, Chomet made a 'French' version of the well-known *Simpsons couch gag* (which opens the Simpson's episodes) that received an enthusiastic reception. Chris Harnick writes:

> This could be the strangest and coolest Simpsons couch gag we've ever seen … The fuse goes out at the Simpsons household and when the lights come back on, everybody's looking a little different and speaking French. Marge can't find Maggie, Bart stuffs a goose to make some pâté, Lisa plays the accordion and everybody is wearing glasses. Yep, that's Homer eating snails. It's pretty neat.
>
> (2014)

Chomet drew upon French stereotypes and the way the 'French' is perceived by others and made something hilarious. The use of stereotypes is transversal to Chomet's works, either French stereotypes or ones deriving from a broader Western culture (see also Floquet, 2006). In his interview with Jennifer Wolfe for Animation World Network, he says:

> To me, it seemed to be the right approach. After all, the American Simpsons is full of stereotypes, it's what makes it funny and Americans are able to laugh at themselves and how others see them through the show. I wanted to do the same for the French – use clichés and French stereotypes such as eating snails, making foie gras, etc., so that we are able to laugh at ourselves and also at how others perceive us.
>
> (Chomet in Wolfe, 2014)

Moreover, Russ Fischer focuses on Chomet's great animation: 'The underlying gag here is that Chomet is involved with the sort of gorgeous animation that we'd love to see more of, but which is a pretty far cry from the cheaper stuff The Simpsons uses now' (Fischer, 2014).

Sylvain Chomet has been engaged with many other projects, such as a theatre play, composing music, painting and many more (see Figure 23). Let us note his endless creativity, the ease with which he expresses himself through many

Figure 23 Sylvain Chomet with one of his paintings depicting his daughter Jinty and his son Ludo.

different media and his never-ending devotion to the principles of quality and collaboration that he embraced ever since he worked as an animator in London, as discussed in Chapter 1.

Sylvain and Sally Chomet's collaboration on the book *Caleb's Cab* (2016) is worth mentioning. It is not their first collaboration, as Sally worked on *The Triplets*, and she was a producer for *The Illusionist*. The noteworthy part is that this time it is a creative collaboration. *Caleb's Cab* was first written by Sally and then illustrated by Sylvain. It is a children's book with a fascinating story. The plot is about the vanishing of Caleb's father and his adventures in his quest to find him, while at the same time, he and his mother struggle to survive under the fear of the 'bad' Money Mongers who trap people in depth to their 'C.A.S.H. scheme'. Chomet's illustrations resemble his animation design style and offer a beautiful visualization of the story.

Interestingly, although Chomet wanted to be an illustrator at the beginning of his career, he rejected many offers. To our knowledge, this is the first time he did illustrations for a book, at least since his animation career began. *Caleb's Cab* is the first book of a series that narrate Caleb's adventures.

Chomet's perception of animation production as a collaborative work remains unaltered, stressing the importance of the feeling of being part of a team and a project. He advises animators not to isolate themselves and, instead of constantly working alone in their place, to form small units because 'even four people is a mini animation studio, but it is still an animation studio!' Chomet has already formed his unit in Bayeux, France (see Figure 26).

When our discussion with Sylvain Chomet took place, he had many projects in various stages of production, including an animated feature film, a live-action feature and his international school of storyboarding for animation. Sylvain Chomet Academy, The SChool, is based in Bayeux, France, and most of the courses will be taught in English (see Figure 24). As Chomet tells Alex Dudok de Wit:

> 'The goal is to secure employment, not to win a diploma,' adds Chomet. 'In that way I tend to think of the course we're offering as an apprenticeship rather than a formal education. My lecturing colleagues are all successful professionals who will continue to work in their areas of expertise as well as teaching at The SChool. They will be mentors, not teachers. They can show how it's done – not just tell.'
>
> (2019)

Chomet has been interested in teaching since the early years of his career, especially to passionate students. At the time of our discussion, he had just

Figure 24 Images from The SChool, Bayeux, France. Courtesy of Sylvain Chomet.

announced the opening of the school and had already received a large number of applications. It seems that this project is very dear to him; maybe the school is a place to pass on his knowledge and legacy and, at the same time, train artists whom he might work with in future projects.

Moreover, he directed the animated music video for the song Carmen by the Belgian artist Stromae (2015). He also co-wrote the Carmen video with French rapper, songwriter and record producer OrelSan. The song is an adaptation of the aria *L'amour est un oiseau rebelle* (Love is a rebellious bird), commonly known as the Habanera, from the opera Carmen by French composer Georges Bizet. The song's video and lyrics are a commentary on Twitter and generally all social media: 'Carmen's bird morphs into an all-too-familiar blue fowl that grows bigger and bigger and all the more menacing, finally consuming everyone – celebrities and everyday people alike – before (literally) expelling them out of its body' (Tsioulcas, 2015). The video clip is important not only for its artistic value, but also because it signifies a change in Chomet's methodology of animation production as it is the first time that Chomet extensively used the referencing technique on one of his animation projects. Chomet clarifies that the referencing technique has nothing to do with rotoscoping, which he despises:

> The first time I did animation like that was for Stromae, in two scenes. One is when he jumps on the big bird, and the other one is the scene where he is with this girl in the bed and they are arguing … And because you can import video footage and have it straight on your table, you can use it as a reference. So, I did a shot with a girl in the studio, and she's got this way of moving, which is very personal. So, I took the footage, and I caricaturised him and her. It is not rotoscoping. I hate rotoscope because, for me, it is not animation, it is cheating, and it is horrible. But referencing is really interesting because you actually use the rigging of the movement. You can change anything you want, change the rigging, but you can keep the volume and the lip sync as well, so you use the soul of the acting of the character … When I see the rigging, I see the points where things are attached, and I can do any kind of character with the same footage. I can do one million characters. You need to be a good animator to do that.
>
> (Appendix 1)

He was reluctant to use references until he realized that even the old animators were using many references, even in his favourite film, *101 Dalmatians* (Geronimi, Luske and Reitherman, 1961):

> The character of Cruella de Vil, for me is one of the best images … I thought that the guy who did that is a genius. And he is a genius! Then I saw the footage which they used … It has nothing to do with rotoscope! Because you see, the actress who plays Cruella de Vil for the reference is very different from what they did.
>
> (Chomet, personal communication, Bayeux,
> 3 to 6 October 2019)

He also mentioned an occasion when he used the same actor to create three totally different characters, concluding: 'You know, it is actually a magic thing to do animation. If you do the trick and nobody sees the trick, that's fantastic!'

Chomet has always been open to changes and has kept pace with technical and technological developments and other methods that might come to his attention and help in producing his films, as discussed in Chapter 3. He notes that technological changes help with the production of 2D animation: 'It all comes in a very exciting time when the technique has become really amazing for 2D animation! You know, we are not stuck … it is the start of something because we have very amazing tools!'

When this discussion took place, Chomet had already made a pilot for an animated film based on the story of the life of Marcel Pagnol, one of France's greatest twentieth-century writers, who excelled in many creative fields, including film making.

While the 2010s were very productive for Sylvain Chomet on many fronts, his last animated feature film, *The Illusionist* (2011), was released over a decade ago. In the meantime, as mentioned above, Sylvain Chomet developed several passion projects and wanted to partner with a producer to make them come to life. At this point, he met Aton Soumache,[2] producer, co-founder and president of ON entertainment. Soumache has produced many animation films: for example, the film *Renaissance* (Volckman, 2006), which won the Cristal for best feature at Annecy Film Festival and the movie *The Little Prince* (Osborne, 2015), which earned a César for Best Animated Feature Film, a BAFTA for Best Animated Feature Film and it was the biggest worldwide success of all times for a French animated movie (120 million US dollars worldwide gross).

Figure 25 Frame from the storyboard of *The Magnificent Life of Marcel Pagnol* movie. Copyright 'Sylvain Chomet' (shading by Chung-Hsuan FAN CHIANG) with courtesy of Whattheprod and OnClassics.

Sylvain Chomet and Aton Soumache first met in early 2020 as Aton Soumache's ON Classics and Ashargin Poiré and Valérie Puech's What the Prod partnered to co-produce Sylvain's next film, *The Magnificent Life of Marcel Pagnol*. Figure 25 is a frame from the storyboard on *Marcel Pagnol* movie. It shows the London studio where Chomet started animation as an in-betweener and fell in love with the media. It was in Goodge Street, at Richard Purdum's studio. This is where he made his first animation, late at night, after work. The studio was located at the two top floors of the tallest building. The tiny light is Chomet working late on a personal animation.

Given the ambition and profusion of Sylvain's projects, Aton quickly had in mind to build an in-house studio, 'a true wonder engine' that would be fully dedicated to Sylvain's projects, with the goal of making it a 'European Ghibli'. In our opinion, Sylvain and Aton met at the right time in their respective careers. The association between one of the greatest animation directors alive and one of the most prolific animation producers in the industry will undoubtedly sparkle and result in many fantastic films in the coming years.

Sylvain Chomet is an artist who constantly creates new things in various media and never ceases to amaze us. Due to the broadness and complexity of his artistic creations, the ending of this chapter will be intentionally left without a strict epilogue to serve as an open invitation to scholars for further research and dialogue on his exceptional and distinctive works.

Appendix 1

In Sylvain Chomet's words

Figure 26 Sylvain Chomet at Bayeux, France. Courtesy of Sylvain Chomet.

Childhood, studies and first drawings

I was born in 1963, in the west suburbs of Paris. My dad was an engineer in a car factory, in Poissy and my mother was a stay-at-home mum taking care of me and my sister. My sister was ten years older than me, so she left home when I was still young. Because I was really tiny, my mother didn't put me in school until I was six years old. So, until I was six, I spent my time just with my mom. She was an artist; she was very skilful. She could paint and she could also rebuild a wall. She could do a lot of things. I remember, one day, she took some plaster and some plastic, and she put the plaster on the plastic and it became a kind of a hard surface and she started to paint a fresco – a prehistoric thing. It was beautiful!

Absolutely beautiful! And it looked like a cave work. I used to watch her creating art and when I was two and a half years old, I asked her for a pencil and some paper and the first time I had this pencil in my hand, I drew the television we had in the lounge. And on the television was a statue of a character with a big moustache. And I drew that too! I even drew the open door of the television cabinet and all the buttons. It's a very basic drawing, but everything is there. My mother kept the drawing and put a date on it, and from then on every time I did a drawing, she put dates on it.

I learnt some music as well, but basically, I was drawing and when I went to school, I was drawing during the courses when I was bored. In France at that time kids were asked what kind of job they wanted to do in the future, and probably as soon as I started going to school ... I went to primary school, we had a great director there and he knew I drew, so he asked me to do this big drawing with all the people from the school, ... I've kept it actually. In France at that time they were asking you what kind of job you want to do in the future I wrote I wanted to be 'designateur humoristique', a cartoonist. During those years my mother used to buy me a magazine. It was fantastic! It was basically a little magazine with a lot of comics stories in it. But really great comics! It had Hugo Pratt! It had some really amazing stuff, all kinds of styles. It's a very French culture, Belgian culture as well. So, I started to get in my head I wanted to be a comic book artist. So, that was it. That's what I wanted to do.

Afterwards, I went to the baccalauréat and then I had to choose a school. There were art schools with normal courses and the option of drawing. Eventually, in the preparatory school, where they teach you how to make a portfolio, I had an amazing teacher. It was fantastic! I learned a lot there. I just realized suddenly that I knew I could draw. After that, I went to the contest and I passed. I arrived in a quite good position but bizarrely, I chose to go in a fashion design school because I saw it on television, it was the beginning of Jean Paul Gaultier and he was a young fashion designer and his shows were like performances, with great people of all shapes ... with the music and everything and I was fascinated by it and I said: 'I want to do that! It's amazing!' So, I went to this school, in Paris, and then realized I was out of my depth there because all the other students knew how to sew! when I was designing my mannequins with the clothes, mine had Tintin heads on. So, they said there is another thing, which is called illustration advertising, which for me was much easier because it's just about drawing ... The teacher, who was a comic book artist as well, was called Pichard and he said to me, 'you know, there is a school which just opened in Angoulême ...' I think he understood what I wanted to do. So, I went to Angoulême but the director told me that I had to do a comic book and come back in six months when there would be new entries.

My parents actually understood so I did this comic book and I was accepted in this school where I spent three years. We basically spent our time drawing and there were other people in the school that we were working together and the guy who did the backgrounds [for *The Old Lady and the Pigeons*] was already in this school. We were a kind of community and we knew each other and apart from the fact that the teachers didn't bring us much, we learnt a lot of things from each other and that was quite a good thing.

While I was at school, I actually published a little book, black and white, which was called *Le secret des libellules*. There was a theatre play for children which was about a book and they said to me: 'invent that book!' Do something about this book. I worked on that and I did my first comic book.

During that period, I did a comic book with the guy who did the backgrounds on *The Old Lady and the Pigeons*. It was a colour book and it was the adaptation of the first novel of Victor Hugo, which is called *Bug-Jargal*. I did 30 per cent of the coloured pictures, and he did the rest. After that I started to work with my friend Hubert, on a comic book series called *Le Pont dans la vase*.

So, I carried on, but at the same time I left France, I went to England. And then animation came into my life and changed everything. So, suddenly I realized it's not fashion design I wanted to do, it's not advertising and it's not comic books, although, if you think about it, when you do animation, you have all that included; you have to design costumes for your characters, advertising, I did commercials, and comic books taught me how to tell a story as well.

Influences

I basically did animated films like I was doing live-action films. My culture for the drawings comes from the French and Belgian comic books; all my influences come from these people. The biggest influence on me and also on other people around me when we were at the school is the French comic book artist Daniel Goossens … And the way he draws, and his stories and his sense of humour, I think he is a genius. I'd say his style, when I was reading his comic books, that's what influenced me to go in my realistic caricaturized style … but most of my culture in cinema didn't come from animation at all. My parents didn't go to the cinema but my mother used to take me to see some animated films when I was a kid, so there would be Warner brothers, and also there were some Disney movies at that time. But otherwise, my cinematographic culture didn't come from going to cinema. It was from television but not the prime-time television – there used to be some late programmes on French television, which were showing repertoire films, amazing stuff! I saw a lot of Fellini films, a lot of Buñuel, at one point they were showing a lot of Tex Avery as well, it was total revolution!

So, my culture is more cinematographic in a way. And to be honest, I started to see more animation, apart from the Disney ones obviously, when I was in Annecy ... When I started to work in London, I didn't really want to do animation. I started working in animation because I had to earn my living, but I still wanted to do comic books! But then I started to discover the world of animation and meet people like Oscar Grillo and Michaël Dudok de Wit, and I became friends with Dominic Buttimore, who was a young producer then ... And we made some beautiful commercials there. Very clever commercials, like the English do so well. They were stylish and very funny ... And it was then that I started to realize that I could have my own style. When I saw Creature Comforts, I saw the power of a good film, what it can give to people ... And, you know, that's the most exciting thing for a director: to be incognito in a theatre and see if people are laughing at the right place, if the thing you've been thinking is actually working.

Recently I did a short live-action film called *Merci Monsieur Imada*, which won the Adami award. We went to Cannes and the audience in Cannes can be really good and very responsive, or very cold. My film was the third one and I was with the other people in a big theatre and during the two first films the atmosphere was really tepid, and people were very cold. That was really harsh and I wanted to leave, because I knew my film was coming in and I didn't know if it was going to work. And when it did, it was really the first-time people started to laugh straight away and never stopped for fifteen minutes! Everything I thought was working. Every little detail! I remember that was really a great feeling! I wrote the music as well, which was great. Comedies don't mean you are going to be laughing all the time, you can bring emotion at one point. To make people laugh, you have to make them cry, but if you make them cry throughout the film, people get bored. You have to be clever in the way you tell things. I always liked the idea that you are telling things in a way people are not expecting. They don't know what the next sequence is going to be, I really love that, to be like a rollercoaster of emotions. That is very interesting!

Interruption: You mentioned Hayao Miyazaki in one of your interviews. Do you like his films?

I've got a lot of respect for Miyazaki, I've seen a lot of Miyazaki's films and when there is one of Miyazaki's films, I will go and see it, because he has something refreshing. His stage and path are quite slow, and I like that because it makes a change from these very eccentric and very American things that are speedy. So, he's got great visuals, great writing. The acting is beautiful and he has these beautiful endings as well. They are not happy endings, like in American movies – sometimes they are really sad. There is a poetry to it [Miyazaki's art] and it is very special. I hope, in a way, I'm also poetical in my way of making films.

You move a lot. Why?

I like to move and I really like to actually live in a place of a different culture. I think Quebec was of a very different culture; although they speak French, they really are North Americans. As I said, when I was in France, I went to a comic books school in Angoulême and I got a diploma, which doesn't mean anything because the publishers don't care about diplomas, they want projects.

There were some animation studios in Angoulême, where they were producing some very bad TV series, but they were very happy to have all these guys coming from the school, because they could draw well. It was a terrible series, but everybody earned his living, and I went there as well. The good thing was that I had my own little room, with a window, looking into the park. I was really frustrated and miserable there, because there is nothing more painful for someone who knows how to draw, to have to work on bad drawings. This is absolutely physically difficult. Really challenging! After some quite disappointing events I felt like a lion in a cage! … So, I said 'I know what to do! I am going to leave France! I'm going to put all my portfolio together and I'm going to go to London and I'm going to do some illustration in England!'

So, it was the middle of the 1980s when I arrived in London and I didn't even know where to sleep. I just took the train and I came; I didn't know where to sleep, it was in the evening; actually, I bumped into a French person who said, 'oh, you can stay at the French institute', which was very cheap, and it was a horrible place, but at least I had a bed and a place to wash, and I slept there. … The next day I went to Soho, bizarrely, because I didn't know that at that time most of the animation studios were there. I didn't even have an address to start searching. I was in Soho Square and I remember myself, sitting on this bench, with my portfolio, and thinking 'What am I doing here? I'm completely mad!' I went up one street and I started to look on the doors and I saw something that had to do with graphic, I didn't know what it was. I rang and I said 'I'm sorry I'm French, I've got a portfolio', and they said 'yes, come in!' These guys actually liked my work and introduced me to some illustration agents who all said: 'You have a very nice style but it is very French, in a way it's not the English style and also it's very difficult to go into illustration, you are very young!' One guy said: 'Have you tried animation? There are a lot of studios in Soho and they are looking for people like you.' I was not very enthusiastic because for me animation was about TV series, but I said 'let's have a try'. I went to Richard Purdum studio and I passed an in-between test and the guy said: 'yes, it's a good test!' … That period was the best ever … I started as an in-betweener and the first job I did was with Michaël Dudok de Wit.

At that time, there were so many animators there who were mostly doing commercials, but very beautiful commercials, very clever commercials, like the English can do, beautiful styles, very funny, very well animated, very artistic. There was one man called Richard Williams. He is Canadian, who actually as a child was fascinated by animation and went to Los Angeles trying to find a job, and became one of the greatest animators of Disney. He came to London and he set up his studio with many people working with him. Some of his employees actually opened their own studios. And there was one other guy, Richard Purdum – he was Richard Williams's assistant. There was a kind of a network, a web, of animation studios which were all related to Richard Williams. And that's why they were actually working in a clever way: instead of being competitive, they would help each other … I think they met every month to talk about the works … and it was very clever! It doesn't exist anymore, unfortunately.

That's where I started to work as an in-betweener and after a year, I started to think … as soon as you understand in-betweens you pass to assisting and then you pass to animation. I started to do my own animation in the evenings. I could use the paper and the line test and I started to do my own things. At one point, because I was still an assistant over there, I decided to take my little animations and go to other studios to become a freelance animator. I easily found a job in one studio, a little studio at that time, and there was a very young producer, Dominic Buttimore, who became my friend, with whom we are going to do *Familiar Things*, the Korean movie. So, he became a very famous producer, he had his own studio in Soho for quite a while. Great studio! …

I was really young and mad and after two years I decided that I can animate in my own style. I had animated in quite a few films so I knew I could adapt my comic book style to animation and it worked! I really love this period, I really love London, I really love English people, my wife is English; England has always been very important to me all my life. I even learned recently from a DNA test that I have 46 per cent of English genes!

I fell in love with animation, really! And it made me even more mad about the way I was treated in France, because I saw the way people were working in London and their dedication about doing their best job, and the level of excellence that was there. It was very uplifting. And I kept that in my studio and in my films. Obviously, when I would open my own school, I would basically keep this English mentality, that mentality from the 1980s.

At that time, when they were doing *Roger Rabbit*, Richard Williams had this big studio and I wanted to go there because for me and everyone else, he was the core of animation. Basically, he was god. His level of animation was fantastic! So, for me, I thought that guy was a god! But I thought I would never meet him because they were still finishing *Roger Rabbit*. They didn't have much animation left to be done, just in-betweens, and I had a director's job in a studio making commercials, so I didn't have the chance to meet him then. So, I thought that guy was a god and I would never meet him but I actually met him once and that's another story, which is really great.

The Old Lady and the Pigeons

So, I was in a park, another park in London, everything started in parks basically, and there were some pigeons around. Suddenly, I saw the pigeons, because when you are an animator, you start to look at things and the way they move ... I was looking at the way pigeons move and I said: 'What ... it's complicated!' because it seems to be like a mechanism. So, there are two head movements for each step ... I'm not even sure there is a rule about it. I did something to make it look like it, so it was basically two head movements for one step.

And there was a guy next to me who also was a very good animator and so we said 'why don't we do an animated film?' ... I did the storyboard of *The Old Lady and the Pigeons*, and I did some designs. So, I had this project, the storyboard and the story, obviously, and some designs of the two main characters and pigeons. I realized that in the UK although I could work on animation and do some really beautiful works, it was very difficult to have my film produced. So, I went back to France, to the south of France, Montpellier, and I worked for some studios over there which were doing TV series, not a very interesting job really, … but you know what, I still wanted to do my film. At that time, I met Didier Brunner. I met him through another friend and he was looking for some projects. He wanted to work with my project and I said 'yes, yes, great!' and we tried to find some money for it. And it took a long time …

[Meanwhile] In Montpellier, they wanted to train some people to work for their studios. So, I said yes, I can do that, I can teach them animation. In a way, that was my first real teaching job and it was really interesting. I tried to inspire my students to make their own films and creations, to experience a higher standard of animation and some of them actually succeeded. Unfortunately the company was not very happy with my initiative so I left after a year.

The producer called me one day and he said: 'We've got money to develop the film!' I can tell you that I was over the moon! I felt amazing! But my film was twenty minutes long and there was probably enough money to do four minutes, so I said to him 'ok, why don't I do the first four minutes and then we use it as a pilot to get the money for the next fifteen minutes'. He said ok, and I did it. I worked in my apartment, I put the storyboard on the wall, I had an assistant, a young girl who was assisting me to do the in-betweens … so we did everything at home and I had a friend who was a comic book artist, I was working with him as well, and he did the backgrounds. We were the three of us and eventually we did the first four minutes of the film, which are actually the four minutes you see on the film – we didn't change anything. The producer took it to the financers in France and it was a 'no' by everybody. Everybody said that's 'weird', 'a bit sinister', 'it won't be fit for children', they don't like the colours, 'it's a little bit too dark'. So I can tell you there were ups and downs. That was another frustration for me; the French cultural mentality at the time was a huge disappointment once again. It changed later on, but that's a very different story. I moved to Canada, to Montreal. I worked in this studio for a couple of years, doing commercials and I was not really thinking that I would make my own films anymore.

What happened basically was that the producer, Didier Brunner, had a great idea to go to England and to talk to the producer Colin Rose, who was the head of BBC Bristol Animation and they were funding animation. He looked at the first four minutes and laughed and said 'that's fantastic! Yes, we are going to help you produce that!' As soon as the BBC got involved, the French TV channels said: 'Oh, yes, we will contribute too.' CNC, the French National Centre of Cinematography, was ok, because CNC gave us the first money to achieve the film. Since I was already working with this commercial animation studio, they agreed to co-produce it, and we opened a studio in Montreal. Then we had a small team and we did *The Old Lady and the Pigeons*. But I wasn't the only animator, there was another guy animating with me, Gérard T. Goulet who did a lot of pigeons as well. There were a lot of pigeons in this film! But the first pack of pigeons was something I did in Montpellier. I'm coming from comic books, so, I've got a sense of illustration, the importance of the light, the dark places, the colours ... It's nice to have a harmony of colours for a scene. So, [the scenes] all have a unity of colours.

The film was finished and we decided to participate in the festivals! We went to Ottawa festival and they didn't want it! That was the festival next door! But you know that there is a 'dispute' between the French-Canadian and the English-Canadian [animation]. They saw the film; they didn't select it. It was a big shock! I said, that's it. It's a bad film. And this lovely person, Colin Rose, came to Montreal and we screened the film and he saw the film and he said: 'Sylvain, you and me know it's a good film.' I wasn't very sure about that because I hadn't made a film for just the two of us. I wanted everybody to like the film. But I thought at least I did it – I got to the end of it. I tried to live the dream. But it's not happening; it's rubbish. Ok, that's it. The end.

At that time, they were recruiting people for an [Disney] animation studio which had just opened in Toronto. I went to work for this big name and there was a big tower and at the top of the tower was the company. Two floors at the top of the building facing the Lake Ontario – in some rooms, mountains of computers boxes and things like were piling. There was so much money! I was there to develop a character and I was working on the sequel of *Hercules*. The first one hadn't been released yet, but people had been working already for six months developing a sequel for *Hercules*. So, I went there and my only job was to develop one character ... I was doing animation, it was nice, it was ok.

While I was still working there, one day I had a call from the producer of *The Old Lady and the Pigeons*, saying: 'Your film has been selected for screening at the World Animation Celebration Festival in Los Angeles!' I said: 'Wait! You didn't tell me that!' He said: 'No ... and tomorrow they will give the award ... and I think you should come!' And I said: 'But I'm working and I don't think I have time to take a plane and come to Los Angeles' ... And we won the first prize! A couple of days later I got a call from Colin Rose who said: 'Congratulations you are nominated for a BAFTA award.' He said: 'Sylvain, you have to understand something. Don't get too excited because all the other films are English films and definitely one of them is going to be chosen because yours is a French film.'

And I said 'It's ok, it's already great to have a nomination. It's great because they recognize my work and it's coming from England.' He said: 'You know, I can go, because I have an invitation.' I said: 'use it. It's a great ceremony' and that was it.

One evening I met Sally, who was working as a PR in Toronto. I met Sally and the next day I had a call from Colin Rose saying 'congratulation! You won a BAFTA!' Actually, I had said to him before he went to the ceremony 'give my regards to the Queen!' as a joke. And he said, 'Congratulations, the Queen is giving you a BAFTA.'

Questions about the *Triplets*

Kirikou (Ocelot, 1998) was released, it was a massive box-office success and everybody at that time in France wanted to do a feature animated film. They started to believe in it. French people are followers, that's the problem. They follow when something works – they try to follow the flow. Brunner wasn't a follower because he took a big chance with *Kirikou* and it actually worked. He was taking a bigger chance with me because I was basically aiming at adults while *Kirikou* was for children. So, he was taking a lot of risk, he wanted to do something, he wanted to show something … and he proved himself as producer.

So, he said, 'You got a short film, do two other short films with the same length and the same character, the old lady.' And I wrote two other stories. I thought the old lady was going to be one of the *Triplets*, she would have two identical sisters. I wanted to use the same character; I wanted to have two identical sisters in different stories. They were born in Paris and actually we could see that in the picture. So, in the beginning you see them in the arms of their mother, in the 1900s, three little girls and I was going to tell three different stories of these three old ladies, one living in Paris, who is the first sister and that's the old lady and the pigeons, another one living in the suburbs, that's the one who would have a nephew who likes bicycles and it was a story about bicycles and the third one living in a remote place in Canada, and it would be a story with frogs. The first one was called: *The Old Lady and the Pigeons*, the second: *The Old Lady and the Bicycles* and the third: *The Old Lady and the Frogs*.

I wrote the story and I started to storyboard the first one, *The Old Lady and the Bicycles*, and BBC was involved again. I took the storyboard to London because Colin was there. And we went to the old BBC building. We had a little room in there and we put the storyboard on the wall and looked at it. And Colin laughed and said to me that what we had could be the material for a feature film! Didier Brunner who was standing behind us thought it was quite a good idea, too. I started to move things around and *The Triplets of Belleville* appeared as big tall ladies, not small ones. The small lady was still a character within a few scenes. I called them *The Triplets of Belleville*, and I said: 'Ok, they are triplets, they are tall and I like these characters, they are very energetic and I am going to call this massive American city Belleville.'

I wrote the story but the French producer had many problems with the Canadian producer for the reuse of the small character, the old lady. I did all the storyboard with this character and I was almost finished with storyboarding when he told me that I couldn't use this character. So, I started drawing and redrawing this little character … She shouldn't be the same, but she should be the same size … and I had to send my drawings to a lawyer in Paris, so he could say 'yes, no' and every time it was going: 'no, it's too similar, no, it's too similar …' and at one point I had almost given up on the idea of this little character when Sally joined me in Montreal and we went to a fantastic Portuguese restaurant, a lovely place with lovely people, the best restaurant I have ever seen. The two owners were absolutely gorgeous; the man had a big moustache and his wife had a very thin voice but she was so lovely! We loved these people! And I said: 'You know what? My character is not going to be a French character, it is going to be a Portuguese.' And I started drawing – I will probably find it for you, the original, first sketch. Most of the time I start with one sketch and then I draw it more and more. And I had the character, and I wanted her to have a clubfoot because this is a very interesting mixture. She is a bit handicap, but she is a very strong character! And then I had the story that this foot was going to solve the whole thing at the end, so it all went together. I did this little character drawing, I sent it to the lawyer and he said, 'Yes that's perfect!'

This restaurant also has a story with the *Triplets* because when the lady, Madame Souza, plays the piano and sings, it's awful. I thought we could use this lady from the restaurant because of her voice – it was obvious she couldn't sing right. We took her to the studio and we asked her to sing something in Portuguese. She did so, I recorded that and it was fantastic! If you are going to create a film you have to integrate all these things.

We did the film in Montreal. We opened a big studio there with a lot of people, Canadian, French, Belgian … We did a lot of work actually in Belgium and *Walking the Dog*, where we made all the crowds in Belleville, all the fat people and it was Benoît Feroumont who actually directed these scenes. He did a very good job; it was really a pleasure to work with him. Then we moved back to France and we finished *The Triplets*, the compositing and everything in a little place in Paris. We had an apartment there, a very tiny apartment but we could escape to Normandy.

My parents had bought a house in Normandy in the countryside. They bought a ruin, something very old, and my mum did everything. She actually turned it into a really nice place. It was a small house, very typical of Normandy. They actually had to let it go later, because nobody was coming anymore there and they were getting old, so they decided to sell the house while I was in Canada. After some time, my wife and I decided to buy it … And we got it! When the film was finished in Paris, we actually lived full time in Normandy. We really liked it over there but it was very remote. It was really in the middle of nowhere.

While we were living in Normandy, the film was an official selection in Cannes. That was a big thing! Everybody was very excited! I don't know if you have been in a screening in Cannes … When you see it from the stage, it's enormous! I think it's a cinema with 5,000 people! Absolutely amazing! So, as we arrived, we were applauded and there was a great feeling about it. But I really saw that the people were looking forward to seeing the film. There was real respect, you know. Suddenly you realize they say thank you for spending all this time in the dark room to do these little characters and it's beautiful, thank you! I could see people react; I could see people laugh … You get the feeling that this is why you do animation and all the hours spent in the dark room are absolutely worth it; it's got something different from comic books. In comic books you never see people laughing. That was really great! Then the film was released right after Cannes and it was amazing! A million in France for adult animated film! It was the first real adult animated film. *Kirikou* was big at the box office but it was for children. So that's all about *The Triplets*. And after that it was the *Illusionist*, which is very different …

What about *The Illusionist*?

I can tell you about the *Illusionist* story. I came with Sally by train to Cannes from Normandy and in the train, I had the original script of Jacques Tati because that's a story which came up during the making of *The Triplets*, and because at one point I wanted the animated characters to watch a live-action film on TV. I quite like this idea – I think it's another kind of art form. And lots of elements of things I like can be embodied. I am a big fan of Tati, so if I could achieve that, you could say that people would be able to virtually watch some Tati – since everything is there. I discussed this with the producer who said that we would have to contact Tati's Estate, holding the copyright. The only one alive was his daughter, Sophie Tatischeff, and she was in Paris. I was in Canada, so the producer got in touch with her, showing her the work we were doing and the storyboard. She agreed to give her permission and she also mentioned of a script of a film that her dad had never made. She didn't want any real actor to play her dad and she thought that it would be fantastic if it was made into an animation film, in the style of *The Triplets*.

The producer told me that we had got the rights and I promised to read the script as soon as I finished *The Triplets*. At first, I wasn't really enthusiastic about adapting someone else's work, even Jacques Tati's, although I really like his work. I had my other project, called *Barbacoa*, a project I never made, which was really close to my heart.

The story was basically about children chasing animals during the commune of Paris, when everybody was starving, because the city was sieged by the Germans. There was a kind of revolution inside the city, so there was no food and people were eating their cats, their dogs, … and the children were chasing animals in the streets … rats, things like that, trying to sell their flesh to the people of Paris. It's quite dark! I had this story about animals escaping from the zoo and it was a kind of a fairy tale because animals would turn into a human shape, and behave like a human. I was working on that and for me that was going to be my next film. It didn't happen like that, it was the *Illusionist*, though.

What happened basically was that the producer gave me the script and he told me to read it while I was coming to Cannes. I read the script which was very short, about thirty pages, and it was written like a little novel. It was very easy to read and very easy to imagine as well. When I finished reading it, I was ecstatic! I already knew that the ending would be a musical piece. So, I read the script in a couple of hours, and I was thinking in my head, 'I hope it's going to be bad, because he didn't do it first, and I don't really want to do it' (laugh). So, I was ready to cheat and I read it with really bad faith, trying to find something wrong about it and I just loved it! And I said: 'it is a beautiful film' and I had everything when I read it, and the ending, already I knew the ending was a musical piece because there was something uplifting in the story as well. It was really amazing! But in the meantime, unfortunately, before I even came back to France, Sophie Tatischeff died. What I'm trying to say is that we had to find some new next of kin holding the rights and that was Sophie Tatischeff's family: Jérôme Deschamps and Mikall Micheff. They are very famous in France because they are doing a lot of things in theatre, and on television as well, they are really nice people, they are real artists and they respect artists. And just because of the fact that it was them, I said yes, I am very willing to do that because I know I am going to be defended by these people.

I went to a film festival in Edinburgh. I was invited to screen *The Triplets* and I had never been to Scotland. I just loved Edinburgh and Scotland: the people, the landscapes, everything. I said to Sally, 'Let's move there, let's move there!' So, we went there; we didn't have children at that time, so it was really easy to move. We found a big old apartment on three floors and we decided to do our own animation studio, a tiny animation studio, with people who had worked with on *The Triplets*: Evgeni Tomov, who was the art director in *The Triplets*, it was this animator called Laurent [Kircher] who arrived as well and some other people. We were five or six people, a small group of people, not yet big, like we had after that. After that it was crazy: sometimes we walked in and we didn't even know some people, which is not a very nice thing. So, we were in this studio, in an apartment, which I really liked, because *The Old Lady and the Pigeons* started in an apartment as well. During that time *The Triplets* was released in the States and it was a big success – the best box-office hit for a French film in the States. So, I had a call from an agent in Hollywood, who asked me if I wanted to be his client. I did not see any reason why not.

So, there was a point when we were developing this animated film *The Tale of Despereaux* and the *Illusionist*.

Around that time, I was contacted by Bob Weinstein. He said that he really liked to do something with me and that he had a film. In fact, that's exactly the producer who wants to have his own toy, you know, who wants to own creators … I realized that if you want to work with the Americans as a director, you are someone for hire. It is all about the money. You can make bad movies and still have a box-office hit, which is mad, because the advertising is so huge. It's not directors that they want; it's technical directors who are going to direct a film.

Meanwhile, as we were developing the *Illusionist*, we developed *The Tale of Despereaux* with Pathé. Pathé is an old French company whose head is Jérôme Seydoux. We got in touch with him and that's how we began to work together. He is the head of the company. He is kind of gentleman, and he came to visit us in the studio. He didn't interfere with anything during the making of the film. He is someone fascinated by drawing and he liked both the *Illusionist* and Tati.

The *Tale of Despereaux* comes from a book by the same title. The book is about a mouse which lives in a castle, in medieval times, and it is a very dark book. It's somewhat old fashioned and it takes place in a dungeon. I said that if you want to keep this darkness, yes, we can do something beautiful. I wanted to be inspired from the paintings of Jérôme Boss and medieval elements. And I started to design the characters. I drew the character of the little mouse. So I drew it, just one drawing and that was it. They had a scriptwriter with whom I was working from distance and he was clever. And then the producer, once again (and this producer is also a director, he is a good live-action director …), he took over the script writing and he came with a script. And it was like he didn't get the book, he lost what was interesting in the book and once again, they bought something and broke it. They actually broke the magical thing that was in the book and became almost like a Disney movie and his references was *The Beauty and the Beast*.

The storyboard was approved but I remember I was really not convinced with the script. In the end there was a serious disagreement concerning a character and I guess that was the last straw. I was doing the storyboard and they sent someone; we had a production director, who they hired to actually come to Edinburgh to supervise the film. And then we started to do storyboard with the team and it was going on very well and then we came to this character and she said: 'yes, but … he wants the character to be a Gaston' and I said: 'but it doesn't work to be a Gaston. Why would he be a weak guy if he is muscular? it doesn't make sense!' …

We had our studio on two floors. On one floor was *The Tale of Despereaux*, the development, where ten people worked at that time and the other floor was the *Illusionist* where different people worked. Both were working on storyboards.

The next day, we saw bodyguards, like big people in black suits, at the front of the studio and we couldn't enter. That was our studio, we were paying for the studio … and they were taking all the computers and everything out. They were really violent. It is quite a shock when you come in the morning and you see security guards there and people cannot get in and are even prevented from going to the top floor where we had the *Illusionist* things. They actually took all the material we had, all the development of the film we had and they did the film somewhere else. And they kept the design because the design was really good! We did it! … Happily, I wasn't involved in the making of the film, but they didn't put my name on the credits! I had to go to the press and say these people are using my designs and they are not even crediting me for that! Sadly, this is how the system works. It's been like that for a long time. Orson Welles was complaining about the same things, and the situation hasn't changed that much since then, even in independent filmmaking movies. However, it shouldn't be like this. Creativity and creation should come first. There are always some terrible stories like that, you know. You could write a whole book about the relation between the director and the producer. But to be honest, in both cases, both Weinstein and the Universal, if they had stuck with my vision, they would be better off with the films. First, they would have a film that would probably be a blockbuster and *Despereaux* would have probably been selected for the Oscars.

But at the same time, we were working on the *Illusionist*. In a way I knew that going with the *Illusionist* was the right thing and we had the whole studio after that.

We did the animatic of the *Illusionist*, a very very precise animatic, almost like posing by posing. It was a very demanding film in 2D animation because I wanted it to be like Jacques Tati's way of shooting. I had realized a special thing about Tati and that was that he didn't move the camera. He just put the camera at (t)his height, in the middle of a big room and then he had the people moving around. If you look at Tati this is very much what it is – the point of view of someone who is actually in a theatre. Because Tati comes from musical and the stage, so basically what you have is a big stage with characters doing things. You can't do that in a normal storyboard because there is no editing there. It's all happening in front of your eyes. On storyboard, it was very precise; if you look at it, you have the film already. I even put the sound and elements of music, so everything was there and it was working. But the problem is that animation takes a lot of time. Because we have a stage, it means that most of the time you see the character in full: you see their eyes, you see their feet. You can't hide elements of the characters. You see the characters walking around and it is the most difficult thing in animation to actually have a character moving away, because of the perspective, most of the time it feels wrong. So, we had a lot of things we had to rework, and it took a lot of time, and the animators really wanted to do their best animation, which they did.

Pathé is a big company and sometimes, the directors and producers change, some left and we started with a producer, who was a live-action producer in Paris, and he didn't know how to do animation. So, we had our own producer in Edinburgh. This guy left at one point and they put us with someone else and he was someone we met at the beginning of the film because we wanted him to be part of the production. And he looked at the film and he was not interested at all. And that was fine. Then, the big boss in Paris gave him the job of French Pathé, so he was in charge of our film. So, we had in charge of our film a guy who didn't want to do the film. And then, he thought that the film was too long. He said,

'We have to cut in the film.' I said: 'Why, what do you want to cut?' He said, 'It's too long.' So, as always, I said to myself: 'I will try to find a solution' and I said: 'Fine. I'm going to make an effort.' So, I agreed to go back and make some cuts into the animatic. And I cut a way big amount of time. He still was not satisfied and brought a live-action editor. This guy started to bring some ideas which were awful. He was absolutely speeding everything!

Fortunately, I had the possibility to actually have a proper talk with Jérôme Seydoux and because he is someone who really likes cinema and knew how badly I was feeling, we managed to talk and agree to start again and make the film that we wanted to do. Had I been with another kind of producer, that would have been a nightmare. When I took back the film, it was edited by this guy, and it was a disaster. It had lost its poesy. He had cut even the slightest gestures between the characters because he thought they weren't helping the action. It's not about the action; it's about the characters, their relation! So, I salvaged a lot of scenes, and I managed to do a film which I am happy with. But there's been a sequence that's been cut. It was a nice scene, where they go to Murrayfield stadium. The girl is with Jacques Tati and they are watching a very funny rugby game and there were all these massive guys and they were really tough on the young lover, and that was the first time she was seeing him. And I believe it was in the original script as well, but because the editor messed up the production, it was not possible … So, that was it. I did all the things I wanted in the end, but there were some beautiful scenes that were cut! He argued that all these little lovely attention scenes were cut because they don't bring anything to the action. But it's not an action movie!

When we were doing *The Triplets*, we were not thinking that it was going to be such a success! But it was! Because it was a very honest film, you know, it was a true film. It wasn't a product. It wasn't something everybody was expecting. On the contrary, every time I do something, I want to do something that people are not expecting.

When I did *Attila Marcel*, I went in live-action and then it was even worse. People in France like people to stay in their box with their etiquette on it, you know, and they said: 'Oh, Sylvain Chomet represents French animation, why is he doing live-action?' Because I like films, that's why I'm doing films.

During the making of the *Illusionist*, I took a small break, to go and shoot *Paris, je t'aime*. And there were some people who didn't understand why I wanted to do live-action; they didn't get it. They thought I wanted to change career. My idea, though, was that if I can do some live-action after two very exhausting and long animation films, I'd be very happy with that! Which I did! But some people are not really very open; they believe that if I am doing live-action, I am a traitor!

Why Tati didn't do the *Illusionist*?

This is a film Tati wrote but didn't make. There were actually many films that he didn't make, because he went to Cannes and he did *Mon Oncle*. It was a big success and he won. In Cannes, he had this script, the *Illusionist*, which he wanted to shoot. It was at the highest point of his career and he decided instead of doing that film to do *Playtime*. *Playtime* was his masterpiece but it cost him all his fortune and he went bankrupt after that because it was a very expensive film. But if he had done this film, the *Illusionist*, it was going to be a very different kind of film, because he didn't use the character of Monsieur Hulot – he used another character. So, the reason why he didn't do the script? I'm not really sure, but we think that at the beginning he wanted to play the role of the magician, which was quite impossible since he had a car accident and had hurt his arm. On top of that, he was a bit clumsy with his hands. Maybe he didn't do the film because he really wanted to be in it and that was not possible. The other reason could be the fact that it might have been too personal to him, because Tati used to be in the musical business and he was really sad that the musical was coming to an end. Unlike all the other musical artists, however, he had the chance to do cinema. So, he was basically saved by that. But he saw a lot of his friends, artists from the musical, getting really poor and he had to help them some times, so, maybe it was too personal for him. And for me, I thought at one point that the film was written for his daughter, Sophie Tatischeff, because he was doing his films and he didn't spend much time with his family and they really liked each other actually. She adored her father and said in an interview that she would like to spend more time with him, but he wasn't always there. So, I dedicated the film to Sophie, first because she gave us the authorization and second because I thought there was a father-daughter bond there worth praising. So, I dedicated it to her.

When I started to do the storyboard, we were in Edinburgh and people knew we are going to do the film. One day I received a very long, hand-written letter by a guy called McDonald. He said that he was Jacques Tati's grandson. He claimed that Tati had an affair with his grandmother during the war and she had a girl. Tati didn't want to have the girl, because he was married at that time, but she kept the child [his mother] … She had a long life and she had a child in Scotland. So that guy was Scottish and he was the grandson of Jacques Tati.

I went to Tati's estate and asked them if they knew this story. They said that they didn't, but with all the details he is giving, there is a big chance it might be true. So, I invited the guy to the studio to show him the storyboard and what the film is about. The guy came and I was at my desk, drawing Jacques Tati. We were doing the development at that time, the storyboard and the animatic, when this guy came in. He was not as tall as Jacques Tati, but he was Jacques Tati! I saw him and I said, yes, yes, definitely! He arrived and the way he was moving was very much like Jacques Tati; it was kind of awkward! I was with the animators in the room and we went: 'Scary! Spooky!'

So, I showed the guy around and then he left. Later, when the film was released, he started to go to the press and say horrible things about Jacques Tati. In fact, he hated Jacques Tati, because he didn't want to recognize his mother. So, he had only bad things to say about Jacques Tati.

When he saw that I dedicated it to Sophie Tatischeff, his daughter, he was angry and thought that it should have been dedicated to his mother. Sorry, but we are making the film and we are deciding who we are dedicating it to. So, he hated Jacques Tati, and he started to think that I intentionally wanted to hurt his mother. I couldn't understand why this young man was doing that. And to be honest, that was not the story I was telling and directing. It's a fiction film, not the story of his life. It was a strange accusation, when I didn't even know he existed. He wrote me the letter and he visited me at the studio when the animatic was almost finished and the story was made. Also, I'm really not sure the script is about that girl! I think Tati wrote it for his daughter! It's a father and daughter relationship and he didn't have a father and daughter relationship with the other girl. He also said that it's a provocation that I was going to Scotland to make this film when he was in Scotland. I didn't know anything about this guy! I didn't go to Scotland because of him. I didn't do the film because of his story! Anyhow, it's just my side of things because when someone makes an accusation, you have to defend yourself. It is his problem, not mine, because I'm not doing an annotation of someone. But there is always something like that – when people are into films and they are successful, people try to claim some crazy stuff …

I read about a *Triplets* prequel. Will you do a prequel?

The films that I like to do are very personal and I've got some really nice projects! I don't mind adaptations – if it's a very good book, it's a good base to tell a story. But I've got my own stories. The problem is that every time I come up with something, I try to challenge a bit the people's habits, I try to do things a bit different and I don't want to be expected to do the same kind of thing. I wouldn't be able to do sequels. And *The Triplets* prequel is not like that because that's a story I wrote at the same time and it's a very different story. You don't have the old lady, or the dog, or bicycles. It talks about something completely different. But I still wanted to develop these characters because I think they are fantastic. I wanted them to carry on their stories. For me they are the main characters in *The Triplets*.

It was a story of the world of *The Triplets of Belleville*, in a different time set, the story when they were babies and young girls with their father before they go to Belleville. Their father was a doctor in a very remote place in North America and he wanted his daughters to become nurses. So, he sends them to a faraway city called Belleville, which at the time is being constructed and the recommendation for them was to go to a nursing school. They arrive in the city and then they see a cabaret, and because we've seen them as children to be dancing and singing all the time, instead of going to the school they go in the cabaret and become those very popular singers in the twenties and thirties. They had to lie to their dad, so they are taking fake pictures as nurses. He believed that they are nurses and this carries on and on for years and years and the story takes place when the daddy is 100 years old. They want to tell him what they have become because he heard their song but he doesn't know it's his daughters who were singing. It's a very touching story and quite funny, too.

Interruption: Is there a good possibility that we will see it?

Well, I don't know, if I find a clever producer, who thinks *The Triplets of Belleville* is well worldwide known – it was really good at the box office, actually it's not much of a risk to take to be honest. But, you know, I think these kinds of producers don't exist anymore, because I need a producer to be willing to go with the project and defend it, something that Didier Brunner did with *The Triplets* and *The Old Lady and the Pigeons*. He also managed to find finances for this film, he made it happen. I think today it's more complicated … So, maybe there is someone, somewhere in the world …

How do you create a film? How does that work, from the first idea?

The way I work, it's much like an archaeologist – someone who goes into a desert and tries to find some prehistoric animals that nobody has ever seen before. So, I go there and then you see a little bone just jutting out of the sand and for everybody it's just another stone. But if you are a good archaeologist, you take a brush and you go around it and you say: 'No, it's a bone actually.' Then you start to find other bones around and then you excavate ... And you've got all these bones but they are all not in the right order, and then you start to put them together and then you realize that this is the jaw. When you finish, you've got a beautiful skeleton of a creature. I think that's how I make films. I find little things like that, some little things that people wouldn't take much notice of. But this is how it works. For example, that's how I got the title for *The Triplets of Belleville*.

Another example is *Attila Marcel*. Well, that's the best example because I was working on *The Triplets* at that time and when I came home Sally wasn't there. I arrived and I had Attila Marcel in my head. Those two words. I wrote them down; I had no idea what those words meant but they were my first little bone. Then, I started to think about it. Attila Marcel ... and I said wait! It has to be something French with Attila and I straight away came up with a guy who was a brut, or he could be a wrestler. I wrote the music for one song in *The Triplets*: Madame Souza is vacuuming the bedroom, and we hear this song about a poor woman who is beaten by her boyfriend but she loves him so much because he is a real man. There's something really goofy about that, which was really funny. The song is imitating the Edith Piaf style of songs, about this man called Attila Marcel, who's beating her and then it developed for years and years ... and it became *Attila Marcel*, which is the film!

But that's the way you find things, you know. You are creating something not because you are intelligent or especially sensitive. You have to be sensitive to find these things and probably you need an eye, but it's not intelligence, it's not thought. I suppose it's that you put the things together and, in the meantime, you've got only a few bones or a few pieces of a big puzzle, but you know it exists and you say 'I want to see this prehistoric animal', 'I want to see the picture, the puzzle of this'. And that's the way it works. I don't believe in creating something from scratch. I think it all comes from things from your life. The film wants to exist and it's there, and if it's not in the right shape, it's going to show you it's not the right shape. If you put the wrong bone at the wrong place, it's not going to be nice to watch. So, it's much more like this. It's got nothing to do with intelligence. You need instinct and a good eye to do that, to be able to know that a little piece that looks like nothing can be something big. I really believe in that.

There is a thrill actually in trying to do your own project, fighting to make it happen and then fighting to produce it. There is a real thrill. And there is a real kind of danger, you know, to put yourself in front of people. It can go both ways, it can be a disaster, or a success. People either like it or are very indifferent, but it is dangerous. If you work all your life in commercials, you are not taking any risks. But life is quite boring then and then you've got things to regret – 'Oh, I could have done that …' – and at the end you start to criticize people who are doing things … People who don't do anything are more critical of people who do things! I respect someone who is going to do a film, even if it is rubbish! I am not judging actually; I just think that this person has done it and even that is a great thing!

Questions about the technique

Since I started animation, it has evolved so much! And it was evolving as I was evolving myself, actually, in filmmaking. For example, when I started working in London, it was the end of 1980s; all the animation studios were doing their commercials in hand-drawn animation. They were doing their commercials with the old technique, which was basically animation on paper, then you photocopied on the cel or you retraced the drawing on a cel and then you painted it at the back with this special paint to actually stick to the celluloid. Then, you would go to do the background on the paper and you would go to a rostrum camera and shoot it. It was a very, very old system! I started in animation like that. I did my first film with the same technique. It was very technical at that time.

When I started in animation, they were using the first video line test. Before that, they used to shoot on the film and use a negative to check the animation. So, when they were checking the animation, they were checking on negative. They were not even doing reverse. It was like black with white lines on it. I never did that. It was the beginning of the video, which everybody thought it was a revolution; there were video line tests. You could actually do line tests without going to a laboratory, so you could have the tests straight away. You shot your drawings and you got your animation. It was taking ages, but, still, it was a revolution. It was brilliant because you could also make it in colour. We had a colour camera, so you could almost do your own little films like that. It was really good.

The thing that was really nice was that at that studio they let us use the materials in the evenings, so that we could make our own films, which I did, and that was great. It was the beginning, you could after that play with the timing; you could play with that and it was really straightforward. Time was of the essence. If you missed something, you had to redo everything from the beginning. But even that was a revolution! Then, they started to have the first really computerized films. I'm talking about the period at the end of the 1980s. We didn't have many computers in the studio. I think at that time Pixar was probably doing their first experimental short films, which I liked. The one with the little lamp [*Luxo Jr*, Lasseter, 1986] is one of the first ones they did and I was following that, when I was learning 2D animation. It was interesting but it seemed to be quite difficult and complicated because it was a very different work.

Then we started to have some computers and some software and now it was much more interesting. So, when I was both in London and in Canada, they were still using rostrum camera. The studio had its own rostrum camera, and a special effects guy. It was really fascinating! At that time, they were still doing special effects on films, with this type of optical effects. And I had a line test, when I did *The Old Lady and the Pigeons*, the first four minutes that I did in the South of France. It was shot in a studio, in a rostrum camera, in a studio in Vallance. So, we basically used the same technique on the old lady and the pigeon [both in France and in Canada]; it was paper and celluloid, painted and rostrum camera and the line tests.

I was animating so much at that time. I remember that I had a team of assistants and the in-betweeners. I work better when people leave the studio, because when they are here, it's very difficult to animate with people constantly asking you questions. I used to arrive in the early afternoon, check things with everybody, and around six o'clock I would sit on my desk and start animating in my office going on until four o'clock in the morning, or something like that.

I remember there was one scene of the old lady, when she arrives with the food on the little trolley. I did the whole animation, but I didn't have time to line test it. I went to bed, and I absolutely remember in my dream seeing the line test! So, I actually made my own line test in my head! And I could see it and I knew it was good! I went to the studio, shot it and it was exactly like that! I think I was becoming a human line test, which was really great!

At that time, it was the early beginning of CGI animation. I didn't plan to have any 3D animation in this film. Even the cars, the trucks, everything is hand animated, which was very boring. That's when I realized that if machines can do it, it would be better (laughter). We decided to use a new 3D software to do just one thing towards the end of the film: when the fat pigeon goes to the window, and we have a view of the glass falling towards us, that was, I remember, the only thing in CGI that we did. Because we were actually working on rostrum camera, we had to print it on paper, then to print it on celluloid and then to paint it on the back, of course. So, there was integration. But it was really cool because at least it was quite effective and it would have taken someone months to do all these little pieces of glass. So that was the first time I put some CGI into one of my films.

Then Pixar's technique was really rocketing, the domestic computers were getting more powerful and the software for CGI was getting cheaper and easier to use. So, when I started on *The Triplets*, I thought that it would be a good idea to use the maximum of that, because I was going to have a lot of vehicles in my film. A lot of bicycles! And I know how terrible they are to actually do. I thought a lot about it because at that time we were not going to use rostrum camera, either. We were going to use hand-drawn animation, paper, and then we would scan it and then it would go into a computer, where we would put things in colour. Much faster! I think it was pretty cool. But the good thing is that it was all digital at that point so it was very easy to integrate CGI. You didn't have to preprint anything; so, we put a lot. We did the boats, the cars, all the bicycles, trucks, lots of things and some stuff like some smoke, and the sea as well. The sea was very interesting. I finally had the tools. I think if I had done *The Triplets of Belleville* before that, without these tools, it would have been much smaller. With these I could have as many levels I wanted! There is no limitation! In the old technique, when you have the celluloids, you can have maximum four layers of celluloid! ... The celluloid affects the colours. They are not really transparent; they are slightly grey. The colour changes if you put layers on top of them. You have to compensate the colours and ... it's madness! Then, we went digital and that was amazingly easy.

Our guy, the one who worked in *The Old Lady and the Pigeons*, was actually working next to my office. He was working on the sea sequence, when the little lady is on the pedalling and she is following the ship in a storm. I could see what he was doing and he was doing the first render of it ... And at one point I was listening to a piece of classical music and I think it was Mozart's C-Minor Mass conducted by John Elliot Gardiner. I was listening to that, working on my animation and then I looked at the render and there was a picture of the sea and I thought to myself: 'Oh, oh, oh wait a minute, wait a minute! I put the volume on and I looked at it and it was so powerful and so beautiful that I said, "Ok, we need that music on that sequence! It's absolutely amazing!"' When we were doing the animatic, I started to put the music, starting with the old lady leaving the beach until her arrival in Belleville and it was matching absolutely everything!

As I said, a lot of things sometimes come from a bit of chance. And you have to take this chance. If you have this feeling that it is working, do it! I said that to the producer and he said that we would need to get its rights. Alternatively, he sent me the same piece performed by four other orchestras because he said the John Elliot Gardiner is really expensive. The other pieces were very nice! But they were not working! I was putting them on and they were not working! It was the same piece! But it didn't work.

There was already a lot of music in the film because it was going to be a musical film and also at that time I was listening to a lot of music. I actually had a friend in Canada who is a physicist; he is an absolute expert in Bach and Glenn Gould. There was a scene with the Tour de France race, where I wanted to have music resonating the sound of a wheel, giving the feeling that it's almost difficult to push the pedals of a bicycle. And I found this Bach part which is a cycling thing. It worked fantastically! This time we had actually a pianist to play this for us and that was very interesting! Music was very important at that time.

Then, when I did the *Illusionist*, I essentially used the same technique, always hand-drawn on paper, because at that time the graphic tablet wasn't really there yet. Maybe the CGI was even better. So, we were still using paper, like in *The Triplets*, a lot of effects were done in compositing as well; in Digital Fusion their compositing was really good and very inventive. I wanted to actually have a reflection very similar to Scotland on the *Illusionist*, to give this same kind of feeling of the Northern lights. The air is always changing there, the light is always changing, so it was a lot of work on that. Imagine you are in a dark room and there is some light coming from outside and you see some particles in the air: you can almost grab the air – that's the feeling I wanted to express. Happily, the art director was from Denmark, which is approximately at the same level as Edinburgh, so he knew exactly this kind of quality of lights. He did a great job because when I watch the film, I can really remember this kind of lights: you can have four seasons in one day. That was the technique I basically used to make my films.

Once my animation god, Richard Williams, asked me how I was doing animation. I had the same kind of questions actually, because I was in the south of France and I wasn't doing animation for a long time. I went to London to see my friend and next to his studio, some young guys who were working on the *Illusionist* had their own little studio. I found five or six of them, and they were in their room, on these tablets. I was curious, so I asked questions as I had been in the countryside. I told him, 'I've been looking at this thing but I always thought the drawing tool was rubbish.' And he said, 'no, no. This is a new thing … take the pencil' and I took the pencil and did some testing. And I said, 'I want one, I want to do animation like this now.' So, now I'm not working with paper at all, you see, there is no paper in my room, it became really a very important thing. And the first time I did animation like that was for *Stromae*, a Belgian pop music video, in two scenes. Because you can import video footage and have it straight on your tablet, you can use it as a reference. It's not rotoscoping. I hate rotoscope; it's not animation, in my opinion. Referencing is really interesting because you actually use the rigging of the movement. You can change anything you want, change the rigging, but you can keep the volume and you can keep the lip sync as well, so you use the soul of the acting of the character – you need to be a good animator to do that. When I see the rigging, I see the points where things are attached and I can do any kind of character. I can do 1 million characters with the same footage. At first I thought that it didn't have the same kind of magic created by the old animators but I realized that the old animators did use a lot of references. And my favourite character of all time, best animation, best film actually, is the *One Hundred and One Dalmatians* animation. I think that the guy who created Cruella's character is a genius! Just look at the way she comes in, waving her fur coat! I saw the actual footage they used and I said 'yes!' It's not rotoscope, at all, because the actress who plays Cruella devil for the reference is very different from what they did. And I just realized, checking with animation, that it was full of reference. So, there was the *Stromae* video and then we did a pilot of an animated film based on the story of the life of Marcel Pagnol. I used that technique for the animation and I saw that I could work ten times faster with it – it's a fantastic technique!

The next thing would be the *Aquarium*. We are going to work with some studios abroad, probably some Belgian studio, probably a studio in London. And in the past, if you wanted to do the in-betweens in Korea, you had to send the drawings by post! On *The Triplets*, I remember there was a problem in the post and we had to fix the actual drawings because they were completely destroyed and it was horrible. Now, it's just a click, you do it online. That's fantastic, so you can have the idea of a worldwide studio, it's really interesting. The way I see the future of this job is that maybe there won't be big studios that everybody works in, but some little units, like the one these guys from the *Illusionist* had, with friends, instead of these massive studios, like the ones we had in Montreal or Edinburgh. I think that is probably the way things are going to happen. However, I wouldn't like the idea of a studio to be lost. Six people consist already a studio.

Working alone is not something I like. On the one hand, I agree that working at home on your own may be quite easy, but, on the other hand, you totally lose the feeling of being part of a team. You need to have interaction. I need to see what people are doing on their desk. I need the interaction. So, my film will be in some studios elsewhere, but we have a unit here. Something's happening when you are part of a project, in a team with other people. It is a mini animation studio, but it's still an animation studio.

When I started animation, it was a very exciting time! Because the technique was changing completely at the same time! Very fast! Before that, the same technique had been used since 1920s and it didn't change. It was exactly the same one! When I started in London, they were doing things exactly as they used to do on *Betty Boop* and *Felix the cat*. That's exactly the same technique. And then, the big boom, with the computer, with everything. And then came CGI, Pixar and everything they do now. And people started to say 2D animation is dead. Now the new 'craze' is 3D CGI, but no, because computers also help to do films like *The Triplets* and so, now I'm really optimistic about the media, the future of the media.

If you look at the first time, I used CGI in *The Old Lady and the Pigeons*. There was a software turning the 3D CGI picture into lines. But when you see closely to the lines, because then it's been scanned and then the scans are printed and painted on celluloid, you see that the line is very dull, it is very straight. It is very computerized. Because it's made of a lot of little tiny elements and they fall, you can't really see it. But then I started to try to integrate all the big ingredients like the cars and bicycles and sometimes you had a CGI bicycle with a 2D character on it. You don't want the discrepancy between the two styles and so with CGI all my struggles in the beginning were to actually break the CGI. I realized that the most difficult thing to do in CGI was to do organic things, to do dirt, to do something which is broken, which is not perfect. The problem with this tool is that at the end, you end up having something which looks like, you know, perfect. But we wanted to have something that looked like it's been hand-drawn. So, we had this rendering software making lines, but they were horrible lines! They didn't have any sensitivity. We started to use them on *Belleville* and then developed them more on the *Illusionist*, but basically, because we had it all digital, we could do whatever we wanted. We took these lines and then we passed them from different filters to actually break them, so, the line is not a perfect straight line but it starts to be a little bit broken and it has some texture on it. I had to go through two or three different filters to actually break the perfection the computer was doing. So, I always had to twist the arm of the computer to make it work for us.

Technique is more. Like my cinematographic technique. When I thought of doing an animated film back in the time, when I was in London, I didn't have any experience in storyboarding or where to put the camera and things like that. So, when I was in Montpellier and we got the money to actually start the film, the first thing I did was to go to Paris and buy a little book. It was written in the 1970s by a live-action director. It's a little technical book about where to put the camera, how to edit the film, and it had little vignettes, live-action vignettes, explaining how to put a shot like this after a shot like that in order to create an emotional effect. And I've learned a lot about that, about cinematographic language, which was very useful when I did my live-action films. Because I already knew where to put the camera, what mistakes you are not supposed to make and how to edit. And when I started to do *The Old Lady and the Pigeons* and all my films after that, I said to myself: 'For me, I'm not doing an animated film, I'm doing a film. So, I'm going to do it exactly as if I were doing a live-action film.' My way of shooting in animation is based on live-action. I love cartoons, but I really want to do something that probably comes from when I was a child and all the characters I was creating. As a child, I was creating my own friends in a way and for me that was real. Every time I was drawing something, it came to life! Every time I started a face, I had to finish it because I didn't want to leave them without a face as I had a feeling that they were real. 'Yeah, they do exist! They do exist! You have to find them, but they exist.' So, you see, for me it's very interactive with live-action and reality.

How did you meet Richard Williams?

That's another story, when I actually met God in person! It was in a festival in Hiroshima. They were screening *The Triplets* and I was invited by the festival. I knew that Richard Williams was there, so I was really scared, because I really wanted to say how much he gave me without even knowing him – in a way, he inspired these animators some of whom actually trained me to become an animator. Everything is thanks to him. Taking all the knowledge from these old people in Disney, Hollywood he actually brought it to England and I had all that in my mind. He was with his wife; I was with Sally and we were at the cocktail party of the festival. He was talking with a lot of people but I am generally too shy to initiate a talk with someone, especially when it's someone I truly respect. Sally started talking to his wife and said: 'You know, my husband is a big admirer of your husband!' She also told her that I was the one who had done *The Triplets of Belleville*. Richard Williams's wife was very enthusiastic and invited us to a restaurant so that we could talk. I felt ecstatic! What had happened was that a friend of Richard Williams had seen my film in Los Angeles and had praised it so, evidently, Williams saw the film.

There was a tiny Japanese restaurant near the festival venue where animators had drawn on the walls and that's where we met. I don't know how old he was at that time, late or mid-sixties, I would say, but he had this amazing energy, he had very blue eyes, you could even see his brain from his eyes. We talked about *The Triplets* and he asked me how I had done it. When I started explaining the animation procedure used – all the new tools, etc., except this one (drawing tablet) that didn't exist yet – he was so interested! It was all about the compositing, the fact that you scan your drawings and then you put the colour in a computer. He still had the old way in mind, the way he had done *Roger Rabbit*, with the celluloids and the paint and there I was in a restaurant in Japan, talking with Richard Williams and having actually to teach him about animation! Richard Williams was someone who, like me, couldn't compromise and he had similar problems with producers. He decided to leave England and went back to Canada in a very remote place next to Vancouver with his wife. He didn't want to talk to anybody. So, he had spent almost ten years in the forest and he was just going back to animation when I met him. He had a childlike enthusiasm with regard to animation and asked me all sorts of questions. It was a beautiful moment! He was a very amazing figure, you know, a very inspiring person, he's been there for quite a long time.

Then we became friends, and he came to Scotland when we were doing the film and we spent some time together, asking more about what kind of computer he has to buy and things like that. The last time we saw him was a couple of years ago, when we were in Bristol visiting our friend, Colin Rose, who lives there. We went with my children because I wanted them to visit the Aardman studio. When we got to the studio, he told me: 'Come on, I want you to meet someone you know.' We went into another little building, like a warehouse kind of building and we opened the door. It was dark in there. I could see tables with tonnes of paper on them, and in the corner, there was a little light coming and Richard Williams was there! He was working on his last film basically, a film he was doing on his own. He was doing everything on his own. And, you know, talking to him was fantastic!

To see him there, at this place, having a rostrum camera in the corner and all his papers everywhere, cels everywhere, was amazing! It was his hub! I asked him if he was using computers but he said they were too complicated for him. He was still using the old method. He took these piles of drawings and he showed me all his animations. Bumping into him was amazing! He was really a passionate person, and he managed to actually transmit his passion to everybody else. To me, he is something of a god in animation!

When I left, I felt a bit sad, though. I didn't want to end up like that, in one room doing my things. There are some limits, you know … I am a social guy as well; I don't really like to be just on my own like that although I love animation. That's why I stopped doing comic books. Comic books are about being on your own as well.

I think he won a special academy award for that film. It was the highlight of his career. He was a very, very fascinating person! Someone like him, with so much passion and energy, can take it to another country, and from that he created all these babies. This big spider went in London and created these baby spiders spreading animation in the UK.

It seems that you could have done many other things than animation …

I could have done things in many different areas. I could have stayed in comic books; I could have done music. I did animation, live-action, I'm interested in theatre as well, I'm going to direct a music performance, next year probably. I would love to write! I find all of these accessible and my biggest desire is to write a book, although it's terribly difficult! I've been trying some stuff but then I realized I became too literate not being able to keep a certain distance. When you write a novel, you need to have a distance from your characters. I'm very close to them … so it doesn't work! Maybe one day I will be able to write it, but I don't have the natural capacities to detach myself from the characters. I have to see them, I have to touch them and draw them. It's very important that it's there. But yes, I could have done many different things, I like all of these. But at the same time when you do films, you actually put all these things together. You have all these things, you have direction, you have design, you have music, you have sound.

Although I'm very passionate about animation and I'm trying to prove that animation is the strongest cinema where you can get the same kind of emotions, I'm not like some major animators who spend their whole lives drawing. I've been doing a lot on my films, so, when I'm not working, I'm not drawing.

When I was living in Scotland, we lived in a village next to the sea, a beautiful place, and we had a visit from Bill Plympton. We met in a festival and then he came and stayed with us. We went for walks on the beach and he was a really sweet guy, a very nice guy. And then he came to my place and he asked me to show him my office. When I told him that I didn't have one he was surprised and wanted to know where I drew. And I said: 'I don't draw. I do music, this is my own little home studio, I don't draw.' He couldn't understand that because he spends his time drawing. He is so productive, he has a fantastic style, you know, he was someone who actually influenced me with his style, with a bit caricature to it; he is a great animator. But he didn't understand that although I am an animator, I would not be completely devoted to drawing.

About animation renaissance

I think the conditions are not rosy at all as far as the way of creating things is concerned. When I say that, people lose their interest. I thought there would be a new generation of animators with great ideas and great styles that can do great things. After *Kirikou*, *Triplets* and *Persepolis* I thought that France was going through a renaissance. Then they started to go back to that old thing. It's basically the producers, the TV people that cover the creation and they started to believe that animation is for children, and it shouldn't be too dark. We proved it; *Kirikou* was for children but it was done in a way that it was also for adults. Michel Ocelot is someone I know and he did also very adult things. His first films are very adult ... There are some [of his] films that are very dark, but very funny at the same time.

That's also why I had to leave France; I wouldn't have been able to do my project because of this mentality, this general animation circuit or industry. We create things, we are inventive but we never manage to actually make it profitable. France invented animation, created it and let it go. France invented animation, invented cinema and there (where) are a lot of things that they never manage to attempt and let them happen. I love to live in France because that's my country and I like the culture. But I really hate a certain mentality [where] it's the wrong people that are ahead of things. It's the wrong people taking the decisions and basically now the producers have become really like kings and they control everything. It was not that way at my time and I am very happy about it. I was one of the first ones to actually learn animation in a real place in London. Also, I was already a scenarist, I could tell stories.

I met a producer that at that time was mad enough to be able to make things happen. He was adventurous. He was the first one to say yes to animation. He said, 'Let's do that!' He did *Kirikou* and while he was doing *Kirikou*, I was doing *The Old Lady and the Pigeons*. Since *Kirikou* was a big blockbuster, we could then do a feature, *Triplets*.

However, things changed afterwards. It seems to me that people don't understand that the ones who create things are the authors, not the money people. And after *Persepolis*, it went down again … We had it and we are losing it. The way that it works in France is so bureaucratic. There is money in France; they give a lot of money to the films. And I think that producers are important. They help the creation; they nourish the creation. They have to be visionaries; they have to believe in something and they have to fight for it. It's a very difficult job. I think we need producers. But the way it is at the moment is quite disappointing. You can't ask producers to be creators. So, speaking about the art production being done in France, there is quite a lot more work done in France right now than in my time as a whole. If you want to talk in industrial capitalistic terms, a lot of people are working for animation. But in terms of creation, it's going down every day, creative needs are dwindling, while the production needs are going up. It's quite weird. Commercial animation is the only thing we see. Everything interesting in a film is gone. I've basically stopped going to see animated films in the cinema. My children now watch them less and less. The frustrating thing is that there aren't films for teenagers because nobody really aims at teenagers or adults in animation. For children, on the other hand, there are a lot of things.

The cinema is at a terrible state at the moment, not only animation but also live-action. Cinema is in the hands of money people, it's in the hands of accountants, in the hands of very uncreative and unimaginative people. That's why it's getting very standardized, always the same stuff … In the past, especially in France, there used to be an element of surprise. You wanted the film to take you by the hand and take you in some uncharted territories, where you are actually going to be living a great experience. But these days, it seems to be like the new generations think that they don't want to take the risk of going to the cinema and watch a film that they don't know anything about. Culturally, this is exactly what is happening at the moment. And not just in animation but in live-action as well. Production counts for nothing without the guy who actually does this film. So, all success is based on the fact that there is someone to actually do the film for the producer.

The *Triplets* was produced with a lot of state money. CNC gave money, but there is a complex cash system related to banks … The whole system is quite complicated and that's why we need producers, but they shouldn't have a say about what should be in the film. For me that's not a producer. That is, you know, a very frustrated director. I used to believe that in France the quality, the moral quality of the people after the war was really high … and that's why we had some really good things in cinema. There was a generation of people who were very cultured, producers at that time were amazingly cultured. However, I think this has changed a lot. Now they all tend to be rolling with what the bank says, what the investors say and at the end … they all look the same. It's not a story you have there, it's basically a product, with people, with pictures moving around, with robots, and monsters and things like that.

And you know, I agree that producers have their head on the chopping board, but they shouldn't stop after production. Making a film is not enough. You have to advertise this film. As for *The Triplets,* they were fantastic! The *Triplets* went well in France, because the film stayed a long time in the cinemas. It was really long. It was all during the summer, and the people I talked to, the people in the cinema, people who actually screen the film, said: 'We are so happy to have *The Triplets* during the summer because it was actually one of the few films making money', but it lasted for four months! A really long life for a film.

The *Illusionist* was also released in a proper way; it had a very good start, first in Paris and then in the rest of the country. So, the word of mouth didn't have time to work. Of all my films, the *Illusionist* had the best start and it was a bigger box-office success in England and Scotland than *The Triplets*. It's very interesting because it's all about Scotland, to be honest.

There's one scene in the film where the hero goes to the cinema and he sees Jacques Tati on the screen. The cinema is called CAMEO. And cameo means when someone is playing his own role in a film. That was an interesting element. But this is a real cinema. It does exist. And actually, they screened the film, *The Illusionist*, in CAMEO for a very long time. The Scottish people were very happy with the film because they said that you truly see a real vision of Scotland. You see the real Edinburgh, you see the real islands and, moreover, tourists flocked to Scotland after the *Illusionist* release. They were really happy to actually see real depictions of Edinburgh and the changing skies. It was a huge satisfaction for me to see that the Scottish people loved the film.

But we didn't seize the opportunity to actually carry on doing things in Scotland, probably because we had the biggest studio on 2D animation at that time in Europe. We had two places, which were in different parts of the city, we had a lot of people and that's when I started to understand that apart from a director, I also had to be a producer or a studio owner, and I didn't really like what it meant for me and the team I was working with because they wouldn't just see me as a director. They would also see me as a producer and I think it's not really good with the relations and that's when I said: 'I will never do that again. That's a mistake. It's quite sad when you actually go to your own studio and you see people working for you that you have never seen before.' Too many people worked in two different places, so that's never something I'm going to do again because I think you can't be a producer and a director at the same time.

Would you share a memory?

When we had this studio in Montreal, in the old town, a very tiny old town, next to the harbour we had this massive 3,000 square feet of open space. It was an old building with old bricks, really nice, it was a very beautiful place. And we were doing paper, and we had a perforator, where you do the holes on the papers. And it was a lot of paper that we used on this film! When I left Montreal there were still some people working, in the animation studio. I moved with Sally back to France, to finish the compositing. Gérard Goulet worked as an animator, he worked on the pigeons with me [in *The Old Lady and the Pigeons*], and did the opening sequence of *The Triplets* and other things during the film as well. And it was very interesting that he actually kept all the little bits of the perforated paper, and when I left, they threw it on me from the building's window! That was fantastic! It was like snowing! That was really nice of him! A thought like that was really crazy! It's been very sweet! It's been very funny! That was a great idea!

Appendix 2

List of Sylvain Chomet interviews

3iS. *César 2011 – Interview de Sylvain Chomet – L'Illusionniste.* (2011). Retrieved from: https://vimeo.com/22576616 (last accessed 20 June 2020).

AlloCiné. *Sylvain Chomet, Jacques Tati Interview: L'Illusionniste.* (2010). Retrieved from: http://www.allocine.fr/personne/fichepersonne-2583/interviews/?cmedia=19117908 (last accessed 20 June 2020).

Amidi, Amidi. (2014). *A Behind-the-Scenes Look at Sylvain Chomet's 'Simpsons' Opening.* Retrieved from: https://www.cartoonbrew.com/tv/a-behind-the-scenes-look-at-sylvain-chomets-simpsons-opening-98434.html (last accessed 20 June 2020).

Arts University Bournemouth. (2018). *Sylvain Chomet: Interview with the 'Bad Boy' of Animation.* Retrieved from: https://aub.ac.uk/latest/sylvain-chomet-interview-title-progress (last accessed 20 June 2020).

Bel, Williams. (2019). *Interview with Sylvain Chomet.* Retrieved from: https://www.youtube.com/watch?v=x0IxpeWCCns (last accessed 20 June 2020).

Basirico, Benoît. (2013). *Sylvain Chomet, Réalisateur et Compositeur de Attila Marcel.* Retrieved from: https://www.cinezik.org/infos/affinfo.php?titre0=20131029170115.

Black, Catriona. (2004). *An Interview with Sylvain and Sally Chomet.* Retrieved from: http://www.artandphilosophy.com/040725b.html.

Borghes, Roberto. (2011). *Remio Amidei a Sylvain Chomet 23 7 2011 con goriziatv copyright.* Retrieved from: https://www.youtube.com/watch?v=DqrVqPTsux4 (last accessed 20 June 2020).

Bullock, Saxon. (2003). *Sylvain Chomet Belleville RendezVous.* Retrieved from: http://www.bbc.co.uk/films/2003/08/27/sylvain_chomet_belleville_rendezvous_interview.shtml (last accessed 20 June 2020).

Caruso, Valerio. (2003). *Sylvain Chomet – Director 'Animation Is like Mime'.* Retrieved from: https://cineuropa.org/en/interview/30891/ (last accessed 20 June 2020).

Cavna, Michael. (2011). *The 'Riffs Interview: 'ILLUSIONIST' filmmaker Sylvain Chomet delves into art, inspiration & Oscars.* Retrieved from: http://voices.washingtonpost.com/comic-riffs/2011/02/the_riffs_interview_illusionis.html (last accessed 20 June 2020).

Challenges.fr. (2010). *Interview Sylvain Chomet – Le tandem d'Edimbourg.* Retrieved from: https://www.challenges.fr/cinema/interview-sylvain-chomet-le-tandem-d-edimbourg_521399 (last accessed 20 June 2020).

Ciment, Gilles. (2003). *Faire flotter des bateaux impossibles. Entretien avec Sylvain Chomet.* Retrieved from: http://gciment.free.fr/caentretienchomet.htm (last accessed 20 June 2020).

Clements, Marcelle. (2003). *Oui, It's a Cartoon. Non, It's Not for Your Kids.* Retrieved from: https://www.nytimes.com/2003/11/02/movies/oui-it-s-a-cartoon-non-it-s-not-for-your-kids.html (last accessed 20 June 2020).

Curiel, Jonathan. *For Caricaturist Chomet, Creator of Triplets of Belleville, It's a Long Way from Disney.* Retrieved from: https://www.sfgate.com/entertainment/article/For-caricaturist-Chomet-creator-of-Triplets-of-2524759.php (last accessed 20 June 2020).

Dailymotion. *Interview de Sylvain Chomet, réalisateur de 'Attila Marcel' avec Guillaume Gouix, Anne Le Ny, Bernadette Lafont et Hélène Vincent.* (2013). Retrieved from: https://www.dailymotion.com/video/x16eujt (video).

Distraction Tactics, *Sylvain Chomet Interview.* Retrieved from: https://www.youtube.com/watch?v=6q_CVNyexz0 (video) (last accessed 20 June 2020).

Doomdee. (2010). *The Illusionist – Extracts and Interview with Sylvain Chomet.* Retrieved from: https://doomdeedoomday.wordpress.com/2010/02/23/the-illusionist-extracts-and-interview-with-sylvain-chomet/ (video) (last accessed 20 June 2020).

Electric Sheep. (VirginieSelavy, 2010). *The Illusionist: Interview with Sylvain Chomet.* Retrieved from: http://www.electricsheepmagazine.co.uk/2010/08/01/the-illusionist-interview-with-sylvain-chomet/ (last accessed 20 June 2020).

ESRA Officiel. (2014). Masterclass *ESRA – Sylvain Chomet.* Retrieved from: https://www.youtube.com/watch?v=rH4CyTzo1aU (last accessed 20 June 2020).

Faelens, Sebastien. (2011). *Sylvain Chomet: La Magie Existe! Interviews.* Retrieved from: http://www.underscores.fr/rencontres/interviews/2011/04/interview-sylvain-chomet-lillusionniste/ (last accessed 20 June 2020).

Fielder, Miles. (2010). *The Illusionist Opens EIFF 2010 – Sylvain Chomet Interview.* Retrieved from: https://edinburghfestival.list.co.uk/article/26048-the-illusionist-opens-eiff-2010-sylvain-chomet-interview/ (last accessed 20 June 2020).

France Net Infos. (2013). *Interview du réalisateur Sylvain Chomet: Attila Marcel.* Retrieved from: https://www.francenetinfos.com/interview-du-realisateur-sylvain-chomet-attila-marcel-56638/ (last accessed 20 June 2020).

Focus on Animation. (2010). *L'illusionniste – Extraits et Interview de Sylvain Chomet.* Retrieved from: https://www.youtube.com/watch?v=Vbru4psfVbA (last accessed 20 June 2020).

Golden Scene, *Belleville RendezVous Interview with the Director.* Retrieved from: http://www.goldenscene.com/bellview/belleview-syn.html (last accessed 20 June 2020).

Hand Drawn Animation. (2010). *Sylvain Chomet Interview.* Retrieved from: http://hand-drawn-animation.blogspot.com/2010/06/sylvain-chomet-interview.html (last accessed 20 June 2020).

Illusionista2010. *L'illusionista – intervista a Sylvain Chomet.* (2010). Retrieved from: https://www.youtube.com/watch?v=g_UirpJaw2w (last accessed 20 June 2020).

Jones, William. (2018). *Sylvain Chomet à propos de La vieille dame et les pigeons.* Retrieved from: https://www.youtube.com/watch?v=noCuqONp5KA (last accessed 20 June 2020).

Jones, William. (2018). *Le Dessin Animé par Sylvain Chomet.* Retrieved from: https://www.youtube.com/watch?v=G1PWQnRFYy4 (last accessed 20 June 2020).

Jones, William. (2018). *Making of Les Triplettes de Belleville.* Retrieved from: https://www.youtube.com/watch?v=RiZVlFExQdw (last accessed 20 June 2020).

Le Quotidien du Cinéma. (2013). *Portrait de Sylvain Chomet.* (1/2). Retrieved from: https://www.youtube.com/watch?v=2Gen6_3BJvQ (last accessed 20 June 2020).

Le Quotidien du Cinéma. (2013). *Portrait de Sylvain Chomet.* (2/2). Retrieved from: https://www.youtube.com/watch?v=Tiet1-_feaA (last accessed 20 June 2020).

Le Court Nous Tient. (2018). *Interview Sylvain Chomet – Festival Le Court Nous Tient.* https://www.youtube.com/watch?v=sBUHMbj53qU (last accessed 20 June 2020).

Meier, Pierre-Michel. (2010). *Sylvain Chomet par PiMi.* Retrieved from: https://www.youtube.com/watch?v=YBFepkBY12I (last accessed 20 June 2020).

Moins, Philippe. (2003). *Sylvain Chomet's 'The Triplets of Belleville'.* Retrieved from: https://www.awn.com/animationworld/sylvain-chomet-s-triplets-belleville (last accessed 20 June 2020).

Mulard, Claudine. (2011). *Sylvain Chomet, des Césars aux Oscars, Le cinéaste Français a remporté vendredi 25 février le César du meilleur film d'animation pour 'L'illusionniste', d'après un scénario inédit de Jacques Tati.* Retrieved from: https://www.lemonde.fr/cinema/article/2011/02/26/sylvain-chomet-des-cesars-aux-oscars_1485459_3476.html (last accessed 20 June 2020).

Nagy, Evie. (2014). *Behind the Scenes of the 'French Simpsons' Couch Gag.* Retrieved from: https://www.fastcompany.com/3029170/behind-the-scenes-of-the-french-simpsons-couch-gag (last accessed 20 June 2020).

Taylor, Drew. (2010). *Exclusive: 'Illusionist' Director Sylvain Chomet Talks Jacques Tati, & Why His Next Film Will Be 3D.* Retrieved from: https://www.indiewire.com/2010/12/exclusive-illusionist-director-sylvain-chomet-talks-jacques-tati-why-his-next-film-will-be-3d-121142/ (last accessed 20 June 2020).

Taylor, Sam. *Sylvain Chomet Talks about Animation.* Retrieved from: https://vimeo.com/12397782 (video) (last accessed 20 June 2020).

The Guardian. (2010). *Why Sylvain Chomet Chose Scotland over Hollywood.* Retrieved from: https://www.theguardian.com/film/2010/jun/10/sylvain-chomet-belleville-rendezvous-illusionist (last accessed 20 June 2020).

The Scotsman. (2010). *Interview: Sylvain Chomet, Film Director.* Retrieved from: https://www.scotsman.com/news/interview-sylvain-chomet-film-director-2460352 (last accessed 20 June 2020).

th1ng. (2014). *Sylvain Chomet's making of 'The Simpsons couch gag'.* Retrieved from: https://www.youtube.com/watch?v=5CgxoNo9_qU (last accessed 20 June 2020).

TIENS TOI BIEN! PRODUCTION. (2014). *Les Triplettes de Belleville – Le spectacle musical – avec Sylvain Chomet et Denis Lafaurie.* Retrieved from: https://www.youtube.com/watch?v=0lNeR_CeYjo (last accessed 20 June 2020).

TIENS TOI BIEN! PRODUCTION. (2014). *Interview de Sylvain Chomet sur le spectacle musical 'Les Triplettes de Belleville dans: Go Ouest'.* Retrieved from: https://www.youtube.com/watch?v=CpmC7sVrHKo (last accessed 20 June 2020).

Tout le cine. (2010). *Interview de Sylvain Chomet sur L'illusionniste.* Retrieved from: https://www.youtube.com/watch?v=rbkkswQk1O4 (last accessed 20 June 2020).

Ville de Paris. (2013). *Attila Marcel un film de Sylvain Chomet.* Retrieved from: https://www.youtube.com/watch?v=zKCTWdEZ51c (last accessed 20 June 2020).

Wilkinson, Amber. (2014). *Drawing on Real Life – Sylvain Chomet Talks about His Live-action Feature Attila Marcel.* Retrieved from: https://www.eyeforfilm.co.uk/feature/2014-09-11-sylvain-chomet-interview-about-making-attila-marcel-feature-story-by-amber-wilkinson (last accessed 20 June 2020).

Notes

Introduction

1   According to the *Literary Terms* definition: 'Anthropomorphism (pronounced ann-throw-poe-MORF-ism) is giving human traits or attributes to animals, inanimate objects or other non-human things. It comes from the Greek words anthropo (human) and morph (form).'

2   Animation production is sometimes characterized by a 'high mobility', meaning that it is not uncommon for a company to be created for the production of an animation feature and, when the production is over, to cease to exist. Additionally, many animators very often work with contracts or as freelancers. This motility sometimes makes the work of animation production scholars more challenging, depending of course on their subject.

Chapter 1

1   'Créé en février 1969, sucesseur de Vaillant, Le Journal de Pif est rapidement devenu un véritable phénomène de presse grâce à ses récits complets d'une part (et non des feuilletons comme on pouvait en lire à l'époque dans les journaux concurrents, Pilote, Tintin, Spirou, *Le Journal de Mickey*, qui cherchaient à fidéliser les lecteurs) et à ses gadgets d'autre part.

Les séries étaient extrêmement variées, allant de l'aventure animalière en couleur (Pif, Placid et Muzo, Pifou), au récit historique de style réaliste en noir et blanc (Rahan, fils des âges farouches; Docteur Justice; Corto Maltese; Teddy Ted, le 'cow-boy aux yeux clairs'; Les Pionniers de l'Espérance; Ragnar le viking …) en passant par l'humour plus adulte comme Gai-Luron ou Corinne et Jeannot. Le jeune lecteur trouvait également chaque semaine une quinzaine de pages de jeux comprenant des tests, des mots croisés, des énigmes …' (Quillien, 2018).

2   Created by Roger Lecureux and Andre Cheret, '*Rahan* is a comic character first published in *Pif Gadget Magazine* in about 1969. Rahan is a hero of more 180 stories … 3500 pages in total' (Rahan.org online).

3   The animator creates the key frames of an animation, and, then, junior animators add frames between the key frames to make the motion smoother. These frames are called 'in-betweens'.

Chapter 2

1   The Cinémathèque Française is a French non-profit film organization founded in 1936 that holds one of the largest archives of film documents and film-related objects in the world.

2   The twelve Disney principles of animation: (1) Squash and Stretch; (2) Anticipation; (3) Staging; (4) Straight ahead Action and Pose to Pose; (5) Follow through and Overlapping Action; (6) Slow in and Slow out; (7) Arc; (8) Secondary Action; (9) Timing; (10) Exaggeration; (11) Solid Drawing; (12) Appeal.

3   Of course, Mickey was not the only victim of commercialization. This also happened to *Betty Boop*, the jazz singer produced by Fleischer. After audience complaints, Betty ended up confined to her house and stripped of all her magic.

4   Limited animation is a technique or process in animation that reuses animated frames, mirrors images (characters) and draws new frames only when necessary to limit work, save on time and, ultimately, reduce the budget (Tetali and Phidi Pulu).

5   However, there is a degree of change in that as although Pixar's films are produced primarily for children, they do also consider the adults in the audience. For example, there has been a notable shift in the age of some Pixar heroes. In many cases, they are adults, dealing with adult problems, unlike Disney heroes, who are mostly children (Shepard, 2012:18, 35–8).

6   Chomet asks his audience to do more than just watch an animation film for adults. He asks them to embrace a different point of view than that of mainstream perceptions and ideologies. For decades, he has differentiated himself from Hollywood conceptions. For instance, when asked about Madame Souza's appearance in *The Triplets of Belleville*, Chomet says: 'Pretty people aren't the point of the film. It's partly a reaction to the new Disney films where the heroes are always handsome and pretty, and the funny characters, or the evil characters, are not. What we think of as pretty girls don't have much character in their faces' (Chomet in Curiel, 2003).

Chapter 3

1   Sally Brown is now married to Sylvain Chomet.

2   Box Office Mojo. *The Triplets of Belleville*. Retrieved from: https://www.boxofficemojo.com/release/rl2255980033/ (last accessed 4 July 2020).

3   Of the 12 million, 9 million was spent in Scotland. It was the most expensive film in the history of Scottish cinema.

Chapter 5

1   During the grand opening ceremony of the American National Exhibition in Moscow, Vice President Richard Nixon and Soviet leader Nikita Khrushchev engaged in a heated debate about capitalism and communism in the middle of a model kitchen set-up for the fair. The so-called 'kitchen debate' became one of the most famous episodes of the Cold War (History.com).

Chapter 7

1   In the end, though, the final judge of each film is its audience. Among many others, a public audience review on Internet Movie Database writes: 'I saw this at the Toronto Film Festival and loved it. The packed audience there also seemed to share my enthusiasm. Funnier, quirkier but more complete than *The Triplets of Belleville*, which I liked. I gave it my vote for the Audience Award. Almost impossible to describe without spoiling so I will just say that it is warm, funny, quirky, scary, melodic, and romantic.' This review is cited because Chomet's films are perceived as a whole and are not labelled as 'animation' or 'live-action'. An analysis of the reviews led us to the preliminary and yet-to-be-proved hypothesis that the contemporary audience's perception has changed more than the industry and the institutions realize.

2   Aton Soumache produced nine animated feature films, a rarity in the animation industry given the time and means required even to make one. He produced the films: *Renaissance* (Volckman, 2006), *The Prodigies* (Charreyron, 2011), *Mune* (Heboyan and Philippon, 2015), *The Little Prince* (Osborne, 2015), *Tall Tales from the Magical Garden of Antoon Krings* (Bouron and Krings, 2017), *Playmobil: The Movie* (DiSalvo, 2019), *Little Vampire* (Sfar, 2020), *Ladybug & Cat Noir: The Movie* (2022) and *Little Nicholas* (Fredon and Massoubre, 2022). Aton Soumache also produced more than fifty seasons of animated series, including five seasons (130 episodes) of the worldwide phenomenon *Miraculous Ladybug: Tales of Ladybug & Cat Noir*.

Filmography

101 Dalmatians. (1961). Dir. Clyde Geronimi, Hamilton Luske, Wolfgang Reitherman. Prod. Walt Disney Productions. USA.

Akira. (1988). Dir. Katsuhiro Otomo. Prod. Akira Committee Company. Japan.

Aladdin. (1992). Dir. Ron Clements and John Musker. Prod. Walt Disney Feature Animation. USA.

Alice in Wonderland. (1951). Dir. Clyde Geronimi, Wilfred Jackson, Hamilton Luske, Jack Kinney. Prod. Walt Disney Animation Studios. USA.

Amélie. (Le Fabuleux Destin d'Amélie Poulain. 2001). Dir. Guillaume Laurant. Prod. Jean-Marc Deschamps, Claudie Ossard. France.

Asterix et Cleopatre. (1976). Dir. René Goscinny and Albert Uderzo. Prod. Belvision. Belgium.

Asterix le gaulois. (1976). Dir. Ray Goossens. Prod. Belvision. Belgium.

Astroboy. (1963–6). Dir. Osamu Tezuka et al. Prod. Mushi Productions. Japan. (TV Series).

Attila Marcel. (2013). Dir. Sylvain Chomet. Prod. Eurowide Film Production. France.

Beauty and the Beast. (1991). Dir. Gary Trousdale and Kirk Wise. Prod. Walt Disney Feature. USA.

Brave. (2012). Dir. Mark Andrews, Brenda Chapman. Prod. Pixar Animation Studios. USA.

Creature Comforts. (1989). Dir. Nick Park. Prod. Aardman Animations. UK.

Fantasmagorie. (1908). Dir. Émile Cohl. Prod. Cohl Émile. France.

Fantastic Planet (La planète sauvage). (1973). Dir. René Laloux. Prod. Argos Films. France-Czechoslovakia.

Felix the Cat. (1919–33). Cr. Otto Messmer, Pat Sullivan. Prod. Pat Sullivan Cartoons. USA. Movie Series.

Finding Nemo. (2003). Dir. Andrew Stanton. Prod. Pixar Animation Studios. USA.

Flaklypa Grand Prix. (1975). Dir. Ivo Caprino. Prod. Caprino Filmcenter. Norway.

Flim Flam Films. (1927). Dir. Otto Messmer, Pat Sullivan. Prod. Pat Sullivan Cartoons. USA.

Flowers and Trees. (1932). Dir. Burt Gillett. Prod. Walt Disney Productions. USA.

Hercules. (1997). Dir. Ron Clements and John Musker. Prod. Walt Disney Pictures. USA.

Jour de fête. (1949). Dir. Jacques Tati. Prod. Cady Films and Panoramic Films. France.

King Size Canary. (1947). Dir. Tex Avery. Prod. Metro-Goldwyn-Mayer. USA.

Kirikou et la sorcière. (1998). Dir. Michel Ocelot. Prod. France 3 Cinéma, Les Armateurs. France.

L'illusionniste. (2010). Dir. Sylvain Chomet. Prod. Pathé, Django Films, Ciné B, France 3 Cinéma. France, UK.

La demoiselle et le violoncelliste. (1964). Dir. Jean-François Laguionie. France.

La Flûte à six schtroumpfs. (1976). Dir. Peyo. Prod. Belvision. Belgium.

La vieille dame et les pigeons. (1997). Dir. Sylvain Chomet. Prod. Les Productions Pascal Blais, Les Armateurs, Club d'Investissement Média. Productions Django, Odec Kid Cartoons, Trans Europe Film. Canada, France, Belgium, UK.

Le diamant. (1970). Dir. Paul Grimault. Prod. Les Gémeaux. France.

Le petit soldat. (1947). Dir. Paul Grimault. Prod. Les Gémeaux. France.

Le Roi et l'Oiseau. (1980). Dir. Paul Grimault. Prod. Les Films Paul Grimault Les Films Gibé France 2.

Les 12 travaux d'Asterix. (1976). Dir. René Goscinny, Henri Gruel, Albert Uderzo, Pierre Watrin Prod. Idéfix. France.

Les passagers de La Grande Ourse. (1941). Dir. Paul Grimault. Prod. Les Gémeaux. France.

Les Triplettes de Belleville. (2003). Dir. Sylvain Chomet. Prod. Les Armateurs, Champion, Vivi Film, France 3 Cinéma, RG Prince Films. France, Belgium, Canada, UK, Latvia, USA.

Lion's King. (1994). Dir. Roger Allers, Rob Minkoff. Prod. Walt Disney Feature Animation. USA.

Lucky Luke. (1976). Dir. René Goscinny. Prod. Belvision. Belgium.

Lucky Luke: La ballade des Dalton. (1976). Dir. René Goscinny, Henri Gruel, Morris, Pierre Watrin. Prod. Idéfix. France.

Mary and Max. (2009). Dir. Adam Elliot. Prod. Melodrama Pictures. Australia.

Merci Monsieur Imada. (2016). Dir. Sylvain Chomet. Prod. Adami. France.

Mon Oncle. (1958). Dir. Jacques Tati. Prod. Specta Films. France.

Monsieur Hulot's Holiday. (Les vacances de Monsieur Hulot, 1953). Dir. Jacques Tati. Prod. Discina Film. France.

Monsters Inc. (2001). Dir. Pete Docter. Prod. Pixar Animation Studios. USA.

Out of the Inkwell. (1918–29). Dir. Dave Fleischer, Max Fleischer. Prod. Max Fleischer. USA.

Paris, je t'aime (segment 'Tour Eiffel'). Dir. Sylvain Chomet. Prod. Victoires International. France, Liechtenstein, Switzerland, Germany, USA.

Playtime. (1967). Dir. Jacques Tati. Prod. Bernard Maurice, René Silvera. USA.

Ratatouille. (2007). Dir. Brad Bird. Prod. Pixar Animation Studios. USA.

Renaissance. (2006). Dir. Christian Volckman. Prod. Aton Soumache. France.

Rio. (2011). Dir. Carlos Saldanha. Prod. Twentieth Century Fox Animation. USA.

Snow White and the Seven Dwarfs. (1937). Dir. David Hand. Prod. Walt Disney Productions. USA.

Spirited Away. (2001). Dir. Hayao Miyazaki. Prod. Studio Ghibli. Japan.

The Debut of Thomas Cat. (1929). Dir. John Randolph Bray. Prod. Bray
    Productions. USA.
The Haunted Hotel. (1907). Dir. Stuart J. Blackton. Prod. Vitagraph Company of
    America. USA.
The Jungle Book. (1967). Dir. Wolfgang Reitherman. Prod. Walt Disney
    Productions. USA.
The Little Prince. (2015). Dir. Mark Osborne. Prod. Aton Soumache. France.
The Magic Violin. (1952). Dir. Ivo Caprino. Prod. Caprino Filmcenter. Norway.
The Magnificent Life of Marcel Pagnol. (In production). Dir. Sylvain Chomet. Prod. Aton
    Soumache. France.
The Newlyweds. (1913). Dir. Emile Cohl. Prod. Éclair. USA.
The Tale of Despereaux. (2008). Dir. Sam Fell and Robert Stevenhagen. Prod. Universal
    Studios. UK, USA.
The Tale of the White Serpent. (1958). Dir. Kazuhiko Okabe, Taiji Yabushita. Prod. Toei
    Animation. Japan.
The Tenacious Tin Soldier. (1954). Dir. Ivo Caprino. Prod. Caprino Filmcenter. Norway.
Tin Toy. (1988). Dir. John Lasseter. Prod. Pixar Animation Studios. USA.
Toy Story. (1995). Dir. John Lasseter. Prod. Pixar Animation Studios. USA.
Up. (2009). Dir. Pete Docter. Prod. Pixar Animation Studios. USA.
Wallace and Gromit: The Wrong Trousers (Park, 1993). Dir. Nick Park. Prod. Aardman
    Animations.
Wallace & Gromit: The Curse of the Were-Rabbit. (2005). Dir. Steve Box, Nick Park.
    Prod. Aardman Animations. UK, USA.
WALL·E. (2008). Dir. Andrew Stanton. Prod. Pixar Animation Studios. USA.
Who Framed Roger Rabbit. (1988). Dir. Robert Zemeckis. Prod. Touchstone
    Pictures. USA.

Bibliography

Adamson, Joe. (1975). *Tex Avery: King of Cartoons*. New York: Popular Library.

Aguilar, Carlos. (2018). *'The Triplets of Belleville' 15th Anniversary: 7 Insights into the Making of a Contemporary Classic*. Retrieved from: https://www.cartoonbrew.com/feature-film/the-triplets-of-belleville-15th-anniversary-7-insights-into-the-making-of-a-contemporary-classic-159630.html (last accessed 22 July 2020).

Alcacer, Juan, David J. Collis and Mary Furey. (2009). *The Walt Disney Company and Pixar Inc.: To Acquire or Not to Acquire?* Harvard Business School, Case 709–462.

Alexandre Alexeïeff in Gianalberto Bendazzi, 1994: xix and xx (preface with title: *In Praise of Animated Film*).

Alexeïeff, Alexandre. (1964). *Reflections on Motion Picture Animation. Film Culture* (32).

Alexeïeff, Alexandre. (1972). Reflections on Motion Picture Animation. In Russett Robert and Cecile Starr (eds), *Experimental Animation*. New York: Van Nostrand Reinold.

AlloCiné. (2013). *'Attila Marcel' : le making–of interactif du film de Sylvain Chomet*. Retrieved from: http://www.allocine.fr/article/fichearticle_gen_carticle=18628934.html (last accessed 22 July 2020).

Anderson, Ross. (2019). *Pulling a Rabbit Out of a Hat: The Making of Roger Rabbit*. Mississippi, USA: University Press of Mississippi.

Animator. (1984). *The Donald Duck Story*. Retrieved from: https://www.animatormag.com/1984/issue-09/issue-9-page-26/ (last accessed 28 August 2022).

Artz, Lee. (2003). *Animating Hierarchy: Disney and the Globalization of Capitalism*. Retrieved from: http://www.globalmediajournal.com/open-access/animating-hierarchy-disney-and-the-globalization-of-capitalism.pdf (last accessed 25 August 2018).

Atkinson, Nikki. (2006). *The Use of Anthropomorphism in the Animation of Animals*. Degree thesis for Bournemouth University National Centre for Computer Animation.

Austin, Christina. (2013). *Pixar's Marketing For 'Monsters University' Is Very Impressive*. Retrieved from: https://www.businessinsider.com/monsters-university-marketing-breaks-the-mold-for-advertising-2013-1?IR=T (last accessed 22 September 2018).

Baird, Merrily C. (2001). *Symbols of Japan: Thematic Motifs in Art and Design*. New York: Rizzoli.

Balkind, Nicola. (2010). *Animation Comes to Life: Anthropomorphism & Wall-E*. Retrieved from: http://filmint.nu/wp-content/uploads/2010/06/FINT_web_june_Balkind.pdf (last accessed 28 August 2018).

Barrier, Michael. (1999). *Hollywood Cartoons: American Animation in Its Golden Age.* New York: Oxford University Press.

Barthes, Roland. (1981). *Camera Lucida: Reflections on Photography.* New York: Hill and Wang.

Barthes, Roland. (1983 [1964]). *Elements of Semiology.* New York: Hill and Wang.

Baudrillard, Jean. (1994 [1981]). *Simulacra and Simulation.* Michigan, USA: University of Michigan Press.

Bazin, Andre. (1967). *What Is Cinema?* Volume 1. Retrieved from: https://archive. org/stream/Bazin_Andre_What_Is_Cinema_Volume_1/Bazin_Andre_What_Is_ Cinema_Volume_1_djvu.txt (last accessed 17 August 2018).

Bell, Elizabeth, Lynda Haas and Laura Sells (eds). (1995). *From Mouse to Mermaid: The Politics of Film, Gender and Culture.* Bloomington: Indiana University Press.

Bendazzi, Giannalberto. (1994). *Cartoons: One Hundred Years of Cinema Animation.* Eastleigh, UK: John Libbey Publishing.

Bendazzi, Giannalberto. (2004). Defining Animation: A Proposal. http://www. giannalbertobendazzi.com/Content/resources/pdf/AnimationEssays/Defining_ Animation-Giannalberto_Bendazzi2004.pdf.

Bendazzi, Giannalberto. (2016). *Animation: A World History: Volume I: Foundations – The Golden Age.* Boca Raton, Florida, USA: CRC Press.

Bendazzi, Giannalberto. (2016). *Animation: A World History: Volume II: The Birth of a Style – The Three Markets.* Boca Raton, Florida, USA: CRC Press.

Bendazzi, Giannalberto. (2016). *Animation: A World History: Volume III: Contemporary Times.* Boca Raton, Florida, USA: CRC Press.

Benkler, Yochai. (2006). *The Wealth of Networks: How Social Production Transforms Market and Freedom.* New Haven: Yale University Press.

Beugnet, Martine. (2014). *An Invention with a Future French Cinema after the End of Cinema. A Companion to Contemporary French Cinema.* New Jersey, USA: John Wiley & Sons, Inc. pp 570–89.

Beylie, Claude. (1964). *La bande dessinée est-elle un art?* revue Lettre et Médecins. January–September 1964.

Bliss, Gillian E. (2017). *Redefining the Anthropomorphic Animal in Animation.* Retrieved from: https://dspace.lboro.ac.uk/2134/27423 (last accessed 26 August 2018).

Boklund-Lagopoulou, Karin. (1984). The Life of Saint Alexius: Structure and Function of a Medieval Popular Narrative. *Semiotica.* 49 (3/4):243–81.

Boklund-Lagopoulou, Karin. (2016). Why Semiotics? In *Changing Worlds & Signs of the Times/Selected Proceedings from the 10th International Conference of the Hellenic Semiotics Society* (pp 88–99). Retrieved from: http://hellenic-semiotics.gr//wp-content/uploads/2016/04/Changing%20Worlds%20&%20Signs%20of%20the% 20Times_WEB.pdf (last accessed 22 September 2018).

Brown, Blain. (2016). *Cinematography: Theory and Practice: Image Making for Cinematographers and Directors.* London: Routledge.

Brown, Steven T. (2008). *Cinema Anime*. New York: Palgrave Macmillan.

Brunner, Didier in Lemercier, Fabien. (2016). *Folivari Aiming to Reach New Heights*. Retrieved from: https://cineuropa.org/en/interview/305868/ (last accessed 8 June 2020).

Buckland, Warren. (2000). *The Cognitive Semiotics of Film*. Cambridge: Cambridge University Press.

Buckmaster, Luke. (2009). *Interview with Adam Elliot, Writer/Director/Designer of Mary and Max*. Retrieved from: https://blogs.crikey.com.au/cinetology/2009/04/10/q-a-with-mary-and-max-writerdirectordesigner-adam-elliot/ (last accessed 2 July 2020).

Bullock, Saxon. (2003). *Sylvain Chomet, Belleville Rendez-Vous*. Retrieved from: http://www.bbc.co.uk/films/2003/08/27/sylvain_chomet_belleville_rendezvous_interview.shtml (last accessed 22 September 2018).

Cairns, David. (2010). *Ce n'est pas une pipe: 'The Illusionist' (Sylvain Chomet, UK)*. Retrieved from: https://mubi.com/notebook/posts/ce-nest-pas-une-pipe-the-illusionist-sylvain-chomet-uk (last accessed 2 July 2020).

Canemaker, John (ed.). (1988). *Storytelling in Animation: The Art of the Animated Image*. Los Angeles: American Film Institute.

Canemaker, John. (1996). *Felix: The Twisted Tale of the World's Most Famous Cat*. New York: Da Capo.

Carbaga, Leslie. (1988 [1976]). *The Fleischer Story*. New York: Da Capo.

Caruso, Valerio. (2003). *Sylvain Chomet – 'Animation Is like Mime'*. Retrieved from: https://cineuropa.org/en/interview/30891/ (last accessed 20 June 2020).

Catmull, Ed. (2008). *How Pixar Fosters Collective Creativity*. Retrieved from: https://hbr.org/2008/09/how-pixar-fosters-collective-creativity (last accessed 20 August 2018).

Cavallaro, Dani. (2011). *Art in Anime: The Creative Quest as Theme and Metaphor*. North Carolina, USA: McFarland.

Chaminade, Thierry, Jessica Hodgins and Mitsuo Kawato. (2007). Anthropomorphism Influences Perception of Computer-animated Characters' Actions. *Scan*. (2):206–16.

Chevillard, Hubert and Sylvain Chomet. (1993). *Le Pont dans la vase. L' anguille*. France: Glénat – Grafica.

Chevillard, Hubert and Sylvain Chomet. (1995). *Le Pont dans la vase. Orlandus*. France: Glénat.

Chevillard, Hubert and Sylvain Chomet. (1998). *Le Pont dans la vase. Malocchio*. France: Glénat – Grafica.

Chevillard, Hubert and Sylvain Chomet. (2003). *Le Pont dans la vase. Barthélémy*. France: Glénat – Grafica.

Chevillard, Hubert and Sylvain Chomet. (2011). *Le Pont dans la vase. Les Intégrales*. France: Glénat – Grafica.

Cholodenko, Alan. (2008). *The Animation of Cinema*. Retrieved from: http://projects.chass.utoronto.ca/semiotics/vol18.2.pdf (last accessed 26 August 2018).

Chomet, Sally. (2016). *Caleb's Cab*. UK: Walker Books.

Chomet, Sylvain. (1986). *Le secret des libellules* (The Secret of Dragonflies). France: Futuropolis.

Sylvain Chomet: Interview with the 'Bad Boy' of Animation. (2018). Arts University Bournemouth. Online. https://aub.ac.uk/latest/sylvain-chomet-interview-title-progress (last accessed 21 August 2022).

Cieply, Michael and Charles Solomon. (2008). *Name Game: A Tale of Acknowledgment for 'Despereaux'*. Retrieved from: https://www.nytimes.com/2008/09/27/movies/27movi.html?_r=1&ei=5070&emc=eta1&oref=slogin (last accessed 26 June 2020).

Collignon Stéphane. (2008). *They Walk! They Talk! A Study of the Anthropomorphisation of Non Human Characters in Animated Films*. Retrieved from: http://hdl.handle.net/2268/172000 (last accessed 27 August 2018).

Comolli, Jean-Louis. (1985). Technique and Ideology: Camera, Perspective, Depth of Field. In Bill Nichols (ed.), *Movies and Methods Vol. 2* (pp 40–58). London: University of California Press.

Costanzo, William V. (2014). *World Cinema through Global Genres*. New Jersey, USA: John Wiley & Sons, Inc.

Courtet-Cohl, Pierre and Bernard Génin. (2008). *Émile Cohl: L'inventeur du dessin animé*. France: Omniscience.

Coyle, Rebecca (ed.). (2010). *Drawn to Sound. Animation Film Music and Sonicity*. London: Equinox Publications.

Crafton, Donald. (1993). *Before Mickey: The Animated Film, 1892–1928*. Cambridge: MIT Press.

Crécy, Nicolas de and Sylvain Chomet. (1989). *Bug Jargal*. Ruçager, France: Éditions Ruçager.

Crécy, Nicolas de and Sylvain Chomet. (1995). *Léon la came*. France: Casterman.

Crécy, Nicolas de and Sylvain Chomet. (1997). *Laid, pauvre et malade: Léon la came*. France: Casterman.

Crécy, Nicolas de and Sylvain Chomet. (1998). *Priez pour nous: Léon la came*. France: Casterman.

Curiel, Jonathan. (2003). *For Caricaturist Chomet, Creator of 'Triplets of Belleville', It's a Long Way from Disney*. Retrieved from: https://www.sfgate.com/entertainment/article/For-caricaturist-Chomet-creator-of-Triplets-of-2524759.php (last accessed 22 September 2018).

David, Bordwell and Kristin Thompson. (2001). *Film Art: An Introduction*. London: McGraw Hill.

Deleuze, Gilles. (1986). *Cinema 1: The Movement-image*. Minneapolis: University of Minnesota Press.

Deleuze, Gilles. (1989). *Cinema 2: The Time-image*. Minneapolis: University of Minnesota Press.

Desowitz, Bill. (2010). *Chomet Talks 'The Illusionist'.* Retrieved from: https://www.awn. com/animationworld/chomet-talks-illusionist (last accessed 12 June 2020).

Desowitz, Bill. (2010). *Chomet Talks 'The Illusionist'.* Animation World Network. Online: https://awn.com/dev/animationworld/chomet-talks-the-illusionist-2/ (last accessed 7 December 2022).

DiCamillo, Kate. (2003). *The Tale of Despereaux.* Massachusetts: Candlewick Press.

Dobson, Nichola. (2020). *Historical Dictionary of Animation and Cartoons.* Maryland: Rowman & Littlefield Publishers.

Dorfman, Ariel and Armand Mattelart. (1975). *How to Read Donald Duck: Imperialist Ideology in the Disney Comic.* New York: International General.

Drotner, Kirsten. (2004). Disney Discourses, or Mundane Globalisation. In Ib Bondebjerg and Peter Golding (eds), *European Culture and the Media* (pp 91–115). Bristol: Intellect Books.

Dudok de Wit, Alex. (2019). *Sylvain Chomet Will Open an Animation School in Northern France Next Year.* Retrieved from: https://www.cartoonbrew.com/ schools/sylvain-chomet-will-open-an-animation-school-in-northern-france-next-year-180567.html (last accessed 12 August 2020).

Eco, Umberto. (1976). *A Theory of Semiotics.* Bloomington: Indiana University Press.

Eco, Umberto. (1985). Articulations of the Cinematic Code. In Bill Nichols (ed.), *Movies and Methods: An Anthology* (pp 590–607). Berkeley: University of California Press.

Edera, Bruno. (1977). *Full Length Animated Feature Films.* New York: Hastings House.

Eisenstein, Sergei. (2016). *Eisenstein on Disney.* Jay Leyda (ed.). London: Methuen.

Electric Sheep Magazine. (2010). *The Illusionist: Interview with Sylvain Chomet.* Retrieved from: http://www.electricsheepmagazine.co.uk/2010/08/01/the-illusionist-interview-with-sylvain-chomet/ (last accessed 12 August 2020).

Eliade, Mircea. (1975 [1958]). *Rites and Symbols of Initiation: The Mysteries of Birth and Rebirth.* Retrieved from: https://archive.org/stream/mircea-eliade-rites-and-symbols-of-initiation-the-mysteries-of-birth-and-rebirth/mircea-eliade-rites-and-symbols-of-initiation-the-mysteries-of-birth-and-rebirth_djvu.txt (last accessed 29 August 2018).

Eliade, Mircea. (1975). *Myths, Dreams, and Mysteries.* New York: Harper & Row.

Eliade, Mircea. (1991 [1954]). *The Myth of the Eternal Return.* Princeton, New Jersey, USA: Princeton University Press.

Ellis, Tiffany A. (2012). *Through the Looking Glass: A Sociolinguistic Analysis of Disney and Disney-Pixar* Retrieved from: http://cardinalscholar.bsu.edu/ handle/123456789/196001 (last accessed 26 August 2018).

Ezra, Elizabeth. (2000). *Georges Melies.* Manchester: Manchester University Press.

Faucher, Yann. (2014). *The Credits of the Simpsons Revisited in French by Sylvain Chomet.* Retrieved from: https://www.lexpress.fr/culture/tele/video-le-generiquedes-simpson-revisite-a-la-francaise-par-sylvain-chomet_1498262.html (last accessed 12 May 2020).

Fiascone, Regan. (2014). *Disney & Pixar: Building a Magic Kingdom of Animation.* Retrieved from: https://sites.duke.edu/iereganfiascone/files/2015/05/DSV-Disney-Case-Study.pdf (last accessed 27 August 2018).

Finch, Christopher. (1973). *The Art of Walt Disney: From Mickey Mouse to the Magic Kingdoms and Beyond.* New York: Harry Abrams.

Fischer, Russ. (2014). *Watch 'The Simpsons' Couch Gag by 'Triplets of Belleville' Director Sylvain Chomet.* Retrieved from: https://www.slashfilm.com/simpsons-couch-gag-by-triplets-of-belleville-director/ (last accessed 27 May 2020).

Fleischer, Richard. (2005). *Out of the Inkwell: Max Fleischer and the Animation Revolution.* Lexington: University Press of Kentucky.

Floquet, Pierre. (2006). What Is (Not) So French in Les Triplettes de Belleville. *Journal for Animation History and Theory.* 1:8–13. Retrieved from: https://journal.animationstudies.org/pierre-floquet-what-is-not-so-french-in-les-triplettes-de-belleville/ (last accessed 29 August 2022).

Foley, Jack. *Belleville Rendez-vous – Sylvain Chomet (Part Two).* Retrieved from: http://www.indielondon.co.uk/film/belleville_rendezvous_chometQ&A2.html (last accessed 11 August 2020).

Foley, Jack. *Belleville Rendez-vous (12A).* Retrieved from: http://www.indielondon.co.uk/film/belleville_rendezvous_rev.html (last accessed 11 August 2020).

Frierson, Michael. (1997). Clay Animation Comes Out of the Inkwell: The Fleischer Brothers and Clay Animation. In Jayne Pilling (ed.), *A Reader in Animation Studies* (pp 82–92). Sydney: John Libbey & Company Pty Ltd.

Furniss, Maureen. (1998). *Art in Motion: Animation Aesthetics.* Eastleigh, UK: John Libbey Publishing.

Furniss, Maureen. (2008). *The Animation Bible: A Guide to Everything – from Flipbooks to Flash.* London: Laurence King.

Furniss, Maureen. (2009). *Animation: Art and Industry.* Eastleigh, UK: John Libbey Publishing.

Furniss, Maureen. (2016). *A New History of Animation.* London: Thames & Hudson.

Furniss, Maureen. (2017). *Animation: The Global History.* London: Thames & Hudson.

Geek Buffet. (2010). *'Magicians Don't Exist' – The Illusionist (2010).* Retrieved from: https://geekbuffet.wordpress.com/tag/triplets-of-belleville/ (last accessed 11 August 2020).

Gifford, Denis. (1990). *American Animated Films: The Silent Era, 1897–1929.* Jefferson, N.C, USA: McFarland.

Giroux, Henry A. (1999). *The Mouse that Roared: Disney and the End of Innocence.* Plymouth: Rowman & Littlefield.

Goldmark, Daniel. (2010). Sonic Nostalgia and Les triplettes de Belleville. In *Drawn to Sound. Animation Film Music and Sonicity* (pp 141–59). London: Equinox Publications.

Goossens, Daniel. (1985). *Laisse Autant le Vent Emporter*. Paris, France: Humanoïdes Associés.

Grant, Joe. (1997). *The Encyclopedia of Walt Disney's Animated Characters*. New York: Hyperion.

Greimas, Algirdas J. (1984 [1966]). *Structural Semantics: An Attempt at a Method*. Nebraska: University of Nebraska Press.

Greimas, Algirdas J. (1987 [1970]). *On Meaning: Selected Writings in Semiotic Theory*. Minneapolis: University of Minessota Press.

Greimas, Algirdas J. and Joseph Courtes. (1979). *Semiotics and Language: An Analytical Dictionary*. Bloomington: Indiana University Press.

Gritten, David. (2010). *Sylvain Chomet on the Illusionist*. Retrieved from: https://www.telegraph.co.uk/culture/film/7928280/Sylvain-Chomet-on-The-Illusionist.html (last accessed 22 July 2020).

Grove, L. (2013). *Comics in French: The European Bande Dessinee in Context*. New York and Oxford: Berghahn Books.

Halas, John. (1987). *Masters of Animation*. Topsfield: Salem House.

Halas, John and Roger Manvell. (1959). *Technique of Film Animation*. New York, USA: Hastings House.

Harnick, Chris. (2014). *The Simpsons Taps Oscar-Nominated Animator for Coolest and Strangest Couch Gag Yet. Is This the Best Simpsons Couch Gag Ever?* Retrieved from: https://www.eonline.com/news/518341/the-simpsons-taps-sylvain-chomet-for-coolest-and-strangest-couch-gag-yet-watch-now (last accessed 22 May 2020).

Hernández, María Lorenzo. (2019). Animated Illustrations – Animated Illustrators. Influences from Traditional Illustration in Outstanding Animated Films. In Alan Male (ed.). *A Companion to Illustration*. New Jersey, USA: John Wiley & Sons, Inc.

Hesmondhalgh, David. (2013). *The Cultural Industries*. Retrieved from: https://www.researchgate.net/publication/261554803_The_Cultural_Industries_3rd_Ed (last accessed 22 September 2018).

Hilty, Greg and Alona Pardo (eds). (2011). *Watch Me Move: The Animation Show*. New York: Merrell Publishers.

Hoffer, Thomas W. (1981). *Animation: A Reference Guide*. Westport: Greenwood Press.

Hugo, Victor. (2004 [1826]). *Bug-Jargal*. Chris Bongie (transl.). Toronto: Broadview.

Jackson, Kathy M. (1993). *Walt Disney: A Bio-bibliography*. Westport: Greenwood Press.

Jardim, Tim. (2011). *Anthropomorphic Character Design in Animation and Sequential Art: The Symbolic Use of the Animal to Portray Personality*. Retrieved from: https://www.academia.edu/976255/Anthropomorphic_character_design_in_animation_and_sequential_art_The_symbolic_use_of_the_animal_to_portray_personality (last accessed 27 August 2018).

Jenkins, Henry. (2006). *Convergence Culture: Where Old and New Media Collide*. New York: New York University Press.

Kanfer, Stefan. (1997). *Serious Business: The Art and Commerce of Animation in America from Betty Boop to Toy Story*. New York: Scribner.

Katsaridou, Maria. (2019). *Social Semiotics of Animation Films*. Retrieved from: http://ikee.lib.auth.gr/record/303239?ln=en (last accessed 21 August 2020).

Kelts, Roland. (2006). *Japanamerica: How Japanese Pop Culture Has Invaded the U.S.* New York: St. Martin's Press.

Kunz, Sahra. (2014). *The Role of Drawing in Animated Films*. Retrieved from: https://www.academia.edu/2352327/The_role_of_Drawing_in_Animated_Films (last accessed 29 August 2018).

Lacassin, Francis. (1971). *Pour un 9ème Art: La Bande dessinée* Paris UGE (coll. 10/18), 1971: 10/18.

Lacassin, Francis. (1982). *Pour un neuvième art: La band dessinée*. Paris, France: Slatkine ressources.

Lagopoulos, Alexandros Ph. (2000). A Global Model of Communication. *Semiotica*. 131 (1/2):45–77.

Λαγόπουλος, Αλέξανδρος Φαίδων και Κάριν Μπόκλουντ-Λαγοπούλου. (2016). *Θεωρία Σημειωτικής: Η παράδοση του Ferdinand de Saussure*. Αθήνα: Πατάκη (in Greek).

Lagopoulos, Alexandros Ph. and Karin Boklund-Lagopoulou. (2021). *Theory and Methodology of Semiotics: The Tradition of Ferdinand de Saussure*. Berlin: De Gruyter.

Lambiek Comiclopedia. (2020). *Daniel Goossens*. Retrieved from: https://www.lambiek.net/artists/g/goossens_daniel.htm (last accessed 12 August 2020).

Lambiek Comiclopedia. (2016). https://www.lambiek.net/artists/g/goossens_daniel.htmcomiclopedia.

Lee, Hye-Kyung. (2010). *Animation Industry at a Crossroads*. Retrieved from: https://kclpure.kcl.ac.uk/portal/files/4682246/lee%20crossroads.pdf (last accessed 22 September 2018).

Lemercier, Fabien. (2009). *An Eminently European Film*. Retrieved from: https://cineuropa.org/en/interview/89643/ (last accessed 8 June 2020).

Lemercier, Fabien. (2012). *Attila Marcel: Sylvain Chomet's New World*. Retrieved from: https://www.cineuropa.org/en/newsdetail/225735/ (last accessed 8 June 2020).

Lenburg, Jeff. (1993). *The Great Cartoon Directors*. New York: Da Capo.

Lenburg, Jeff. (1999). *The Encyclopedia of Animated Cartoons*. New York: Checkmark Books.

Lent, John A. (1994). *Animation, Caricature, and Gag and Political Cartoons in the United States and Canada: An International Bibliography*. Westport: Greenwood Press.

Leslie, Esther. (2002). *Hollywood Flatlands: Animation, Critical Theory and the Avant-Garde*. London: Verso.

Levi, Antonia. (1996). *Samurai from Outer Space: Understanding Japanese Animation*. Illinois: Carus Publishing Company.

Levi-Strauss, Claude. (1955). Structural Study of Myths. *The Journal of American Folklore*. 68 (270): 428–44.

Literary Terms. *Anthropomorphism*. Retrieved from: https://literaryterms.net/anthropomorphism/ (last accessed 8 June 2020).

Lo Duca, Giuseppe-Maria. (1982 [1948]). *Le Dessin animé: Le dessin animé: histoire, esthétique, technique*. Paris: L'Harmattan.

Lord, Peter and Brian Sibley. (1998). *Creating 3D Animation: The Aardman Book of Filmmaking*. New York: Harry Abrams.

Male, Alan (ed.). (2019). *A Companion to Illustration*. New Jersey, USA: John Wiley & Sons, Inc.

Maltin, Leonard. (1987). *Of Mice and Magic – A History of American Animated Cartoons*. New York: Penguin Books.

Manovich, Lev. (2001). *The Language of New Media*. Cambridge: MIT Press.

Marr, Merissa. (2006). *Pixar to the Rescue?* Retrieved from: https://www.wsj.com/articles/SB113772713632051651 (last accessed 28 August 2018).

Maskell, Peter, Harald Bathelt and Anders Malmberg. (2006). Building Global Knowledge Pipelines: The Role of Temporary Clusters. *European Planning Studies*. 14 (8):997–1013.

McCall, Douglas L. (1998). *Film Cartoons: A Guide to 20th-century American Animated Features and Shorts*. Jefferson: McFarland.

McClean Shilo, T. (2007). *Digital Storytelling: The Narrative Power of Visual Effects in Film*. Cambridge: MIT Press.

McGowan, David. (2019). *Animated Personalities: Cartoon Characters and Stardom in American Theatrical Shorts*. USA: University of Texas Press.

Merritt, Russell and J. B. Kaufman. (1993). *Walt in Wonderland: The Silent Films of Walt Disney*. Baltimore: The Johns Hopkins University Press.

Moins, Philippe. (2003). *Sylvain Chomet's 'The Triplets of Belleville'*. Retrieved from: https://www.awn.com/animationworld/sylvain-chomet-s-triplets-belleville (last accessed 22 August 2020).

Μπόκλουντ-Λαγοπούλου, Κάριν. (1983). Τι είναι η Σημειωτική; *Διαβάζω* (71):15–23.

Napier, Susan J. (2005). *Anime from Akira to Howl's Moving Castle: Experiencing Japanese Animation*. New York: St. Martin's Press.

Nelmes, Jill. (2012). *An Introduction to Film Studies*. New York: Routledge.

Neupert, Richard. (2005). The Triplets of Belleville (Les triplettes de Belleville). *Film Quarterly*. 58 (3):38–42.

Neupert, Richard. (2011). *French Animation History*. New Jersey, USA: John Wiley & Sons, Inc.

Nilaya, Josh. (2017) *The Serious, Subversive (And Sometimes Shocking) History of Cartoons*. Retrieved from: https://www.wnpr.org/post/serious-subversive-and-sometimes-shocking-history-cartoons (last accessed 7 June 2020).

O'Rourke, Michael. (1998). *Principles of Three-dimensional Computer Animation*. New York: W. W. Norton & Company.

Onstand, Katrina. (2008). *Pixar Gambles on a Robot in Love*. Retrieved from: https://www.nytimes.com/2008/06/22/movies/22onst.html (last accessed 28 August 2018).

Orwall, Bruce. (2004). *Can Disney Still Rule Animation after Pixar?* Retrieved from: https://www.wsj.com/articles/SB107567970352817493 (last accessed 20 August 2018).

Pallant, Chris. (2010). Neo-Disney: Recent Developments in Disney Feature Animation. *New Cinemas: Journal of Contemporary Film*. 8 (2):103–17.

Pallant, Chris. (2011). *Demystifying Disney. A History of Disney Feature Animation*. London: Bloomsbury.

Pathé Distribution. (2010). *The Illusionist*. Retrieved from: https://pathefilms.ch/libraries.files/20100073_en_1_The_Illusionist_Englisch.pdf (last accessed 3 August 2020).

Pilling, Jayne (ed.). (1986). *That's Not all Folks! A Primer in Cartoonal Knowledge*. London: British Film Institute.

Pilling, Jayne (ed.). (1992). *Women & Animation: A Compendium*. London: British Film Institute.

Pilling, Jayne (ed.). (1997). *A Reader in Animation Studies*. Eastleigh, UK: John Libbey Publishing.

Pixar. (2003). *Finding Nemo*. Retrieved from: https://www.pixar.com/feature-films/finding-nemo/#nemo-main (last accessed 29 August 2018).

Poitras, Gilles. (1999). *The Anime Companion: What's Japanese in Japanese Animation*. Berkeley: Stone Bridge Press.

Price, David A. (2009). *The Pixar Touch: The Making of a Company*. New York, USA: Vintage Edition.

Propp, Vladimir. (1968 [1928]). *Morphology of the Folk Tale*. Austin: University of Texas Press.

Raffaelli, Luca. (1997). Disney, Warner Bros. and Japanese Animation. In Jayne Pilling (ed.), *A Reader in Animation Studies* (pp 112–35). Sydney: John Libbey & Company Pty Ltd.

Robin, Allan. (1999). *Walt Disney and Europe: European Influences on the Animated Feature Films of Walt Disney*. London: John Libbey.

Quillien, C. (2018). *Pif Gadget - L'album des 50* ans (synopsis). https://www.bandedessinee.info/Pif-Gadget-L-album-des-50-ans-bd.

Saussure, Ferdinand de. (1983 [1916]). *Course in General Linguistics*. Illinois: Open Court Publishing Company.

Schoales, John. (2006). Alpha Clusters: Creative Innovation in Local Economies. *Economic Development Quarterly*. 20 (2):162–77.

Schodt, Frederik L. (1996). *Dreamland Japan: Writings on Modern Manga*. Berkeley: Stonebridge.

Scott, Allen J. (2000). *The Cultural Economy of Cities: Essays on the Geography of Image-producing Industries*. London: Sage.

Shepard, Iris G. (2012). *Ideology in Popular Late Twentieth and Twenty First Century Children's and Young Adult Literature and Film*. Retrieved from: http://scholarworks.uark.edu/cgi/viewcontent.cgi?article=1556&context=etd (last accessed 28 August 2018).

Smoodin, Eric (ed.). (1994). *Disney Discourse: Producing the Magic Kingdom*. London: Routledge.

Sok-yong, Hwang. (2017). *Familiar Things* (Natikeun Sesang). Sora Kim-Russell (transl.). London: Scrive Publications.

Solanki, Hiren. (2013). *Excuse Me, Who Are You ... and Do You Speak Animese? The Distinctive Language of Animation*. Retrieved from: http://fansconf.a-kon.com/dRuZ33A/wp-content/uploads/2013/04/Distinctive-Language-of-Animation-by-Hiren-Solanki.pdf (last accessed 26 August 2018).

Solomon, Charles. (1987). *The Art of the Animated Image: An Anthology*. Los Angeles: American Film Institute.

Sony Pictures Classics. (2010). *The Illusionist*. Retrieved from: https://www.sonyclassics.com/theillusionist/presskit.pdf. (last accessed 26 June 2020).

Stam, Robert, Robert Burgoyne and Sandy Flitterman-Lewis. (1991). *New Vocabularies in Film Semiotics. Structuralism, Post-structuralism and Beyond*. London: Routledge.

Stergiou, Makis. (June 2020). *Chomet's Films as Charts*. Personal Communication with Maria Katsaridou, Brussels.

Surman, David. (2003). *CGI Animation: Pseudorealism, Perception and Possible Worlds*. Retrieved from: https://www.academia.edu/168038/CGI_Animation_Pseudorealism_Perception_and_Possible_Worlds (last accessed 26 August 2018).

Terry Ramsaye in the MOTION PICTURE HERALD, February 28, 1931 quoted in Maltin, Leonard. (1987). *Of Mice and Magic: A History of American Animated Cartoons*. New York: Plume.

Tetali, Phani and Phidi Pulu. *Limited Animation*. Retrieved from: http://dsource.in/sites/default/files/course/limited-animation/downloads/file/limited-animation.pdf (last accessed 5 July 2020).

Thomas, Bob. (1991). *Art of Animation*. New York: Hyperion.

Thomas, Bob. (1994 [1976]). *Walt Disney: An American Original*. New York: Hyperion.

Frank, Thomas and Ollie Johnston. (1981). *Disney Animation: The Illusion of Life*. New York: Abbeville.

Tsioulcas, Anastasia. (2015). *Stromae, 'Carmen'*. Retrieved from: https://text.npr.org/s.php?sId=396789203 (last accessed 2 July 2020).

Turner, Victor W. (2017 [1967]). *The Ritual Process: Structure and Anti-structure*. New York, USA: Cornell University Press.

Turner, Victor W. (1967). Betwixt and between: The Liminal Period in Rites of Passage. In *The Forest of Symbols: Aspects of Ndembu Ritual* (pp 93–111). New York, USA: Cornell University Press.

Urban Cinefile. (2004). *Chomet, Sylvain: The Triplets of Belleville.* Retrieved from: http://www.urbancinefile.com.au/home/view.asp?a=8748&s=Interviews (last accessed 15 August 2020).

Van Gennep, Arnold. (1960). *The Rites of Passage.* Chicago: University of Chicago Press.

Wasko, Janet. (2001). Challenging Disney Myths. *Journal of Communication Inquiry.* 25:237–57.

Wasko, Janet. (2001). *Understanding Disney. The Manufacture of Fantasy.* Cambridge: Polity Press.

Wasko, Janet, Mark Phillips and Eileen R. Meehan. (2001). *Dazzled by Disney? The Global Disney Audiences.* New York: Bloomsbury.

Watts, Steven. (1995). Art and Politics in the American Century. *Journal of American History.* 3:84–110.

Wells, Paul. (1998). *Understanding Animation.* New York: Routledge.

Wells, Paul. (2002). *Animation and America.* New Jersey: Rutgers University Press.

Wells, Paul. (2002). *Genre and Authorship.* New York: Wallflower Press.

Wells, Paul. (2007). *Basics Animation: Scriptwriting.* Switzerland: AVA Publishing.

Wells, Paul. (2008). *Re-Imagining Animation: The Changing Face of the Moving Image.* Switzerland: AVA Publishing.

Wells, Paul. (2008). *The Animated Bestiary: Animals, Cartoons, and Culture.* New Jersey: Rutgers University Press.

Whiteley, Aliya. (2016). Caleb's Cab. *Sally and Sylvain Chomet Interview.* Retrieved from: https://www.denofgeek.com/books/calebs-cab-sally-and-sylvain-chomet-interview/ (last accessed 21 August 2020).

Wilkinson, Amber. (2014). *Drawing on Real Life. Sylvain Chomet Talks about His Live-action Feature Attila Marcel.* Retrieved from: https://www.eyeforfilm.co.uk/feature/2014-09-11-sylvain-chomet-interview-about-making-attila-marcel-feature-story-by-amber-wilkinson (last accessed 21 August 2020).

Williams, Richard. (2002). *The Animator's Survival Kit.* London: Faber and Faber.

Wilshin, Mark. (2014). *Attila Marcel (2013).* Retrieved from: https://www.dogandwolf.com/2014/09/attila-marcel-review/ (last accessed 21 August 2020).

Wolfe, Jennifer. (2014). *Q&A: Director Sylvain Chomet Talks 'Simpsons' Couch Gag.* Retrieved from: https://www.awn.com/news/qa-director-sylvain-chomet-talks-simpsons-couch-gag (last accessed 21 August 2020).

Wozny, Michaela. (2014). *Creating an Emotional Impact without Dialogue: The Case Study of Pixar's 'Up'.* Retrieved from: https://research.shu.ac.uk/aces/enquiry/index.php/enquiry/article/download/42/45 (last accessed 25 August 2018).

Yoon, Hyejin, Edward J. Malecki. (2009). Cartoon Planet: Worlds of Production and Global Production Networks in the Animation Industry. *Industrial and Corporate Change.* 19 (1):239–71.

Index